THE ARMY AND THE LAW

Gift of Herbert F. West '22

THE ARMY AND THE LAW

By GARRARD GLENN

Revised and Enlarged by

A. ARTHUR SCHILLER

New York
COLUMBIA UNIVERSITY PRESS
1943

Gift of Herbert F. West '22

COPYRIGHT 1943
COLUMBIA UNIVERSITY PRESS, NEW YORK

Foreign Agents: OXFORD UNIVERSITY PRESS, Humphrey Milford, Amen House, London, E.C. 4, England, AND B. I. Building, Nicol Road, Bombay, India

MANUFACTURED IN THE UNITED STATES OF AMERICA

Nov. 12, 1943
Gift
344
G487a

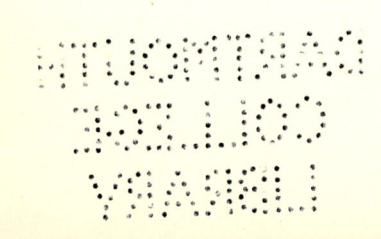

PREFACE TO THE FIRST EDITION

THIS book deals with the army only in its relation to the common law which governs the general public, and with the soldier only in so far as his activities are, in point of law, of interest to non-military persons. It is an endeavor simply to assemble the principles of law which impose duties upon the civilian, citizen, or enemy, quite as much as they give him rights which the army must observe. Hence I do not treat of the rules governing the internal affairs of the army except in so far as they bear on its rights and obligations with respect to people who are not members of its personnel. For the same reason, I have avoided mention of the laws of war, and matters of strict international law, beyond such passing reference as might be necessary to indicate the boundaries of the jurisdiction of common law courts. Jurisdiction, as the Supreme Court has said, means simply the power to decide a case;[1] and many controversies are possible with respect to the army which common law courts cannot decide. All such matters I have endeavored to classify as non-justiceable, and to say no more about them than might be necessary for purposes of classification. Such is my appointed path, and for all deviations from it my apologies are tendered in advance.

My thanks are due to all those who took a kindly interest in this work during its progress, including my partners and Dean Stone of Columbia Law School. My brother-in-law,

[1] The Fair v. Kohler Die Co., 1913, 228 U.S. 22, 33 S.Ct. 410, 57 L.Ed. 716.

Colonel S. J. B. Schindel, U.S.A., and my partner, Mr. C. R. Ganter, were also kind enough to read the advance proofs and make valuable suggestions thereon.

GARRARD GLENN

New York
July, 1918

PREFACE TO THE REVISED EDITION

WHEN, in April, 1941, Professor Glenn offered me the opportunity of preparing a second edition of his book, it was understood that pressure of other activities would prevent him from doing more than reading the manuscript and suggesting changes. Unfortunately, due to ill health, Professor Glenn has been able to read and revise only the first two chapters. Consequently the sole responsibility for the book as it now stands rests upon my shoulders. Although, wherever possible, I have attempted to retain the text of the first edition, nevertheless, in a number of places I have rephrased it in a way which might not be acceptable to the first author and in a few instances I have taken a position contrary to that expressed by him.

The relation of the army to the common law in the present conflict reflects the same general tendencies that have developed in the course of our history, but several factors of primary importance in the years following the termination of World War I have shifted the emphasis of some of the topics considered in this volume. More space has been devoted to the conscript at the expense of the chapter concerning martial law in time of peace. The reviser has, in the annotations, attempted to substitute decisions during and subsequent to World War I for those dating from the time of the Civil War. Further, cognizance has been taken of all the statutes, regulations, and decisions pertinent to the subject matter which date

1. INTRODUCTORY

THE protection of the state from the public enemy, using that term in its broadest aspect, as distinguishing the public enemy from the casual malefactor, has always belonged to an organized force of armed men who in their collective aspect embody the physical force of the nation. This implies several things. First, the actions of this collective body must be governed by some sort of directions issuing from some power of state; and for convenience these directions are disseminated, through repetition or amplification, by various subordinate agents forming part of the force. Hierarchy is, therefore, inseparable from the idea of control. From this logically flows a duty of obedience to these directions on the part of the various members of the force.[1] Finally, an army,

---

[1] The following expressions from the Army Regulations of 1913 contain the whole duty of man in this respect:

"Command is exercised by virtue of office and the special assignment of officers holding military rank who are eligible by law to exercise command. Without orders from competent authority an officer can not put himself on duty by virtue of his commission alone, except as contemplated in the twenty-fourth [now 68th] and one hundredth and twenty-second [now 120th] articles of war. (§ 13)

"All persons in the military service are required to obey strictly and to execute promptly the lawful orders of their superiors. (§ 1)

"Military authority will be exercised with firmness, kindness, and justice. Punishments must conform to law and follow offenses as promptly as circumstances will permit. (§ 2)

"Superiors are forbidden to injure those under their authority by tyrannical or capricious conduct or by abusive language. (§ 3)

"While maintaining discipline and the thorough and prompt performance of military duty, all officers, in dealing with enlisted men, will bear in mind

whether created for a particular purpose, standing as a skeleton organization, or with all its *cadres* filled, is a necessity. It may not be a permanent institution with depots and headquarters in time of peace, but if it be dissolved it will, in case of subsequent need, be succeeded by another body of like organization.

It is obvious that the existence of any such body, whether regular or intermittent, will result in certain customs, being more or less recognized as governing the conduct of the members of the force in matters not covered by express directions or orders. And thus a system of precedent, custom, or tradition, call it what you will, evolves, which plays its part in the government of the army.

Such a body of law will naturally vary in application according to the activities of the army. In short, there may be a

---

the absolute necessity of so treating them as to preserve their self-respect. Officers will keep in as close touch as possible with the men under their command and will strive to build up such relations of confidence and sympathy as will insure the free approach of their men to them for counsel and assistance. This relationship may be gained and maintained without relaxation of the bonds of discipline and with great benefit to the service as a whole. (Change No. 35)

"Courtesy among military men is indispensable to discipline; respect to superiors will not be confined to obedience on duty, but will be extended on all occasions. (§ 4)

"Deliberations or discussions among military men conveying praise or censure, or any mark of approbation, towards others in the military service, and all publications relating to private or personal transactions between officers, are prohibited. Efforts to influence legislation affecting the Army, or to procure personal favor or consideration, should never be made except through regular military channels; the adoption of any other method by any officer or enlisted man will be noted in the military record of those concerned." (§ 5)

Much the same, in greatly abbreviated form, is now to be found in AR 600–10 and AR 600–20.

military law governing the army in time of peace and an additional law which comes into existence when the activities of the army extend into the field of war.

Wherever we have what can be called law of any sort we cannot go far without the idea of its enforcement, by means of some court's having power to hear anyone accused of a breach of the law and to order his punishment in case he is adjudged guilty. The army could not exist without that power any more than a court could exist without the self-protective right of punishing for contempt.

The proper understanding of such orders, the best interpretation of tradition, and the wisest discernment of customs obviously would belong to those who are members of this force. It would, therefore, seem that courts created from among the personnel of the organization should be left alone in their administration of its system of law. Nor has it ever been doubted by the common law that entry into the army is more than a matter of contract; it is a change of status on the part of the entrant and means his subjection to the laws and customs governing the army.[2] These factors make powerfully for segregation and the creation of a system of jurisprudence administered exclusively by military courts.

There is such a system, and it forms no part of that common law which governs the community at large and is enforced by courts of general jurisdiction. But the law governing the army is not all to be found in the decisions of military courts, the Articles of War and other federal enactments or the Army

[2] In re Grimley, 1890, 137 U.S. 147, 11 S. Ct. 54, 34 L. Ed. 636; In re Morrissey, 1890, 137 U.S. 157, 11 S. Ct. 57, 34 L. Ed. 644; Iroquois Iron Co. v. Industrial Commission, 1920, 294 Ill. 106, 128 N.E. 289, 12 A.L.R. 924.

for it."[6] But that does not mean that civil courts are excluded from all questions which savor of the international. As has been well said: "The rules of international law have not infrequently become the subject of inquiry by courts in order to determine the rights of litigants, in which case, of course, the rules of international law are ascertained and applied by the courts in the same way as rules of private law, and international law thus has to that extent a complete and formal sanction. Our own federal courts, for example, have been called upon at various times to interpret treaties, to determine in a given case whether a state of war existed, whether a blockade existed, what was lawful prize and contraband, the rights of neutrals and belligerents, and many other questions of purely international law."[7] From this we can gather that the boundaries of the common law courts are not a matter of angles and squares; yet the courts must respect these boundaries, and they are important factors in any consideration of the army's place in our law.

Such then is our task, to define the army's relation to the common law. The naval establishment occupies a position equal to that of the army as a part of our national defense, and many of the principles hereinafter discussed apply to it as well—in fact all the fundamental principles do—but clarity of presentation will be best preserved, it is believed, by confining this discussion to the army.

[6] Marshall, C. J., in United States v. Palmer, 1818, 3 Wheat. 610, 634, 4 L. Ed. 471; cf. Jones v. United States, 1890, 137 U.S. 202, 212, 11 S. Ct. 80, 34 L. Ed. 691. Thus the public acts of foreign governments, in matters of international relations, are proven by the records of our State Department rather than by independent judicial inquiry, Underhill v. Hernandez, 1897, 168 U.S. 250, 18 S. Ct. 83, 42 L. Ed. 456.
[7] Stone, *Law and Its Administration* (1915), pp. 84–85.

2. THE CONSTITUTION OF THE ARMY

CONGRESS has power to raise and support armies, but no appropriation for that purpose shall be for more than two years.[1] In the exercise of that power, the Army of the United States at the present time consists of the Regular Army, the National Guard of the United States, the National Guard while in the service of the United States, various reserve elements, and persons inducted under the Selective Training and Service Act.[2] The Regular Army is the standing army of this country, recruited by voluntary enlistment.[3] In addition, able-bodied male citizens and male aliens who have declared their intention of becoming citizens, between the ages of eighteen and forty-five, make up the militia, the enrolled or active portion of which, organized, armed, and equipped in accord with federal statutes, and federally recognized under the terms of the National Defense Act, is known as the "National Guard of the Several States, Territories and the District of Columbia."[4] Since by the provisions of the Constitution the

[1] Constitution, Art. I, sec. 8, clause 12.
[2] National Defense Act, sec. 1, 10 U.S.C.A. § 2.
[3] In earlier days, notably in 1812, in the Civil War, and in 1898, Volunteer regiments were raised, and often armies were composed almost wholly of such units, but since the National Defense Act in its present form makes no provision for such a force, discussion of this subject is omitted from this book.
[4] National Defense Act, sec. 57, 32 U.S.C.A. § 1. The stages in the development of the militia in the history of this country are presented by Ansell, 1917, 26 Yale L.J. 471–80, and Wiener, 1940, 54 Harv. L. Rev. 181–220. For further

militia is subject to the government of the respective states unless and until it is called forth into national service "to execute the laws of the Union, suppress insurrection and repel invasions," it was found expedient in recent years to create that body known as the National Guard of the United States.[5] This

---

details of the ever-increasing "federal recognition" of militia units, see Colby, 1925, 98 Cent. L.J. 240–44, and the language of such cases as Bianco v. Austin, 1922, 204 App. Div. (N.Y.) 34, 197 N.Y.S. 328; United States ex rel. Gillett v. Dern, 1934, 64 App. (D.C.) 81, 74 F. 2d 485.

[5] Although the constitutional limitation of federal service of the militia, Constitution, Art. I, sec. 8, clause 15, was held not to preclude the conscripting of the individual members of the National Guard (United States v. Sugar, 1917, D.C. Mich., 243 F. 423), nevertheless the opinion of Attorney General Wickersham of Feb. 17, 1912, 29 Op. Atty. Gen. 322, was considered authoritative in preventing the calling forth of the National Guard as units for service abroad during World War I. The act of June 15, 1933, 48 Stat. 155, 32 U.S.C.A. § 4a, establishing the "National Guard of the United States," gave Congress the power to authorize the President to "order" the units thereof to federal service; this makes the individual Guardsman primarily a federal reservist, secondarily a state militiaman, cf. note, 1941, 89 U. Pa. L. Rev. 1065, 1068. Although the National Defense Act, as amended, 32 U.S.C.A. §§ 81, 81c, contemplated the express declaration of a national emergency by Congress before the Guard could be ordered to extended federal service, Congress dodged this responsibility in authorizing the President to order out the National Guard, along with other reserve components, in the present emergency, Public Resolution of Aug. 27, 1940, 54 Stat. 858, 50 U.S.C.A. App. § 401, though in the Selective Training and Service Act, sec. 1c, 50 U.S.C.A. App. § 301c, it is declared that "it is the intent of the Congress that, whenever the Congress shall determine that troops are needed for the national security in excess of those of the Regular Army and those in active training and service under section 3(b) [draftees], the National Guard of the United States, or such part thereof as may be necessary, shall be ordered to active federal service and continued therein so long as such necessity exists." As a result the court, in Kennedy v. Cook, 1940, 285 Ky. 9, 146 S.W. 2d 56, 132 A.L.R. 251, considered the federal training and service of an officer of the Guard merely as an extension of the normal fifteen-day period. The Congress has now, Act of Aug. 18, 1941, 55 Stat. 626, 50 U.S.C.A. App. § 351, declared "that the national interest is imperiled" and has authorized the President to extend the period of training and service.

CONSTITUTION OF THE ARMY 9

is a reserve component of the Army of the United States, made up of federally recognized units and organizations and persons of the National Guard of the various states.[6] Within its restricted orb of action each state uses its militia, and more particularly its National Guard, for the same purposes of self-protection as the national government uses the army, and the common law's views with regard to such a state force coincide with its views with regard to the national army. It is not necessary, therefore, for us to concern ourselves with the functions of the state militia when existing, as a separate body, in times of peace; in time of war or national emergency, when the militia is at the disposition of the federal government, the state is authorized to provide itself with a Home Guard.[7]

Among further reserve elements of the army are the Officers' Reserve Corps, the Organized Reserves and the Enlisted Reserve Corps.[8] The members thereof are subject to active duty upon Presidential call, normally for not more than fifteen days

---

[6] The distinction between the National Guard and the National Guard of the United States is further displayed in the provisions respecting the organization thereof, National Defense Act, sec. 58, 32 U.S.C.A. §§ 4, 4a; the discharge of officers and the withdrawal of federal recognition, National Defense Act, secs. 76–77, 32 U.S.C.A. §§ 114–15; and the calling forth of the National Guard, Act of Jan. 21, 1903, 32 U.S.C.A. §§ 81a–81b, contrasted with the drafting of the National Guard of the United States, National Defense Act, sec. 111, 32 U.S.C.A. § 81.

[7] Act of Oct. 21, 1940, 54 Stat. 1206, 32 U.S.C.A. § 194. Although the act specifically provides that such state troops (home guards) shall not be called forth into the military service of the United States, it is questionable whether this proviso is constitutional.

[8] National Defense Act, sec. 1, 10 U.S.C.A. § 2. Statutory enactments respecting these reserve elements are collected in 10 U.S.C.A., chap. 20, and Mil. Laws, chap. 25. Officers retired from active service and the recently re-established Regular Army Reserve, Act of April 25, 1938, 52 Stat. 221, 10 U.S.C.A. § 343, constitute elements of the Regular Army that may be called to active service.

a year, but for longer periods of time when a national emergency has been expressly declared by Congress.[9] Since members of these reserve components are only subject to military law when called to active duty, and since the laws and regulations affecting them when in such service are no whit different from those applying to officers and men of the Regular Army, it is unnecessary to dwell in particular on their relation with the common law.[10]

Our constitutional theories prohibit the use of the national army for any purpose not distinctly federal. It, of course, may be used in time of war or national emergency; and it may be used in any case where the maintenance of the federal government's power is in question, or where some duty is charged upon the national government for the discharge of which the use of the army is necessary. Congressional legislation on this subject all bears to that end.[11] In general outline, the use of the army, in connection with the functions of the national government, is governed by substantially the same considerations as control the use of the British army in similar connections. There

[9] National Defense Act, secs. 37a, 55b, 10 U.S.C.A. §§ 369, 426. As indicated in note 5, *supra*, Congress authorized the President to order reserve components of the Army to active service without expressly declaring an emergency, Public Resolution of Aug. 27, 1940, 50 U.S.C.A. App. § 401; more recently, Act of Aug. 18, 1941, 55 Stat. 626, 50 U.S.C.A. App. § 351, Congress has declared "that the national interest is imperiled."

[10] Although by law reserve officers are subject to military law only when on active service, due to the fact that they are at other times public officers on inactive status, nevertheless a number of perplexing problems have arisen, primarily in connection with the doctrine of incompatibility of office; full discussion by Colby, 1925, 98 Cent. L.J. 312–19, and 1937, 21 Minn. L. Rev. 162–80.

[11] Statutory enactments respecting the use of the army are conveniently collected in Mil. Laws, chap. 4; discussion of the same in Davis, *Treatise on the Military Law of the United States* (3d ed. 1915), pp. 323–38.

CONSTITUTION OF THE ARMY

is, however, with us one restriction which must be noted, that the army shall not be used "as a posse comitatus or otherwise," for the purpose of executing the laws, except in such cases and under such circumstances as its employment may be expressly authorized by the Constitution or by act of Congress.[12] Since the Railroad Strike of 1894 this restriction has largely been academic, for in that period of stress, when the United States marshal was unable to carry out the laws, he was instructed to so certify to Washington, whereupon President Cleveland sent troops to the area of disturbance. However, the troops were not placed under the marshal but rather were a substitute for his posse and performed their duties exclusively under the military officer in command. Such procedure has been followed ever since. As a matter of fact, there is grave doubt as to the constitutionality of the Posse Comitatus Act of 1878, when it provides "that the Army of the United States shall not be used for the purpose of executing the laws, in view of the fact that the Constitution expressly makes the President the Commander-in-Chief of the Army and Navy, and expressly makes it his duty to take care that the laws are faithfully executed." [13]

According to our national scheme, "power to declare war is confided to Congress. The executive power, and the command of the military and naval forces, is vested in the President." [14]

---

[12] Act of June 18, 1878, 20 Stat. 152, 10 U.S.C.A. § 15.

[13] Lorence, 1940, 8 U. Kan. City L. Rev. 164, 186. This article contains not only a full treatment of the constitutional question but also a study of the historical background and particulars of the enactment of the Posse Comitatus Act, the author concluding that there is no longer any reason for the act to be on the books.

[14] Hamilton v. Dillin, 1874, 21 Wall. 73, 87, 22 L. Ed. 528. The war powers of the President, particularly in view of his position as commander in chief of the army and navy (see Berdahl, *War Powers of the Executive* (1920),

THE ARMY AND THE LAW

The President is always the commander in chief of the army, and he is also the supreme head of the National Guard when called or drafted into the service of the United States.[15] In matters of command he acts through the War Department, at whose head is a cabinet officer, the Secretary of War. Beneath him come successive ranks of command extending from the highest general officers down through the various grades of commissioned officers. A commission is not a contract of any sort; the President, by and with the advice and consent of the Senate, has the power of appointment of military officers.[16] Removal from military office is regulated by the Articles of War and statutory enactments, which provide for such a thing in case of a conviction of a military offense by a court-martial or by order of the President normally on the advice of various special boards.[17] Lowest in rank are the non-commissioned of-

---

pp. 43 ff., 101 ff.), have again become a question of moment, cf. Patch, *Military Service*, Editorial Research Reports (1941), and Commager, New York *Times*, Sunday Magazine Section, Oct. 19, 1941. But this subject is not within the scope of this book.

[15] Constitution, Art. II, sec. 2, clause 1.

[16] Constitution, Art. II, sec. 2, clause 2.

[17] A.W. 118, 10 U.S.C.A. § 1590, provides that no officer shall be dismissed from the service except by order of the President or by sentence of a general court-martial, and in time of peace no discharge except in pursuance of the sentence of a general court-martial; but it has long been held (Blake v. United States, 1880, 103 U.S. 227, 26 L. Ed. 462) that this did not withdraw from the President the power, with the advice and consent of the Senate, of superseding a military officer by the appointment of another in his place. The holding in Myers v. United States, 1926, 272 U.S. 52, 47 S. Ct. 21, 71 L. Ed. 160, as interpreted in Morgan v. T.V.A., 1939, D.C. Tenn., 28 F. Supp. 732, approved in Morgan v. T.V.A., 1940, C.C.A. Tenn., 115 F. 2d 990, certiorari denied, 1941, 312 U.S. 701, that the President may dismiss an officer appointed by him, regardless of whether that officer engaged in quasi-judicial or quasi-legislative functions, would seem to indicate that the President is entirely free in dismissing military officers. Whether an officer dismissed

CONSTITUTION OF THE ARMY

ficers, appointed from among the private soldiers. So the manner and form of one's joining the ranks as an enlisted man will be our next inquiry.

Save in periods of stress an essential quality of both the Regular Army and the National Guard has been that no man need elect to serve in either except by his own choice. To leave out of question the National Guard, this made of our Regular Army a "standing army" of the kind with which English history has made us so familiar since the days of the Stuarts. In its support, outside of the reserve corps created by enactments of the last three decades, there stood nothing but the state militia. This system, whose utter inadequacy has been faithfully shown by competent critics on both sides of the Atlantic,[18] has been a characteristic of Anglo-Saxon institutions for three centuries. In England, at least prior to the Territorial and Reserve Forces Act of 1907, there were the regular army and the militia, and the statute just mentioned did not repeal the various militia acts which go back to the time of Charles II.[19] "Historically," says a standard writer, "the militia is an older institution than the permanent army, and the existence of a standing army is historically, and according to constitutional

---

by order of the President has a right to court-martial, as provided by R.S. § 1230, 10 U.S.C.A. § 573, has not been entirely settled, for Wallace v. United States, 1920, 55 Ct. Cl. 396, which held that R.S. § 1230 was inoperative since it had been superseded by A.W. 118, was affirmed on different grounds in the Supreme Court, Wallace v. United States, 1922, 257 U.S. 541, 42 S. Ct. 221, 66 L. Ed. 360, leaving the constitutional question open.

[18] Upton, *Military Policy of the United States* (1917), pp. 105, 180, 434; Wiener, 1940, 54 Harv. L. Rev. 181, 188; War Office (Great Britain), *Manual of Military Law 1929*, pp. 187 f.; but cf. Clode, *Military Forces of the Crown*, vol. I (1869), p. 48.

[19] Dicey, *Law of the Constitution* (9th ed. 1939), pp. 295 ff.

theories, an anomaly. Hence the standing army has often been treated by writers of authority as a sort of exceptional or subordinate topic, a kind of excrescence, so to speak, on the national and constitutional force known as the militia. As a matter of fact, of course, the standing army is now the real national force, and the territorial force is a body of secondary importance." [20]

The same thing happened with us. Taking over the English fear of the standing army, our Constitution adopted the English conception of the annual Mutiny Act (of which more will be said hereafter) by providing that no appropriation for the support of the army shall be for a longer period than two years. At the same time we are told that "a well-regulated militia is essential for the security of a free people." General Upton, in his *Military Policy of the United States*, has shown that, whatever may be the value of militia as against an overweening sovereign, its essential worth as security for a free people against a foreign invader is a very doubtful quality, because, to speak only of our war of 1812, a small force of regulars defeated a much larger force of militia at Bladensburg, took Washington, and burned the Capitol. It is also noteworthy that two satires on militia training, so alike as to have raised the charge of plagiarism, are to be found in Longstreet's *Georgia Scenes*, published long before our Civil War, and Thomas Hardy's *Trumpet Major*, published in our own time.

Over against this theory of a small standing army and the militia, stands the idea of universal service, an idea to the acceptance of which the exigencies of national emergencies have forced both England and this country. But as our scheme of

[20] Dicey, *op. cit.*, p. 296.

CONSTITUTION OF THE ARMY

universal service has been limited, by the terms of the Selective Service Act of 1917 to the period of the war, and by the terms of the Selective Training and Service Act of 1940 to May 15, 1945, it might not be out of place to point out certain historical considerations. These are so obvious, and concerning them so much has been said, that the only claim for their presentation is the fact that the end of a national emergency always brings problems, and that among the greatest of these will be the question whether we shall return to the complex army-militia system of olden time.[21]

We hear much of universal service as a German idea. May we point to the fact that, as a practical matter, it originated (as opposed to the idea of standing armies), with the French Republic at its birth? On February 21, 1793, France, having relied during the previous year on volunteers, now that England and Holland had joined the ranks of her enemies, enacted through the decree of the National Convention as follows: "Tous les citoyens français, depuis l'âge de 18 ans jusqu'à 40 ans accomplis, non mariés ou veufs sans enfants sont en état de réquisition permanente jusqu'à l'époque du complément du recrutement effective des 300,000 hommes de nouvelle leveé, décréteé ci-après." [22]

Thus originated, in the words of one of France's soldierly

---

[21] For a comprehensive summation of the pros and cons of compulsory military service in connection with the present emergency, see J. E. Johnsen, *Compulsory Military Training* (The Reference Shelf, Vol. 14, No. 6, 1941); noteworthy arguments are also to be found in the Hearings before the Committee on Military Affairs, House of Representatives, 76th Congress, 3d session, on H.R. 10132 (1940), and Hearings before the Committee on Military Affairs, United States Senate, 76th Congress, 3d session, on S. 4164 (1940).

[22] Caron, *La Défense nationale*, p. 8.

enemies, "the conscription, that mighty staff on which France leaned when all Europe attempted to push her down—the conscription, without which she could never have sustained the dreadful war of antagonist principles entailed upon her by the revolution—that energetic law which he [Napoleon] did not establish, but which he freed from abuse and rendered great, national and endurable, by causing it to strike equally on all classes—the conscription made the soldiers the real representatives of the people." [23] It is a commonplace how Prussia, in the bitter years that followed Jena, elaborated the proposition of universal service, and how France, in the epoch that lay between Waterloo and Sedan, departed more and more from its rigid enforcement; but the basic idea of the enrollment of a nation's manhood in her defense is essentially French.

Prior to this titanic stroke of the beleaguered French Republic, the idea of a standing army had been very fashionable on the continent of Europe, attaining, indeed, its full flower about the middle of the eighteenth century. The philosophical tendency at that time was to regard war as an affair of kings, not of the people, and the idea thus germinated was shared by minds the most diverse. Thus both Rousseau and his Dutch contemporary Vattel advanced the suggestion that war is merely a relation of state to state, in which the individual citizens have no interest, except as they may be hired soldiers.[24] To the same view came finally Frederick the Great, despite the fact that a crude theory of universal service, in the shape of allotted districts for recruiting purposes, had existed in Prussia

[23] Napier, *Peninsular War*, Bk. 22, chap. 4.
[24] See passages quoted in Bordwell, *Law of War between Belligerents* (1908), p. 47.

even in his father's time. "The old King saw with satisfaction," says the admiring Treitschke, "how his unfortunate land was being strengthened agriculturally, and now defined the ideal of the army with the astounding words, 'The peaceful citizen shall not even notice when the nation is at war.' So one of the pillars which upheld the edifice of state—universal service— began slowly to totter." [25] A little earlier in the century an incident of the kind Frederick fondly prefigured had actually occurred. A peaceful citizen of England, the Rev. Laurence Sterne, tells us how he got as far on his *Sentimental Journey* as Paris, in sheer forgetfulness that his nation was then at war with France. And, finally, if we want the very pitch and climax of this idea—the peaceful citizen going about his business in comfortable calm while his country's sovereign and standing army hold off the foe—let us read what Paley, whose part in contemporary English and American thought has been recognized by many writers of much diversity of opinion has to say on the subject. His *Moral Philosophy* contains a chapter [26] treating "Of War and of Military Establishments." After pointing out that it is not unlawful for a Christian to bear arms, and that a nation should go to war if just cause compels it (with which we all agree), he proceeds to discuss the system of a standing army. Showing first the inefficiency of militia as against a standing army, with which we must agree if we read General Upton's book, he concludes that the standing army is the only thing to have. That, in the face of the examples afforded, first by the campaigns of revolutionary and Napoleonic France, and later of Prussia in 1866 and 1870, is a *non sequitur*,

[25] Treitschke, *Life of Frederick the Great* (Putnam ed. 1915), pp. 183 f.
[26] Bk. 6, chap. 12.

because most assuredly, as against a nation with a system of universal service, a small standing army, however excellent, cannot prevail.

But this conclusion of Dr. Paley's is not as interesting as his additional reflections on the subject. In them lies imbedded a historical fact of great value, namely, that at one time, and not so very far back in our common history, the idea of universal service was accepted; the only difference being that this idea was then applied to the militia. From the terms of the English statute regulating the militia, enacted in 1663,[27] Professor Dicey draws the conclusion that "in the Seventeenth Century Parliament apparently meant to rely, for the defense of England, upon this national army raised from the counties and placed under the guidance of country gentlemen." [28] It was the standing army, composed partly of foreign mercenaries and devoted to the service of the king, of which Parliament was jealous, not the national army proposed by the Act of 1663.[29] The standing army, in short, was part of that royal appanage of which Parliament was distrustful. Therefore, after the revolution of 1688, Parliament adopted the expedient of an annual Mutiny Act, which made offenses against discipline in the regular army punishable by court-martial, only for the period of one year; thus making it necessary for Parliament annually to provide for the continuance of a regular army. But an astonish-

[27] 14 Car. II, c. 3.   [28] Dicey, *op. cit.*, p. 296 n. 1.
[29] See the *Federalist*, parts 24–26. Thus during the Protectorate the case of Paradine v. Jane, 1647, Aleyn 26, 82 Eng. Rep. 897, the pioneer case on the operation of war as vis major in excusing non-performance of contract was decided. The defendant, the owner of lands over which Prince Rupert's army had passed, described in his plea the Prince as "a certain German Prince, by name Prince Rupert, an alien born, enemy to the King and his Kingdom, who did invade this realm with a hostile body of men."

CONSTITUTION OF THE ARMY

ing change came with the successful operations of the new army, in the campaigns of Marlborough; a change which Addison reflects in the 165th essay of the *Spectator*. The standing army then became popular with the middle and upper classes, and those who expressed their philosophy of life, among whom was Dr. Paley. So, to return to Dr. Paley's observations of war and the military establishment, we find him saying this: "Moreover, as such a militia must be supplied by rotation, allotment, or some mode of succession, whereby they who have served a certain time are replaced by fresh draughts from the country, a much greater number will be instructed in the use of arms, and will have been occasionally embodied together, than are actually employed, or than are supposed to be wanted at the same time. Now what effects, upon the civil condition of the country, may be looked for from this general diffusion of the military character, becomes an inquiry of great importance and delicacy. To me it appears doubtful whether any government can be long secure, where the people are acquainted with the use of arms, and accustomed to resort to them . . . To which we may subjoin, that in governments like ours, if the direction and officering of the army were placed in the hands of the democratic part of the constitution, this power, added to what they already possess, would so over-balance all that would be left of regal prerogative, that little would remain of monarchy in the constitution, but the name and expense: nor would these probably remain long." [30]

Now, there is a complete Tory argument against universal

---

[30] Paley, *Moral Philosophy*, Bk. 6, chap. 12. To somewhat the same effect writes another eighteenth-century philosopher, but of a far more liberal complexion, Adam Smith, *Wealth of Nations*, Bk. 6, chap. 1.

service, so complete as to leave no doubt in the mind of any democrat of the wisdom of a system of universal service; for, so far from its being incompatible with a democratic state, Dr. Paley, the spokesman of the eighteenth-century High Tories, shows that it is an abhorrent thing and wholly incompatible with the system of government of which George III was a shining exemplar. The fathers of our Constitution grasped a part of that idea, when they put the provisions of the Mutiny Act into our Constitution, but, like our English ancestors of the Whig school, they never thought of wiping out the dual system of standing army plus militia and establishing in its place a single national army based on universal service, in which only the corps of officers should have permanency. The democratic statesmen of modern English times have followed the same line, keeping the dual system of a small standing army with a nebulous militia. Both nations, therefore, long ignored the fact that the idea of universal service had germinated in England, and burgeoned in France, as already shown. Perhaps at the conclusion of the present war there will still be found people in English-speaking countries who will maintain that the idea of universal service belongs wholly to Prussia, blinding their eyes to the fact that its genesis comes from far more liberal sources.

Let us remember that the idea of conscription is not a strange thing to us. In the time of our Civil War this country, in both sections, knew what it meant to have the enemy at the gates. And previously, in the war of 1812 an armed enemy took a part of our domain in the far North,[31] resulting in the British occupation of Castine; another force won on our soil the battle of Bladensburg and captured Washington; and still another

[31] See United States v. Rice, 1819, 4 Wheat. 246, 4 L. Ed. 562.

landed in Louisiana and retired only after the battle of New Orleans.

It is no wonder that as far back as 1841 Mr. Monroe, Secretary of War, advocated compulsory service.[32] In our Civil War both sides resorted to conscription. The Confederate Congress, by its Acts of April 16, 1862, and September 27, 1862, authorized the Confederate President "to call out and to place in the military service of the Confederate States, for three years, unless the war shall have been sooner ended, all white men, who are residents of the Confederate States" between certain ages, who were not legally exempt from military service.[33] The constitutionality of this legislation was upheld in such courts of the Confederate States as it came before, and particularly is to be commended the decision of the Supreme Court of Georgia.[34] The United States government was authorized by Congress to take men selected by a system of lottery or draft, for military purposes, by the Act of March 3, 1863.[35] The constitutionality of this Act unfortunately was not tested in the Supreme Court, but its validity was upheld in the highest court of the State of Pennsylvania.[36]

The Selective Service Act of May 18, 1917, provided for the immediate raising of the Regular Army and the National Guard to the full strength that had been authorized by the

---

[32] Cited in Jeffers v. Fair, 1862, 33 Ga. 347, 369.

[33] Matthews, *Public Laws of the Confederate States* (1862), 1st Congress, 1st session, chap. 31, and 2d session, chap. 15.

[34] Jeffers v. Fair, 1862, 33 Ga. 347. See also Ex parte Coupland, 1862, 26 Tex. 386; Burroughs v. Peyton, 1864, 16 Gratt. (Va.) 470. Cf. Robinson, *Justice in Gray* (1941), pp. 436, 519.

[35] 12 Stat. 731.

[36] Kneedler v. Lane, 1863, 45 Pa. 238; the arguments advanced and the opinions delivered in this lengthy case are well summarized by Pomeroy, *Introduction to the Constitutional Law of the United States* (9th ed. 1886), pp. 390 ff.

National Defense Act, and in addition provided for the formation of a National Army by empowering the President to draft the required number of men, up to 1,000,000, from the male citizenry and aliens who had declared their intention of becoming citizens, within the ages of eighteen and forty-five.[37] Presidential proclamations provided for the registration of the citizenry and alien declarants within these ages, and executive regulations set up draft boards and established rules for the selection of men therefrom to make up the National Army. It was not long before the constitutionality of the Selective Service Act was questioned, and a series of cases followed in which the act was upheld in all its particulars in the face of a host of objections based on constitutional grounds.[38] The Supreme Court upheld the validity of draft legislation, among other reasons, on the authority found in the federal Constitution for the national government to "raise and support armies," [39] while decisions of the lower federal courts disposed of arguments that conscription was involuntary servitude, denial of due process, or ex post facto legislation, and that the regulations providing for the draft boards were a delegation of legislative power and an encroachment on judicial power, and the like.[40]

[37] 40 Stat. 76, 50 U.S.C.A. App. §§ 201–2.
[38] All the cases concerned with the validity of the act are cited in 50 U.S.C.A., annotations pp. 172 f.; the most significant of these are treated in 129 A.L.R. 1172–81.
[39] Selective Draft Law Cases, 1918, 245 U.S. 366, 38 S. Ct. 159, 62 L. Ed. 349, Ann. Cas. 1918B, 856, L.R.A. 1918C, 361.
[40] Involuntary servitude, class legislation, executive tribunals exercising judicial powers, delegation of legislative and judicial powers upon the President, not an exercise of power conferred on Congress, calling out militia for purpose not authorized are all considered in United States v. Sugar, 1917, D.C. Mich., 243 F. 423; the due process question is treated in Angelus v. Sullivan, 1917, C.C.A. N.Y., 246 F. 54; religious freedom in United States v. Stephens,

CONSTITUTION OF THE ARMY

At the present time the Selective Training and Service Act of September 16, 1940, as amended, provides for the registration of male citizens and male residents between the ages of eighteen and sixty-five, and for the subsequent training and service of such persons as are selected by draft boards established by presidential regulations.[41] A public resolution of August 27, 1940, had authorized the President to order to active service any or all reserve components of the Army of the United States and retired personnel of the Regular Army.[42] Though enacted in time of peace, in contrast to the conscription act of 1917, the constitutionality of the 1940 act has been upheld in a number of the lower federal courts, in great part on the grounds asserted in the earlier decisions, some cases with added observations on the peacetime nature of the enactment.[43]

The historical and constitutional matters which have already been considered induced our courts long ago, in common with those of England, to view the army as having a distinct status in the governmental system, indeed as occupying the position practically of an estate of the realm. The cardinal necessities of its existence, command on the one side and obedience on the other, can lead to no other conclusion on the part of a common law court, if it is to recognize the lawfulness of having an army

---

1917, D.C. Del., 245 F. 956; ex post facto legislation in United States ex rel. Pfefer v. Bell, 1918, D.C. N.Y., 248 F. 992.
[41] 54 Stat. 885, 50 U.S.C.A. App. §§ 301 ff.
[42] 54 Stat. 858, 50 U.S.C.A. App. §§ 401 ff.
[43] United States v. Cornell, 1940, D.C. Idaho, 36 F. Supp. 81; Stone v. Christensen, 1940, D.C. Ore., 36 F. Supp. 739; United States v. Rappeport, 1941, D.C. N.Y., 36 F. Supp. 915, affirmed 1941, C.C.A. N.Y., United States v. Herling, 120 F. 2d 236; United States v. Garst, 1941, D.C. Pa., 39 F. Supp. 367; United States v. Lambert, 1941, C.C.A. Pa., 123 F. 2d 395; Local Draft Board v. Connors, 1941, C.C.A. Mont., 124 F. 2d 388.

at all. Matters connected with the army are, therefore, in the common law view, essentially things of status rather than contract. This is not the only instance of common law acceptance of status as an actual proposition. Marriage, for example, with its accompanying restrictions in points of evidence and of property right, is in our law, wholly a matter of status. Just so it is with the army, and, therefore, we find the law fully admitting that entry into the national service effects, for the soldier or officer concerned, a "change of status." [44]

The Selective Training and Service Act of 1940 can make no difference in this respect, because no valid distinction can be made between a voluntary assumption of military status and its imposition by operation of law. In the words of the Supreme Court, which upheld the similar statute of 1917, compulsory service simply amounts to "the exaction by government from the citizen of the performance of his supreme and noble duty of contributing to the defense of the rights and honor of the nation," and any contention that this imposes involuntary servitude is refuted by its mere statement.[45]

For that reason, a minor's enlistment, so far as the common law was concerned, was not voidable, from his standpoint or that of his parents, though it could be avoided by the state at any time.[46] For any modification of this broad view that may obtain at present, therefore, we must look to statutes, and ours on the subject have had a long and changeable history.

The earliest statutory enactments fixed the enlistment age as between eighteen and thirty-five or forty-five. After the Civil

[44] In re Morrissey, 1890, 137 U.S. 157, 11 S. Ct. 57, 34 L. Ed. 644.
[45] Selective Draft Law Cases, 1917, 245 U.S. 366, 390.
[46] Commonwealth v. Gamble, 1824, 11 Serg. & R. (Pa.) 93; In re Morrissey, 1890, cit *supra;* Ex parte Beaver, 1921, D.C. Ohio, 271 F. 493.

War the age limits had generally been fixed at sixteen and thirty-five. The act of March 2, 1899, raised the minimum age to eighteen and such apparently is the law today.[47] But the proviso requiring the consent of parents or guardian to the enlistment of minors, which had seen varying age limits set, was stated in the National Defense Act of 1916 in terms forbidding the enlistment of a person under the age of eighteen without the consent of parents or guardian.[48] In spite of a decision to the contrary, the most recent adjudication as well as the practice of the War Department considers that "indirectly, but none the less explicitly, Congress recognizes and authorizes enlistments of all minors under 18 years of age with the consent of parents or guardians. The effect of this is to repeal the minimum limit of 18 years provided in section 4, even if it does not restore and re-enact the limit of 16 years originally found in R.S. §§ 1116 and 1118. Moreover, in the event the 18-year minimum is repealed, and the 16-year minimum is not restored, then the common law applicable to the enlistment of minors under 18 years of age will be in force."[49] Whatever

[47] 30 Stat. 978, 10 U.S.C.A. § 621. The earlier statutes and cases construing them are to be found in the annotations to Mil. Laws § 246 and 10 U.S.C.A., § cited.

[48] National Defense Act, sec. 27, 39 Stat. 185, 10 U.S.C.A. § 627. The present Army Regulations, AR 600-750.9, of Sept. 30, 1942, prohibit the enlistment of minors under eighteen and relate the proviso regarding the necessity of parental consent to the years between eighteen and twenty-one, although no statutory authority for such a construction exists.

[49] Ex parte Beaver, 1921, D.C. Ohio, 271 F. 493, 497. The contrary holding is Hoskins v. Pell, 1917, C.C.A. Miss., 239 F. 279, L.R.A. 1917D, 1053, one judge dissenting, which has expressly been disapproved in an opinion of the Judge Advocate General of May 11, 1918, 1918 Op. J.A.G. 357, and which is frowned upon in Ex parte Beaver. Nevertheless Hoskins v. Pell is cited, and Ex parte Beaver is not mentioned, in the annotation to sec. 27 of the 1940

the minimum age may be, it would follow that the enlistment of a minor having parent or guardian, without the latter's consent, could be effected only by his making to the recruiting officer untruthful statements as to his age, or presenting a false certificate as to the consent of his parent or guardian. In any such case, the only one logically entitled to complain would be the parent or guardian thus defrauded, by the minor's act, of his services. Certainly the minor, the perpetrator of the fraud, should not be allowed to complain. Such is the view of the courts. They consider the law as intended, not for the minor's protection, but rather for the benefit of the parent or guardian. The enlistment, of its own force, made the minor "not only *de facto*, but *de jure*, a soldier—amenable to military jurisdiction." [50]

And then it must be remembered that there is another innocent party in the transaction, the government; and the courts felt that they could not allow the statutory right of the parent or guardian to operate to the prejudice of the government. Hence the demand of the parent or guardian for the return of the minor should be promptly made, and any delay will be construed as a consent, operating by way of an estoppel on the demandant.[51] Also it is just as clear that the avoidance of the en-

---

edition of the National Defense Act, prepared for the use of the Committee of Military Affairs of the United States Senate.

[50] In re Morrissey, cit. *supra*, note 44, at p. 159.

[51] Ex parte Dostal, 1917, D.C. Ohio, 243 F. 664, 670: "Furthermore, the written consent required of the parents or guardian of a minor is primarily for the benefit of such parents or guardian. It is designed, not merely to protect an immature minor from improvident action, but to preserve the parent's or guardian's right to his custody and service. The parent or guardian may undoubtedly waive the requirement that the consent be in writing. This written consent may undoubtedly be given after, as well as at the time of, the en-

listment must await, for its operation, the consequences of any military offense which the minor may have committed with, or after, his enlistment. All of this, when coupled with the statute enacted in 1892, whose provisions now form part of the Articles of War,[52] makes fraudulent enlistment and the receipt of pay or allowances thereunder a military offense. The result is that the minor's very act of deception in enlisting, if followed by the receipt of a dollar of pay, is an offense for which the government may exact punishment, prior to his being handed over to the parent or guardian.[53]

The same propositions apply to other matters of disqualification. The statutes reject as applicants aliens, insane and intoxicated persons, deserters, and convicted felons.[54] The case of one *non compos mentis*, such as an insane or intoxicated per-

---

listment. It follows, as a consequence, that the parent or guardian may, by acquiescence, with knowledge, after the enlistment, waive all right to relief because written consent was not previously given. This waiver will result from silence or acquiescence while a minor is continuing in the service and drawing pay from the government." Cf. Ex parte Dunakin, 1913, D.C. Ky., 202 F. 290. The so-called ratification of the enlistment of a minor is further considered in an unreported case, In re O'Dell, 1918, D.C. S.C., in which a father sought the release of his son under eighteen years of age, who had enlisted without his consent; the court held that the acceptance by the father of an allotment of $15 per month out of the son's pay and of a government allowance of $10 a month was a clear ratification of the son's enlistment in the army.

[52] A.W. 54, 10 U.S.C.A. § 1526.

[53] In re Cosenow, 1889, D.C. Mich., 37 F. 668; United States v. Williford, 1915, C.C.A. N.Y., 220 F. 291. In Ex parte Avery, 1916, D.C. N.C., 235 F. 248, a minor, even though held in arrest, was released on petition for writ of habeas corpus on the part of his parents, for charges had not been prepared and preferred to bring him before a court-martial for fraudulent enlistment, at the time the writ was filed.

[54] Act of Aug. 1, 1894, 28 Stat. 216, 10 U.S.C.A. § 625; R.S. § 1118, act of Feb. 27, 1877, 10 U.S.C.A. § 622.

son, takes care of itself, because his mind did not accompany his act and he did not make a change of status. But if the government should be satisfied to keep in its service an alien or deserter, again the common law idea of status prevails over the statutory definition, and the soldier cannot escape by showing that his enlistment should not have been accepted.[55]

Since the qualifications with regard to enlistment in the Regular Army flow from federal enactment, there are necessarily no such limitations upon enlistment in the organized militia of the several states unless provided for by the statutes of the state. Consequently a minor who enlisted in the National Guard without the consent of his parents cannot be discharged upon the application of the parent.[56] When the National Guard, however, is called or drafted into the service of the United States the question arises whether the law of the state or that of the federal government is to apply. A decision early in the last war refused to grant the petition of the parent of a minor who had enlisted without consent when the unit to which he belonged was called into federal service, stating: "No provision will be found in the statutes relating to [the] National Guard of the District of Columbia enabling the parent to annul a lawful enlistment entered into by a member of the

---

[55] Regarding aliens, see United States v. Cottingham, 1843, 1 Rob. (Va.) 615, 40 Am. Dec. 710; 1854, 6 Op. Atty. Gen. 474, 484; Ex parte Dostal, 1917, D.C. Ohio, 243 F. 664, 671. For deserters, see In re McVey, 1885, 23 F. 878; and the opinion of the Judge Advocate General that a deserter from the naval service in time of war may be enlisted in the army, 1919 Op. J.A.G. 847. Deserters and convicted felons may now be enlisted with the authorization of the Secretary of War, 10 U.S.C.A. § 622.

[56] Acker v. Bell, 1911, 62 Fla. 108, 57 So. 356, 39 L.R.A. (n.s.) 454, Ann. Cas. 1913C, 1269; Birdsong v. Blackman, 1921, 127 Miss. 693, 90 So. 441.

National Guard; and in the absence of such statute the court's conclusion is that the petitioner cannot avail herself of the provision of the federal statute, although her son may be temporarily in the military service of the United States. He is in such service by virtue of his enlistment as a member of the National Guard of the District of Columbia, and it is his eligibility in the last-named service that determines his liability to be mustered into and retained in the military service of the United States." [57] In *Hoskins v. Dickerson*, however, where a person under eighteen had enlisted, without consent, in the National Guard of the United States and of the state of Mississippi, the enlistment was declared voidable at the instance of his father.[58] The cases may be distinguished in that the latter concerns an enlistee of a reserve component of the Army of the United States, but the language of the court itself, that the federal law will apply to "a member of the National Guard while in the service of the United States," may well be deemed to include not only the National Guard of the United States when drafted, but also the National Guard of the several states when called forth under the constitutional provision.[59] In the authority given by Congress, in the present emergency, for the draft of the National Guard of the United States, care was taken to except therefrom members thereof who were under the age of eighteen.[60]

[57] Ex parte Winfield, 1916, D.C. Va., 236 F. 552, 554.
[58] 1917, C.C.A. Miss., 239 F. 275, L.R.A. 1917D, 1056, Ann. Cas. 1917C, 776. In accord, Ex parte McCollam, 1942, D.C. N.J., 45 F. Supp. 759.
[59] On the distinction between National Guard called into federal service, and National Guard of the United States drafted into federal service, see *supra*, notes 5-6.
[60] Public Resolution of Aug. 27, 1940, sec. 1, 50 U.S.C.A. App. § 401.

The calling forth or drafting of the militia into federal service effects a change of status, in the case of a call from the time that the terms of the call require response thereto, in the case of a draft from the date of the order; a refusal to obey is a military offense, and punishable as such.[61] When the militia was called forth in 1812, the Supreme Court at first considered that the Act of Congress made the officers and members of the militia a part of the national forces only from the time of their arrival at the appointed place of mobilization, whereas Mr. Justice Story thought that the status was imposed from the date when the soldier received notice of the call. But in the end this made no difference, because all the judges agreed that it was competent to make the date of the call the time when the officers and members of the militia became subject to the military control of the government.[62] If any subtle shade of distinction in this respect had remained, it was obliterated in the later decision of *Martin v. Mott*.[63] In the Civil War, indeed, Congress, to remove any doubt on the subject, provided, by its Act drafting the militia into the national forces, that anyone failing to report should be deemed a deserter, subject to trial by court-martial of the national army.[64] A recusant of this class was held to be in the national service from the date of the call, and hence his failure to report made his offense desertion from

[61] National Defense Act, secs. 101, 111, 32 U.S.C.A. § 81; 50 U.S.C.A. App. § 402. Cf. 1912-40 Dig. Op. J.A.G. § 293(1) (Feb. 20, 1923).
[62] Houston v. Moore, 1820, 5 Wheat. 1, 5 L. Ed. 19.
[63] 1827, 12 Wheat. 19, 6 L. Ed. 537, reversing the decision of the N.Y. Court of Errors, Mills v. Martin, 1821, 19 Johns. (N.Y.) 7. Incidentally Martin v. Mott firmly established the principle that the President is sole judge of the existence of the exigency which results in his calling forth the militia to federal service.
[64] Act of July 17, 1862, 12 Stat. 597.

CONSTITUTION OF THE ARMY

the national army.[65] The same result has been reached under the present law.[66]

In passing, it should be noted that the similar problem of the date of change of status from a private person to a soldier exists in the case of a conscript. The provisions of the Selective Service Act of 1917 were somewhat ambiguous in this respect, and there resulted a series of decisions, some contradictory in effect, but the rule was finally established that proof of the mailing of the notice of induction was sufficient to warrant holding that a draftee who failed to report, was a deserter subject to court-martial.[67] Selective Service Regulations at the present time do not attempt to fix a definite time for this change of status.[68]

---

[65] McCall's Case, 1863, D.C. Pa., Fed. Cas. No. 8669, 5 Phila. 259.

[66] Ex parte Dostal, 1917, D.C. Ohio, 243 F. 664, 673.

[67] Franke v. Murray, 1918, C.C.A. Mo., 248 F. 865, L.R.A. 1918E, 1015, Ann. Cas. 1918D, 98; United States ex rel. Helmecke v. Rice, 1922, D.C. Tex., 281 F. 326; United States v. McIntyre, C.C.A. Mont., 4 F. 2d 823. Two earlier opinions to the contrary, Farley v. Ratliff, 1920, C.C.A. W. Va., 267 F. 682, and Ex parte Caplis, 1921, D.C. Tex., 275 F. 980, are expressly disapproved in the latest determination, United States ex rel. Bergdoll v. Drum, 1939, C.C.A. N.Y., 107 F. 2d 897, 129 A.L.R. 1165, certiorari denied, 1940, 310 U.S. 648, 60 S. Ct. 1098, 84 L. Ed. 1414.

[68] S.S.R. (2d ed.) § 633.9: "At the induction station, the selected men found acceptable will be inducted into the land or naval forces." In United States ex rel. Diamond v. Smith, 1942, D.C. Mass., 47 F. Supp. 607, the court notes that neither the Selective Service Act nor the Regulations set forth the procedure for induction; according to AR 615–500 of Sept. 1, 1942, the court says: "it seems if a man successfully passes the physical examination and is accepted by the Army for training and service, he is inducted into the Army whether he takes the oath administered to him or not." To the same effect, Ex parte Billings, 1942, D.C. Kan., 46 F. Supp. 663, 667.

3. MILITARY LAW AND MILITARY COURTS

JUST as today the lawyer interested in any branch of practice finds part of his law in the shape of legislation and part still in the flux of case law, so military law—using the term in its broadest sense—presents itself today partly by way of statute and partly by way of tradition and precedent. With us the statutory portion is primarily to be found in those federal enactments known as the Articles of War. The Constitution allows Congress to "make rules for the government and regulation of the land and naval forces." [1] The Articles of War governing our army were first prepared in the years immediately preceding the outbreak of the Revolutionary War [2] and survived the adoption of the Constitution, being continued in force by successive statutes, "so far as the same are applicable to the Constitution of the United States." [3] By the Act of April 10, 1806, a legislative overhauling was made; [4] save for amendments made from time to time and for a restatement in 1874, the re-enactment of the Articles of War made in 1806 constituted the code of laws governing the relations of officers and men, and their conduct as affecting the good of the service,

---

[1] Art. I, sec. 8, clause 14.
[2] Enacted by the Second Continental Congress, June 30, 1775, revised and superseded by the Code of Sept. 20, 1776, see Callan, *Military Laws of the United States* (1863), pp. 63–76.
[3] Act of March 3, 1795, sec. 14, 1 Stat. 340.
[4] 2 Stat. 359, Comp. Stat. 1913, §§ 2305–448.

MILITARY LAW AND MILITARY COURTS

until 1916. In that year a complete revision was made, eliminating obsolete matter and introducing many modifications and changes looking to a scientific and modern statement of military law.[5] As a result of the experiences encountered in World War I and in part as an answer to the harsh criticism directed against the Code of 1916,[6] a revised and supplemented Code of 1920 was enacted, as Chapter II of the amended National Defense Act,[7] which, together with minor amendments, is the present Military Code.[8]

This Code applies only to those who can be considered part of the army's personnel, including members of the Army Nurse Corps, field clerks, and other persons lawfully called, drafted, or ordered into service, so far as the army at home and in time of peace is concerned.[9] When the army is abroad, without the territorial jurisdiction of the United States, the Articles apply as well to all retainers and persons accompanying or serving

---

[5] Act of Aug. 29, 1916, 39 Stat. 619.
[6] Notably by Ansell, 1919, 5 Cornell L.Q. 1; 1919 Pa. B.A. 280; 1920 Ohio B.A. 134; cf. also Morgan, 1919, 29 Yale L.J. 52, and 1919 Md. B.A. 197; Bogert, 1919, 5 Cornell L.Q. 18. The other side of the picture was presented by Maj. Gen. Crowder, J.A.G., *Military Justice during the War* (1919); Wigmore, 1919 Md. Bar Assoc. 188, 218.
[7] 41 Stat. 787, 10 U.S.C.A. §§ 1471–1593, Mil. Laws §§ 354–479.
[8] The successive codifications, 1775–1874, are reprinted in Winthrop, *Military Law and Precedents* (2d ed. rep. 1920), pp. 953–96, while a comparative table of the sections of the Code of 1874 and those of 1916 and 1920 is to be found in Mil. Laws, introductory annot. to chap. 3.
[9] A.W. 2, 10 U.S.C.A. § 1473. The drafted man is subject to the Articles of War, Franke v. Murray, 1918, C.C.A. Mo., 248 F. 865, L.R.A. 1918E, 1015, Ann. Cas. 1918D, 98; but a man not lawfully inducted into the service is not, Ver Mehren v. Sirmyer, 1929, C.C.A. Iowa, 36 F. 2d 876. Further, the WAACS are subject to the Articles of War by Act of May 14, 1942, 10 U.S.C.A. § 1714. Note also that "all persons under sentence by courts-martial" are within the scope of the Articles of War, Kahn v. Anderson, 1921, 255 U.S. 1, 41 S. Ct. 224, 65 L. Ed. 469.

with the forces, and in time of war "all such retainers and persons accompanying or serving with the armies of the United States in the field, both within and without the territorial jurisdiction of the United States, though not otherwise subject to these articles." [10]

Historically, the American Articles of War find their source in the corresponding British Articles, and the latter go back in turn to the Revolution of 1688.[11] The device of an annual Mutiny Act, first adopted in the time of William III,[12] had for its object to deprive the Crown of an army for more than a year at a time. To accomplish this, the Act, annually passed, provides two things: first, an appropriation for the army's support, for only one year, and second, authority to define offenses against discipline and punish them through courts-martial, also for only one year. Thus, at the end of each year not merely will

---

[10] A.W. 2(d), 10 U.S.C.A. § 1473(d). Among civilian retainers or persons accompanying or serving the forces "in the field" have been held: a mate on an army transport, Ex parte Gerlach, 1917, D.C. N.Y., 247 F. 617; a superintendent in the Quartermaster Corps serving on the Mexican border, Ex parte Jochen, 1919, D.C. Tex., 257 F. 200; a stenographer employed in the construction quartermaster's office at a U.S. post, Hines v. Mikell, 1919, C.C.A. S.C., 259 F. 28, reversing Ex parte Mikell, 1918, D.C. S.C., 253 F. 817; officials of the American Red Cross in France during World War I, 1917 Op. J.A.G. 273. Among the more recent works on the amenability of civilians to military jurisdiction, see Fletcher, 1917, 2 Minn. L.R. 110, 126; Warren, 1919, 53 Amer. L. Rev. 195; Morgan, 1919, 4 Minn. L. Rev. 79; Underhill, 1923, 12 Calif. L. Rev. 75, 81.

[11] Further on the history of the Articles of War, see Winthrop, *Military Law*, pp. 17 ff.; Davis, *Military Law*, pp. 2 f., 342 f.; Hoover, "Army Courts-Martial," in *Legal Essays to Orrin Kip McMurray* (1935), pp. 165, 166 ff. On the British articles, see War Office (Great Britain), *Manual of Military Law 1929*, pp. 10 ff., with further references.

[12] Effective April 12, 1689, Statutes of the Realm 55, 1 W. & M., c. 5; reprinted Winthrop, *Military Law*, p. 929.

MILITARY LAW AND MILITARY COURTS

the army be without pay unless the Act be renewed, but it will also be without any lawful rules of discipline, much less the means of enforcing breaches of discipline.[13]

The Mutiny Act, however, did not contain a complete code of regulations. While it made mutiny and desertion punishable by court-martial, it left all other matters affecting discipline to be regulated by the royal prerogative, and, therefore, indeed, sanctioned such regulations as had previously existed for the government of the British forces. We thus are led back historically to the Articles of War which had been issued by James II in 1686;[14] their origin in turn may be found in various regulations drawn up for the conduct and discipline of the army, as far back as the "Statutes, Ordinances, and Customs" of Richard II, issued by him to his army in 1385.[15] In the course of time the Articles took a form not unlike that which they bore in more modern times, and the Prince Rupert Articles, issued by the commander in chief under the authority of a commission from Charles II, in 1672,[16] formed the groundwork for the Articles of War issued in 1878, which were consolidated with the Mutiny Act in the Army Discipline and Regulation Act of 1879; this was re-enacted as the Army Act, and is still in force throughout the British Empire.[17]

The double aspect of the English statute, consisting of an

---

[13] Dicey, *Law of the Constitution* (9th ed. 1939), p. 309.
[14] Clode, *Military and Martial Law* (2d ed. 1874), p. 53; the articles are reprinted in Winthrop, *Military Law*, pp. 920 ff. (incorrectly dated 1688).
[15] Grose, *Military Antiquities* (1786), vol. II, pp. 64 ff.; Winthrop, *Military Law*, p. 904.
[16] *Parliamentary Papers*, XV (1867), p. 238; Davis, *Military Law*, pp. 567 ff.
[17] War Office (Great Britain), *Manual of Military Law 1929*, pp. 418 ff., with supplemental amendments to date.

appropriation of money for the army's support for only one year and also conferring authority to punish offenses against discipline, though recognized by all having occasion to examine the subject,[18] was overlooked by the framers of our Constitution. They provided that no sums should be voted for the support of the army for a longer period than two years, but they did not provide a time limit for statutory provisions concerning the discipline of the army. Therefore, the Act of 1806 and its amendments, last recodified by the Code of 1920, constitute that permanent statutory code which the British Army, in theory, lacks. But there is no practical difference in the fundamentals of the two establishments, because, despite the permanence of our military code, as a practical matter there would be no army for its governance unless Congress, every two years, should appropriate the funds necessary for that purpose.

As these Articles apply only to persons who may be considered part of the military machine, so most of the offenses they prescribe are offenses which only such persons would have the faculty of committing. There are, however, two exceptions. Whosoever relieves or attempts to relieve, correspond with or aid the enemy, either directly or indirectly, shall suffer death or such other punishment as a court-martial or military commission may direct.[19] And, in time of war, the Articles extend to the case of a spy, as therein defined, whether or not the accused person wear our uniform, be entitled to wear it,

[18] See, for example, the dissenting opinion of Woodbury, J. in Luther v. Borden, 1849, 7 How. 1, 60, 12 L. Ed. 581.
[19] A.W. 81, 10 U.S.C.A. § 1553; traceable back to the earliest American articles of war, and further back to British and Swedish articles of war, Winthrop, *Military Law*, p. 629.

MILITARY LAW AND MILITARY COURTS

or be a citizen or alien.[20] These two Articles are now marked as exceptions to the proposition that the Articles of War apply only to persons who, as therein defined, compose the army's personnel, and have no relation to persons who have not assumed the status of soldier or assumed some other connection with the army as above defined.

For a classification of these Articles we need go no further than the Code itself. The first two are articles of definition, then we have a number of articles relating to the composition, jurisdiction, and procedure of courts-martial,[21] and then come the punitive articles. These have been divided according to the following headings, which speak for themselves: [22] first, Enlistment, Muster, Returns; second, Desertion, Absence without leave; third, Disrespect, Insubordination, Mutiny; fourth, Arrest, Confinement; fifth, War offenses; sixth, Miscellaneous crimes and offenses. The Code of 1920 concludes with articles devoted to courts of inquiry [23] and miscellaneous provisions.[24]

In addition to the Articles of War and other federal statutes which provide in part for the administration of the military

---

[20] A.W. 82, 10 U.S.C.A. § 1554; superseding R.S. § 1343, which in turn in earlier form is to be found in the Code of 1806 and the resolution of the Continental Congress of Aug. 21, 1776, Winthrop, *Military Law*, pp. 765 f.

[21] A.W. 3–53, 10 U.S.C.A. §§ 1474–1525.

[22] A.W. 54–96, 10 U.S.C.A. §§ 1526–68; the most important of these articles are further discussed in the official *Manual for Courts-Martial, U.S. Army, 1928* (1936 ed.), pp. 138–91. For further treatment in the various textbooks on military law, see notably Winthrop, *Military Law*, passim; Davis, *Military Law*, chap. 19. For cases and opinions regarding offenses, see the annotations to U.S.C.A. §§ cited; Mil. Laws §§ 412–454 [in the 1929, 1939 editions and the 1940 Supplement]; Schiller, *Military Law and Defense Legislation* (1941), pp. 498–526; 1912–40 Dig. Op. J.A.G. §§ 412–454 (pp. 263–367), Supp. I thereto, and 1 Bull. J.A.G., same sections.

[23] A.W. 97–103, 10 U.S.C.A. §§ 1569–1575.

[24] A.W. 104–121, 10 U.S.C.A. §§ 1576–1593.

establishment,[25] there are the Army Regulations.[26] These are said to have the "force of law" but, in so far as they are departmental regulations,[27] or are made by the President in the exercise of authority conferred by act of Congress,[28] they cannot conflict with the federal statutes.[29] It is to be noted, however, that the President, under his constitutional prerogative as commander in chief of the army and navy, has the right to issue rules and regulations for the guidance thereof; [30] and the

[25] These are conveniently collected in *Military Laws of the United States* (8th ed., 1939), with Supplement I thereto (1940).

[26] Lieber, *Remarks on the Army Regulations* (1898); Winthrop, *Military Law*, pp. 27 ff. At various times in the history of our country there have been compilations of the existent Army Regulations, notably that promulgated in 1881, the last revision of which appeared in 1913. The so-called "pamphlet system" of Army Regulations was instituted in 1920, whereunder all administrative regulations for the military service, whether general or special in character, are published in a single system of numbered pamphlets, superseded by new pamphlets when necessary; this is the system in force at the present time. The description of the content of Army Regulations is to be found in AR 1–15, a listing of the titles in AR 1–10, and an alphabetical arrangement thereof in AR 1–6.

[27] R.S. § 161, 5 U.S.C.A. § 22.

[28] So, for example, the regulations governing units and members of the National Guard under a call into federal service, AR 130–10.135, which carry out the provisions of the National Defense Act, sec. 101, 32 U.S.C.A. § 82, and the Public Resolution of Aug. 27, 1940, 50 U.S.C.A. App. § 402.

[29] United States v. Webster, 1840, D.C. Me., Fed. Cas. No. 16,658, 2 Ware 46; In re Griner, 1863, 16 Wis. 423; United States v. Eaton, 1892, 144 U.S. 677, 688, 12 S. Ct. 764, 36 L. Ed. 591; Laurey v. United States, 1897, 32 Ct. Cl. 259, 265.

[30] Kurtz v. Moffitt, 1885, 115 U.S. 487, 503, 6 S. Ct. 148, 29 L. Ed. 458. Cf. Lieber, *Remarks on Army Regulations*, pp. 6 ff., where Army Regulations are classified as (1) those which have received the sanction of Congress, (2) those that are made pursuant to, or in execution of, a statute, (3) those emanating from, and depending on the constitutional authority of the President as commander in chief, and (4) departmental regulations, made by virtue of the authority conferred by R.S. § 161; so also In the Matter of Major William Smith, 1888, 23 Ct. Cl. 452, 460.

MILITARY LAW AND MILITARY COURTS

Secretary of War may act as his representative in so doing.[31] Nor may Congress "in the disguise of 'rules for the government' of the Army impair the authority of the President as Commander-in-chief." [32] Consequently an Army Regulation emanating from and depending on the authority of the President as commander in chief (and by far the greater number are of this type) would seem to prevail over a Congressional enactment, where the legislature had attempted to regulate matters outside its constitutional jurisdiction.[33] In the same category as Army Regulations may be placed the General Orders, "general in application, and of permanent duration but not readily susceptible of immediate incorporation in established forms of regulations"; [34] these frequently relate more to matters of administration than to rules of conduct.

In time of war there is a certain amount of additional formulated law governing the army in its relations with the enemy, both armed and non-combatant. Outside of the scanty enactments afforded by the Declaration of Paris, the first code of the

[31] United States v. Eliason, 1842, 16 Pet. 291, 301, 10 L. Ed. 968.

[32] Swaim v. United States, 1893, 28 Ct. Cl. 173, 221.

[33] A possible conflict might have arisen in the event of an Army Regulation or General Order effecting the movement of draftees or the recently mobilized National Guard or Reserve officers beyond the limits of the Western Hemisphere; the movement of troops is an essential element of command, and has always been considered exclusively within the power of the President as commander in chief, Fleming v. Page, 1850, 9 How. 603, 615, 13 L. Ed. 276. The attempted limitation, by Congress, of service of draftees and the mobilized reserve components to the Western Hemisphere, Selective Service and Training Act of 1940, sec. 3(e), 50 U.S.C.A. App. § 303(e); Resolution of Aug. 27, 1940, sec. 1, 50 U.S.C.A. App. § 401, would therefore be unavailing. The territorial restriction was removed by Congress itself by the Act of Dec. 13, 1941, 50 U.S.C.A. App. § 731.

[34] AR 310–50.2. As intimated, General Orders are of the same status as Army Regulations, and frequently have later been issued as regulations, Maddux v. United States, 1885, 20 Ct. Cl. 193.

laws governing the conduct of an army in the field emanated from this country in the stress of the Civil War. That war will be remembered, among other things which have placed it on the pages of history, "for the issuance of the Instructions for the Government of the Armies of the United States in the Field, prepared by Dr. Francis Lieber and revised by a board of officers of the United States Army." [35] These instructions constituted, to use the language of the writer last quoted, the first comprehensive codification of the laws of war. Published in 1863,[36] by General Order No. 100 of the War Department, this code was made obligatory on the armies of the United States in their operations against the South, and was so recognized by the United States Supreme Court.[37] In 1899 the First Peace Conference codified many of the rules of war, utilizing Leiber's work to a considerable extent, and the revised code of the Second Peace Conference, known as the 1907 Hague Regulations, has been used by many of the signatory powers as the basis of instructions framed for their respective forces.[38] Our War Department issued, in 1914, Rules of Land Warfare incorporating both the written rules of war of the Hague Regulations, and unwritten rules defined by well-recognized authorities on international law and established by the custom and usage of civilized nations.[39] According to the 1940 revision,

[35] Bordwell, *Law of War between Belligerents* (1908), p. 73.
[36] Reproduced in *Regulations of the Army of the United States*, 1881, § 1319; O'Brien-Diefendorf, *General Orders of the War Department, 1861, 1862, & 1863*, II (1864), pp. 104 ff.; Birkhimer, *Military Government and Martial Law* (3d. 1914), appendix II.
[37] Ex parte Vallandigham, 1864, 1 Wall. 243, 248, 17 L. Ed. 589.
[38] Oppenheim, *International Law,* II (6th ed., 1940), pp. 178 ff., with further references.
[39] "The Rules of Land Warfare, 1914, simply consolidate the Lieber instructions, the Hague regulations, and the British Manual," Colby, 1925, 23 Mich.

although "technically each of the written rules is binding only between powers that have ratified or adhered to . . . the treaty or convention by which the rule is prescribed. . . . As a general rule they will be strictly observed and enforced by United States forces in the field, as far as applicable there, without regard to whether they are legally binding upon all of the powers immediately concerned"; [40] "the unwritten rules are binding upon all civilized nations. They will be strictly observed by our forces, subject only to such exceptions as shall have been directed by competent authority by way of legitimate reprisals for illegal conduct of the enemy." [41]

It is of interest to note that the Digest of Justinian included materials not only with respect to the governance of the army,[42] but also some provisions concerning the enemy and captured property.[43] There have always been additional laws of war, for Grotius, in this respect, was more a pioneer of progress than a law-giver of any sort. The reader need be neither of the profession of arms nor of the bar to find their mention. One has

---

L. Rev. 482, 493. Already in 1903 the British War Office had published *The Laws and Customs of War on Land,* compiled by Professor Holland; in 1912 there was issued *Land Warfare: an Exposition of the Laws and Usages of War on Land,* compiled by Colonel Edmonds and Professor Oppenheim, which was incorporated in the *British Manual of Military Law 1914;* the present British instructions are to be found in Amendment 12 (Jan. 1936) to the (War Office) *Manual of Military Law 1929.*

[40] *Rules of Land Warfare* (Basic Field Manual, FM 27-10), prepared under the direction of the Judge Advocate General.

[41] Secs. 5b, 5a.

[42] Sherman, 1919, 13 Ill. L. Rev. 581-91; Taubenschlag, "Militärstrafrecht," in *Paulys Real-Encyclopädie der classischen Altertumswissenschaft,* Vol. XV (1932), col. 1668 ff.

[43] Bordwell, *Law of War between Belligerents,* pp. 9-10; Phillipson, *International Law and Custom of ancient Greece and Rome,* II (1911), pp. 223 ff., 234 ff.

only to pick up Caesar's *Commentaries* to find Ariovistus, the German king, unctuously reminding the great Roman of certain of the customs of war then obtaining;[44] Montaigne's *Essays* are full of reflections upon the customs of war as they obtained in the days before Grotius wrote.[45] The regulations which Henry V promulgated for the guidance of the semifeudal army which he took to the field of Agincourt and the resulting occupation of large portions of France are still extant.[46] There has been growth in this body of jurisprudence of course, but it would be no true and healthy body did it not grow. From one point of view, one of our judges may be right when he says that "the rules introduced into modern warfare constitute so many voluntary relinquishments of the rights of war."[47] But, *mutatis mutandis*, the same may be said of growth in the common law. Still, no one attempted to codify this law until 1863. Lieber's Code, therefore, however open to criticism though it may be in minor points, deserves all praise as a pioneer model, and as one of the best fruits of our Civil War. The Rules of Land Warfare, superseding Lieber's Code in 1914, were the guiding principles in the relation of our forces with the enemy in World War I and undoubtedly will be faithfully observed on similar occasions in the future.[48]

[44] Caesar, *Gallic War*, Book I, chap. 44.
[45] Particularly the Fifteenth Essay.   [46] Bordwell, *Law of War*, p. 23.
[47] The Rapid, 1814, 8 Cranch 155, 161, 3 L. Ed. 520.
[48] The view has been advanced that the so-called laws of war are no laws at all, discarded by belligerent powers whenever it is to their advantage to do so, are a "mere narrative of the thwarted aspirations of people in an age-long struggle against the arbitrary and irresponsible action of governmental power," Edmunds, *The Laws of War: Their Rise in the Nineteenth Century and Their Collapse in the Twentieth*, 1929, 15 Va. L. Rev. 321. The thesis that the laws of war lose their binding force in case of extreme necessity, a view which has been generally accepted in German military circles since the

MILITARY LAW AND MILITARY COURTS 43

Let us now turn to the uncodified portions of the law. Here, once and for all, let it be noted that the common law courts fully recognize the existence of what Mr. Justice Story called "the customary military law." [49] It is not for the writer to define or classify this body of law; he would rather call to mind the words of an English colonial judge, whose view has been adopted by our Supreme Court,[50] that "of questions not de-

---

time of Clausewitz, and which apparently is still guiding today, has undoubtedly, in part, given rise to this opinion; see the German General Staff's *Kriegsbrauch im Landkriege* (1902); Garner, *German War Code* (1918), pp. 7 ff.; Oppenheim, *International Law*, II (6th ed. 1940), pp. 183 ff. If "extreme necessity" is contemplated to include instances "when violation of the laws of war alone offers, either a means of escape from extreme danger, or the realisation of the purpose of war, namely, the overpowering of the opponent" (Oppenheim, *loc. cit.*), then it may well be said that there is no such thing as the "laws" of war, Baty and Morgan, *War: Its Conduct and Legal Results* (1915), pp. 166 ff., 169. But it is to be pointed out that English, American, French, Italian, and even some German authorities on international law do not accept this principle of "military necessity," Oppenheim, *op. cit.*, p. 184 n. 1. The other escape from the laws of war, namely, the doctrine of reprisal, has also persuaded many that the laws of law are a thing of the past, Oppenheim, *op. cit.*, pp. 446 ff. It is to be hoped that the recent revisions of both the English and American rules of land warfare mean that these countries, at least, intend to faithfully observe the established laws and customs of war, whether written or unwritten. Violations thereof, cf. Garner, *International Law and the World War* (1920), *passim*, have nothing to do with the fundamental validity of the laws of war.

[49] Martin v. Mott, 1827, 12 Wheat. 19, 35, 6 L. Ed. 537.
[50] Smith v. Whitney, 1886, 116 U.S. 167, 178, 6 S. Ct. 570, 29 L. Ed. 601, quoting from Porret's Case, Perry's Oriental Cases, 414, 419. To the same effect is Kirkman v. McClaughry, 1908, C.C.A. Kan., 160 F. 436, where the court, in upholding, on habeas corpus, the validity of a cumulative sentence inflicted by a court-martial, said, at p. 439: "Doubtless, in actual practice, many common-law rules, deemed applicable to the proceedings of courts martial, have become incorporated into the customary military law, but nothing has been brought to our notice indicating that the rule relied upon by the appellant was deemed applicable to such proceedings in England, the home of the common law, or that it is recognized as a part of the customary military law

pending upon the construction of statutes, but upon military law or usage, within the jurisdiction of courts-martial, military or naval officers, from their training and experience in the service, are more competent judges than the courts of common law. This is nowhere better stated than by Mr. Justice Perry in the Supreme Court of Bombay, saying: 'And the principle of the noninterference of the courts of law with the procedure of courts-martial is clear and obvious. . . . Now this procedure is founded upon the usages and customs of war, upon the regulations issued by the Sovereign, and upon old practice in the army.' " If even "common-law judges have no opportunity, either from their law books or from the course of their experience, to inform themselves," [51] it would be presumptuous for the writer to attempt a description of this actual body of law.[52] All that can be done is to indicate its reaches.

Thus, matters of court-martial procedure not covered by the Articles of War are governed by the custom of the service. We

---

of the United States. On the contrary, we learn from recognized sources of authority that, in the military service, it is a well-established and long-continued practice to regard sentences of courts martial, such as are here under consideration, as cumulative, and to execute them consecutively, one upon the expiration of another in the order of their imposition." This decision, and the language there used, is cited with approval in Mosher v. Hudspeth, 1941, D.C. Kan., 37 F. Supp. 173, affirmed, 1941, C.C.A. Kan., 123 F. 2d 401, a case likewise involving cumulative sentences.

[51] Perry, J., in Porret's Case, quoted in Smith v. Whitney, *supra*.

[52] It is, however, doubtless true, as stated in Kirkman v. McClaughry, *supra*, note 50, "that many common law rules, deemed applicable to the proceedings of courts-martial, have become incorporated into the customary military law"; and it is interesting to see how in this connection the Anglo-American instinct for precedent has shown itself. One has only to read such standard works on military law as Winthrop or Davis to note how, over and over, precedents are cited from actual decisions or opinions rendered by the Judge Advocate General.

MILITARY LAW AND MILITARY COURTS 45

need give but a few instances.[53] The 19th Article of War does not prescribe by whom the oath shall be administered to witnesses before a court-martial; by custom it is administered by the trial judge advocate.[54] Cumulative sentences are inflicted by courts-martial, although no express authority to do so appears in the Articles of War.[55] The 96th Article of War provides for the punishment of conduct prejudicial to good order and military discipline, or of a nature to bring discredit upon the military service, although such conduct is nowhere defined in the Articles; reference must therefore be had to the unwritten law and custom of the army.[56] And again, the extent of the offense of conduct unbecoming an officer and a gentleman is determined upon the basis of military precedents and usages.[57]

To conclude the outline of the branches of military law, mention should be made of that body of law, more properly termed military government, which is applicable to the enemy, whether soldier or civilian. "Military government is the domin-

---

[53] Winthrop, *Military Law*, pp. 41 ff.; Davis, *Military Law*, pp. 10 ff.; Young, *Constitutional Powers and Limitations* (1941), pp. 80 f.

[54] Davis, *Military Law*, p. 10; Mil. Laws (5th ed. 1917), p. 586, n. 2. The capacity of the trial judge advocate to administer oaths is recognized by the act of July 27, 1892, sec. 4, 27 Stat. 278, and by A.W. 114, 10 U.S.C.A. § 1586.

[55] Kirkman v. McClaughry, 1908, C.C.A. Kan., 160 F. 436; Mosher v. Hudspeth, 1941, D.C. Kan., 37 F. Supp. 173, affirmed C.C.A. Kan., 123 F. 2d 401. In this instance there occurs an illustration of the frequent practice, today, of incorporating usages and customs in the written regulations, see AR 600–375. 15e concerning consecutive execution of sentences.

[56] *Manual for Courts-Martial*, § 152. Cf. Swaim v. United States, 1893, 28 Ct. Cl. 173, 228, 233; Winthrop, *Military Law*, pp. 720 ff., with instances of offenses within A.W. 96 [old A.W. 62] collected, pp. 726 ff.

[57] Fletcher v. United States, 1891, 26 Ct. Cl. 541, 562; 1930 Dig. Op. J.A.G. 11, 1912–40 Dig. Op. J.A.G. § 453 (6); instances of offenses under this article collected by Winthrop, *Military Law*, pp. 713 ff.

ion exercised by a belligerent power over invaded territory and the inhabitants thereof. Such a government performs its functions and discharges its obligations by what is known as martial law." [58] This distinct branch of law covers not merely the duties and obligations of the inhabitants of the captured territory, so far as the same may not be expressed in the established rules of land warfare previously referred to, but also guides our army in its government of occupied territory.[59] And lastly we have what is called by many martial law at home, or as a domestic fact, which has officially been termed [60] the exercise of military jurisdiction "by a government temporarily governing the civil population of a locality through its military forces, without the authority of written law, as necessity may require (martial law)." The enforcement of all such law is committed to military courts, but the nature of these courts must vary according to the persons subject to them.

For the punishment of all offenses committed by persons comprising part of the military establishment as defined by the Articles of War,—we have already noted the classifications of these offenses made by the Articles—the statutory code provides a system of courts whose personnel is drawn from the

---

[58] Magoon, *Law of Civil Government under Military Occupation* (1902), p. 12.

[59] Dealt with at length in chapters 6 and 7, *infra*.

[60] *Manual for Courts-Martial* (1928), p. 1. Martial law had been defined in an earlier edition of the *Manual*, 1921 ed., p. 3, as "military power exercised in time of war, insurrection or rebellion in parts of the country retaining their allegiance, and over persons and things not ordinarily subjected to it. This is an application of the doctrine of necessity to a condition of war, springing from the right of self-preservation." But it is to be noted that the nature and extent of "martial law at home" has been variously defined by the courts and text writers, most of which are conveniently collected by Rankin, *When Civil Law Fails* (1939), pp. 173 ff.

MILITARY LAW AND MILITARY COURTS 47

commissioned officers of the army. These courts are defined respectively by the Articles as general, special, and summary courts-martial.[61] A general court-martial has power to try any person subject to military law for any offense made punishable by the Articles of War, and any other person who by the law of war is subject to trial by military tribunals.[62] A special court-martial has power to try any person subject to military law for all save offenses made capital by the Articles.[63] A summary court-martial's jurisdiction is still more restricted by eliminating therefrom not merely capital offenses, but also the trial of officers, members of the Army Nurse corps, warrant officers, field clerks, privates holding a certificate of eligibility to promotion, and objecting non-commissioned officers.[64]

The procedure of these courts is prescribed by the Articles of War and by military usage.[65] Needless to say, its existence has but little of the flavor of the common law. These courts, as did all others whose origin lay without the domain of the common law, borrow their forms of procedure from the civil law, and thus trace back to Roman sources. The practice of Roman courts of justice has never departed from the memories of men of the law. Its accents persist not merely in our courts of probate and of admiralty, but in the fundamentals of equity practice;[66] and it is not strange that the procedure of courts-martial faintly shadows the same mighty tradition. Indeed, in

---

[61] A.W. 3, 10 U.S.C.A. § 1474.
[62] A.W. 12, 10 U.S.C.A. § 1483; cf. *Manual for Courts-Martial*, §§ 12–13.
[63] A.W. 13, 10 U.S.C.A. § 1484; cf. *Manual*, §§ 14–15.
[64] A.W. 14, 10 U.S.C.A. § 1485; cf. *Manual*, §§ 16–17.
[65] See Winthrop, *Military Law*, pp. 110 ff.; Davis, *Military Law*, pp. 61 ff.
[66] A comprehensive treatment of the relation of the court of chancery to civil law principles in Spence, *Equitable Jurisdiction of the Court of Chancery*, I (1846), particularly pp. 205 ff., 322 ff., 346 ff.

its early days the court-martial, the court of the Constable and Earl Marshal, enjoyed the assistance of three doctors of the civil law.[67]

This, coupled with the fact that the jurisdiction of the court-martial is essentially criminal, gives its procedure an added interest. The practice in equity is a daily reminder of the civil form of action by which the grievances of Roman citizens were redressed. But, outside of the practice in church courts, the procedure of the court-martial is the only image, in any common law country, of the practice which prevailed in the criminal prosecutions of the days of the Empire.[68] It is also interesting to note that the dual position of the judge advocate, the prosecutor in the military court, as not merely counsel for the government but also the adviser of the court, in the way of doing justice to the prisoner, is reflected by the modern office of district attorney or state prosecutor, an institution peculiar to this country. Finally, it is a matter of gratification to the common law practitioner that these courts are to follow the rules of evidence generally recognized in the trial of criminal cases in the District Courts of the United States, so far as not otherwise prescribed by Presidential regulation or act of Congress,[69] and also to follow the common law in the definition of

[67] On the history of this predecessor of the court-martial, see Hale, *History of the Common Law* (1779), pp. 33 ff.; Bacon, *Abridgement*, II (Amer. ed. 1813), pp. 151 ff.; War Office, *Manual of Military Law 1929*, pp. 7 ff.; Sherman, *Roman Law in the Modern World* (3d ed. 1937), I, p. 365.

[68] For Roman military procedure, see Mommsen, *Römisches Strafrecht* (1899), pp. 33 ff.; Costa, *Crimini e pene da Romolo a Giustiniano* (1921), pp. 183 ff.

[69] It is especially interesting to note that the chapter on evidence in both the 1917 and 1921 *Manual for Courts-Martial* had the benefit of the labors of Professor Wigmore, at those times a Reserve officer in the Judge Advocate's

MILITARY LAW AND MILITARY COURTS

crimes, so far as such crimes may also be punishable by the Articles of War.[70]

Nothing of a civil nature attaches to the jurisdiction of courts-martial, they having no power to entertain a civil suit for the redress of any injury whatsoever.[71] As long ago stated by Mr. Justice Lawrence,[72] "a court-martial cannot give damages for injurious conduct, as a jury can." It is true that if a member of the forces feels injured by the conduct of another member, a request may be made for the offices of another form of military tribunal, the court of inquiry, which, after investigating the matter, reports its conclusions; if such conclusions demonstrate to the officer convening the court of inquiry the commission of a military offense, the accused is then brought before a regular court-martial for trial.[73] But in the end all such procedure gets back to the question of criminal prosecution, and thus the idea of reparation of wrong by damages or restitution is wholly excluded.

Another essential feature of the jurisdiction of such a court is that its judgment has merely an advisory effect and no operation until it has received the approval of the officer, or his

---

Department; in the present 1928 *Manual for Courts-Martial* the chapter has been reorganized and considerably reduced.

[70] See *Manual for Courts-Martial* (1928), pp. 188 ff.; *Manual for Courts-Martial* (1921), p. 408; Winthrop, *Military Law*, p. 721.

[71] The procedure provided by A.W. 105, 10 U.S.C.A. § 1577, for the assessment of damages against persons subject to military law as redress for injuries to property, after findings by a board of investigation, has nothing to do with courts-martial and is directed to the relief of civilians injured as a result of military operations. This is but supplementary to the liability of persons in military service to civil suits for damages, dealt with in the following chapter.

[72] Warden v. Bailey (1811), 4 Taunt. 67, 78, 128 Eng. Rep. 253.

[73] A.W. 97–103. See further Winthrop, *Military Law*, pp. 516 ff.

successor in command, through whose order of appointment the court-martial received its fiat of creation.[74] In some cases there must also be confirmation by the President or some other military authority.[75] Under the present system in this country, the court does not "cease to exist" after reporting, as an English common law court held,[76] for provision has been made for reconvention of the court for the purposes of revision of its action.[77] In addition to the possibility of a rehearing before a differently constituted court-martial,[78] there is always an automatic appellate review by independent legal authority. This latter, in that the record of a trial by a general court-martial has to be referred to a staff judge advocate, and occasionally to the Judge Advocate General, to assure that the court-martial as well as the reviewing and confirming authorities comply with the law.[79] Furthermore, in cases requiring approval or confirmation by the President, the record must have been examined and an opinion rendered by a Board of Review and by the Judge Advocate General before action by the President.[80] Sentences of a general court-martial involving the penalty of

---

[74] Under A.W. 46 ff., 10 U.S.C.A. §§ 1517 ff., the appointing authority, acting in his capacity as reviewing authority, may approve or disapprove the whole or any part of a sentence, or remand a case for revision or rehearing; within the power to order the execution of a sentence is contained the power to mitigate, remit, or suspend the whole or any part thereof.

[75] A.W. 48–49, 10 U.S.C.A. §§ 1519–20. Cf. United States v. Fletcher, 1893, 148 U.S. 84, 13 S. Ct. 552, 37 L. Ed. 378.

[76] Matter of Poe (1833), 5 B. & Ad. 681, 110 Eng. Rep. 942; this is not the rule of British military practice today, for reconvention of the court for revision is authorized, War Office, *Manual of Military Law 1929*, pp. 62 ff., 652 ff.

[77] *Manual for Courts-Martial*, § 83, and p. 75.   [78] *Manual*, §§ 84, 89.
[79] *Manual*, p. 74 f.   [80] A.W. 50½, 10 U.S.C.A. § 1522.

death, dismissal not suspended, dishonorable discharge not suspended, or confinement in a penitentiary, may not be executed unless and until a Board of Review has held that the record of the trial upon which the sentence is based is legally sufficient to support the sentence.[81] Finally, the record of trials by general courts-martial are submitted to the Judge Advocate General's Office, and if found legally insufficient, are examined by the Board of Review, and ultimately submitted to the Secretary of War for action by the President.[82] Thus, it can be said that there is no final judgment in the case until there has been independent examination of the proceedings and approval of the sentence of the court-martial.

The underlying reason for this is very interesting. The military court, in effect, renders no judgment, it merely recommends that a judgment be rendered. Strictly speaking, a court-martial is not a court in the full sense of the term, certainly not as understood in the civil phraseology. True, facts are judicially determined according to established rules of evidence which reflect the criminal procedure of the civil federal courts, and the safeguards afforded the civil accused are substantially those provided the accused soldier.[83] But courts-martial are

---

[81] A.W. 50½, 10 U.S.C.A. § 1522.

[82] A.W. 50½, 10 U.S.C.A. § 1522. The safeguards afforded by the requirement of reference to the staff judge advocate and the automatic review by a Board of Review are among the most important revisions of the 1920 Articles of War, cf. Ansell, 1922, 32 Yale L.J. 146; Taylor, 1926, 12 Va. L. Rev. 463. Descriptive treatment of the "appellate" procedure of courts-martial, recently by Hoover, *Legal Essays to Orrin Kip McMurray* (1935), pp. 165, 176 ff.; King, 1941 Wisc. L. Rev. 311, 334 ff.

[83] Privilege against self-incrimination, A.W. 24, 10 U.S.C.A. § 1495; against double jeopardy, A.W. 40, U.S.C.A. § 1511. See generally Sabel, 1941, 25 Minn. L. Rev. 323.

not part of the federal judiciary within the Constitution, but are rather instrumentalities of the executive power.[84] Essentially, therefore, the powers of judgment and of punishment are intertwined with the power of direction. The common law conception of a court whose judgments are self-executing is wholly lacking. There is, of course, the fact that originally by custom and, since the first Mutiny Act in England, by statute the soldier has the right to a reference of his case to a court-martial, and to go free of punishment unless that body finds him guilty of the acts for which punishment is eventually awarded. But obviously the mere fact, that a court-martial derives its power from statute, does not alter its essential character as a referee rather than a court of oyer and terminer.[85]

The Articles of War are careful not to exclude from their prescriptions relating to courts-martial as above defined, "mili-

---

[84] Dynes v. Hoover, 1857, 20 How. 65, 79, 15 L. Ed. 838: "These provisions [Constitution, Art. 1, sect. 8; Art. 2, sect. 2; 5th Amend.] show that Congress has the power to provide for the trial and punishment of military and naval offences in the manner then and now practiced by civilized nations; and that the power to do so is given without any connection between it and the 3d article of the Constitution defining the judicial power of the United States; indeed, that the two powers are entirely independent of each other"; cf. Kurtz v. Moffitt, 1885, 115 U.S. 487, 500, 6 S. Ct. 148, 29 L. Ed. 458; State ex rel. Lanng v. Long, 1914, 136 La. 1, 66 So. 377, L.R.A. 1915E, 235, Ann. Cas. 1917B, 240. See generally Winthrop, *Military Law*, pp. 48 ff.; Hoover, *Essays to Orrin Kip McMurray*, pp. 165, 172 ff.

[85] In passing it should be noted that the American military law does not know the "drum-head" court-martial, now the field general court-martial of the English law. For the summary trial of offenses without written charges, originally no record was kept unless capital sentence was imposed; this practice was the vital issue in Rex v. Wall, 1802, 28 How. St. Tr. 51. Now, however, "such written record as seems practicable must be kept," Rules of Procedure, § 107 [War Office, *Manual of Military Law*, p. 681]. Generally on the field general court-martial of present-day Britain, see the War Office *Manual*, pp. 67 f., 476 f., 680 ff.

MILITARY LAW AND MILITARY COURTS

tary commissions, provost courts, or other military tribunals of concurrent jurisdiction in respect of offenders or offenses that by statute or by the law of war may be triable" by such courts.[86] The jurisdiction of these courts relates to matters of military occupation and martial law of which we shall hereafter speak. It is enough to say here that in all matters of procedure, they are governed by the practice obtaining in regular courts-martial of the class above described.

[86] A.W. 15, 10 U.S.C.A. § 1486.

4. THE ARMY'S RIGHT OF SELF-REGULATION

OUR investigation has shown, it is to be hoped, that so far as its laws and the correlative rights of its members are concerned the functioning of the army should be a matter of self-control. The commission of offenses against the law and custom of the army, on the part of persons who are members of it, is to be judged by the governing powers of that organization, sitting in that respect in a judicial capacity; and the sanction of such laws is also a matter entirely within the control of the organization. One's first impression, therefore, might be that a common law court can find no starting point of review in a controversy involving the commission of a military offense if all the parties to that controversy are members of the army.

But the question whether a particular controversy was one within this exclusive jurisdiction or not might well involve a question of fact or of law. The jurisdiction of a court-martial depends upon whether the particular delinquent was or was not a member of the forces. Likewise the decision or act of a commander would depend for its immunity from common law adjudication upon whether or not it was justified by the powers conferred upon that commander by the custom and statutes governing the organization of the army.

Now the determination of that question cannot be left to

the military court or to the commander, because to do that would be to deny the very proposition that there are limits to the court-martial's jurisdiction or the commander's powers, which of course there are. Consequently it is for the common law court to decide, in the particular case, whether the military court had jurisdiction or the commander had power to act. Naturally the common law court will not make such a decision unless somebody having interest in the premises invokes its decision.

That can be done in a number of ways. First, as to the court-martial: If a party is imprisoned under the judgment of a special court, he has the right by means of a writ of habeas corpus to test the question whether the special court had the power so to commit him.[1] If the court has not yet proceeded to judgment, the application for the writ of habeas corpus will ordinarily not be entertained.[2] Further, the alleged delinquent may bring an action for damages against the officer of the court who

[1] Of the numerous instances of such a method we may mention Rose ex rel. Carter v. Roberts, 1900, C.C.A. N.Y., 99 F. 948; Deming v. McClaughry, 1902, C.C.A. Kan., 113 F. 639, 649, affirmed McClaughry v. Deming, 1902, 186 U.S. 49, 22 S. Ct. 786, 46 L. Ed. 1049; Collins v. McDonald, 1922, 258 U.S. 416, 42 S. Ct. 326, 66 L. Ed. 692; United States ex rel. Harris v. Daniels, 1922, C.C.A. N.Y., 279 F. 844. Further cases digested, Mil. Laws (1929 ed.), pp. 568 ff.

[2] In re Davison, 1884, C.C. N.Y., 21 F. 618; United States ex rel. Wessels v. McDonald, 1920, D.C. N.Y., 265 F. 754. Some cases, like Ex parte Houghton, 1904, C.C. Me., 129 F. 239, have held that the civil court, having first got jurisdiction by reason of the writ, supersedes subsequent proceedings by the military authorities to punish for military offenses committed either before or after the writ issued, but the majority view now is that arrest and confinement, preparatory to trial by court-martial, is a good answer to the writ, Ex parte Lewkowitz, 1908, C.C. N.Y., 163 F. 646; United States v. Williford, 1915, C.C.A. N.Y., 220 F. 291. Note that a writ will not issue where there is merely moral restraint, rather than actual confinement, Wales v. Whitney, 1885, 114 U.S. 564, 5 S. Ct. 1050, 29 L. Ed. 277.

executes its judgment of punishment upon him.[3] Second, as to the act of an officer: If the person injured by that act believes that it was not justified by any lawful authority, he may bring an action for damages against the officer in question.

In this connection, however, our dual system of federal courts and state courts intrudes itself. The state courts have no power by means of habeas corpus to take the body of a prisoner, held for court-martial, from the custody of the officer detaining him, and hence they must dismiss the writ when a return is made showing that the prisoner is held under the authority of the United States or color thereof.[4] And in like manner our statutory Articles of War provide [5] that any civil or criminal prosecution, commenced in a state court "against any officer, soldier, or other person in the military service of the United States on account of any act done under color of his office or status, or in respect to which he claims any right, title, or authority under any law of the United States respecting the military forces thereof, or under the law of war," may be removed for trial into the United States District Court in the district where the suit or prosecution is pending. But the federal courts also administer the common law; so the statutes give only a choice of civil courts, nothing more.

Now, as to the case where an inferior claims that he has been injured by the conduct of a superior: the defendant must show whether he acted by the explicit order of one still higher, or

---

[3] Instances of such actions may be found in Wise v. Withers, 1806, 3 Cr. 331, 2 L. Ed. 457, and Dynes v. Hoover, 1857, 20 How. 65, 15 L. Ed. 838.

[4] In re Neill, 1871, D.C. N.Y., Fed. Cas. No. 10089; Tarble's Case, 1872, 13 Wall. 397, 20 L. Ed. 597; and generally Ableman v. Booth, 1858, 21 How. 506, 16 L. Ed. 169.

[5] A.W. 117, 10 U.S.C.A. § 1589.

ARMY'S RIGHT OF SELF-REGULATION

under the general authority of standing orders, the regulations, or the Articles of War.[6] In the latter case the question he presents is whether his act was within his jurisdiction or *ultra vires;* but in the former case his act was purely ministerial and must be justified as such.

Considering the case of acting under explicit orders, the defendant is in no different position from any other person acting in a ministerial capacity, and is entitled to the same measure of protection that the common law gives in such cases.

The common law view of such a matter is clear. The orders of a superior to commit a wrong do not excuse the commission of it. But the duty of obedience must carry a certain weight, at least when that duty springs from the obligation of public service rather than of contract. From this consideration has grown the rule that a ministerial officer, when executing an order or process "fair on its face," is not liable in damages should it develop that the process or direction should in fact not have been issued.[7]

There is no reason, according to the weight of authority, why this rule should not apply to the soldier, as concerns a ministerial rather than a discretionary act. Obedience is, as we have seen, recognized by common law courts as of the very essence of military service. If, then, the orders on their face show the authority of the power which issued them to issue them and are invalidated only by some extraneous fact to

---

[6] Summaries of the cases involving liability of soldiers *inter sese* in the annotations in L.R.A. 1915A, 1148, 1157; Ann. Cas. 1917C, 23; most recently, 135 A.L.R. 27, 31, 45. See also Winthrop, *Military Law*, pp. 880 ff., and for English law, War Office, *Manual of Military Law 1929*, pp. 149 ff.

[7] See Chegaray v. Jenkins, 1851, 5 N.Y. 376; Curtiss v. Witt, 1896, 110 Mich. 131, 67 N.W. 1106; Board of Education v. Jeppson, 1929, 74 Utah 576, 280 P. 1065.

which they bear no reference, then the officer who acts under them is protected from an action by the inferior who is injured by the operation of these orders when carried into effect. That is the decision of Mr. Justice Willes, one of the greatest of common law judges, in *Keighly v. Bell*,[8] where the plaintiff, a captain in the British service, sued the defendant, a major general therein. In granting a non-suit Mr. Justice Willes expressed the opinion that "a soldier, acting honestly in the discharge of his duty—that is, acting in obedience to the orders of his commanding officer—is not liable for what he does, unless it be shown that the orders were such as were obviously illegal. He must justify any direct violation of the personal rights of another person by showing, not only that he had orders, but that the orders were such as he was bound to obey." The rule in our country seems to be to the same effect. Despite the rather broad language in *Little v. Barreme*,[9] the soldier, like any other public officer, is protected by orders not palpably illegal.[10] There seems to have been no case in this country directly concerning civil suit by a member of the military forces against his immediate superior for injuries suffered as a result of the execution of an apparently legal order by the superior.[11] As a

[8] 1866, 4 F. & F. 763, 805, 176 Eng. Rep. 781.
[9] 1804, 2 Cranch 170, 178, 2 L. Ed. 243.
[10] Riggs v. State, 1866, 3 Cold. (Tenn.) 85; McCall v. McDowell, 1867, C.C. Cal., 1 Abb. (U.S.) 212, 218, Fed. Cas. No. 8673; United States v. Clark, 1887, C.C. Mich., 31 F. 710; Neu v. McCarthy, 1941, 309 Mass. 17, 22, 33 N.E. 2d 570, with further citation of cases and comment, and notes thereto in 1941, 36 Ill. L. Rev. 361, and 21 Boston U. L. Rev. 564.
[11] Almost in point are the cases involving the liability of an officer executing the sentence of a court-martial which did not have jurisdiction of the plaintiff: thus in Barrett v. Crane, 1844, 16 Vt. 246, a quartermaster was held liable in a civil suit for the execution of a sentence where the plaintiff was an alien and consequently not within the court-martial's jurisdiction; in the reverse

matter of fact, civil suit where both plaintiff and defendant are military personnel turns upon the second of the situations presented above, whether the defendant acted under the general authority of army orders or regulations, Articles of War, and the like, to which matter we now turn.

The liability of an officer who is acting within the exercise of discretionary power is wholly a question of *ultra vires* or *intra vires*—a question, in short, of jurisdiction. That question, from the viewpoint of a common law court, depends entirely upon the scope of the defendant's powers as defined by the law of the army, whether that law be found in the Constitution, or in the codified or the uncodified portions of the military law. This rule applies to all persons in the service, from the President, its commander in chief, down through the noncommissioned officer.

When Congress has conferred upon the President power to draft the militia into the national service, whenever a national exigency requires it, then the President is vested with jurisdiction to decide whether an emergency has arisen of a nature justifying his calling the draft. Such was the decision in *Martin v. Mott*,[12] where Mr. Justice Story, speaking for the court,

---

situation, where the court-martial had jurisdiction, there was no liability of the officer levying on the plaintiff's property for a fine imposed, Brown v. Wadsworth, 1843, 15 Vt. 170, 40 Am. Dec. 674. However, it is to be noted that in these cases the plaintiff considers himself a civilian, and thus the matter has little to do with self-regulation within the military forces. Likewise, actions against a civil official for executing an illegal sentence of a court-martial are not in point, Hutton v. Blaine, 1815, 2 Serg. & R. (Pa.) 75; Mills v. Martin, 1821, 19 Johns. (N.Y.) 7; and the leading case of Dynes v. Hoover, 1857, 20 How. 65, 15 L. Ed. 838.

[12] 1827, 12 Wheat. 19, 6 L. Ed. 537, approving the like holding in Vanderheyden v. Young, 1814, 11 Johns. (N.Y.) 150, and thus contradicting the principle laid down in 1812 by the Justices of the Supreme Judicial Court of

said: "that the authority to decide whether the exigency has arisen, belongs exclusively to the President, and that his decision is conclusive upon all other persons. . . . If a superior officer has a right to contest the orders of the President upon his own doubts as to the exigency having arisen, it must be equally the right of every inferior officer and soldier; and any act done by any person in furtherance of such orders would subject him to responsibility in a civil suit, in which his defence must finally rest upon his ability to establish the facts by competent proofs. Such a course would be subversive of all discipline, and expose the best disposed officers to the chances of ruinous litigation."

It is so all the way down: The defendant must show, to avoid the condemnation of a common law court, that the act which he directed, or the decision which he made, was within the scope of the powers conferred upon him. He must derive those powers from one or the other of the sources of law and authority governing the existence and operations of the army. If he cannot do so, there is but one view that the common law court can take. The act, not being justified by any portion of military law or regulation, naturally cannot find any justification in any principle of common law. So, for example, the captain of a militia company is liable in trespass for having issued a warrant against a private soldier in that company, for a fine "legally imposed," where nothing appeared on the face of the warrant to show that he had jurisdiction to

---

Massachusetts, 8 Mass. 548, that the right to call forth the militia was exclusively vested in the commanders in chief of the militia of the several states, namely, the governors thereof, and neither Congress nor the President had any rights therein.

do so;[13] and a member of a National Guard company is entitled to damages for false imprisonment where the officer, in times of peace, summarily punished him without having recourse to the procedure provided by the military code of the state.[14]

If, however, the act directed or the decision taken is within the scope of the officer's authority, then the injured inferior has no cause of action in the civil courts. A commander is not liable for assault and battery for restraining the plaintiff by tying him to a gun for failure to perform military duties, since such method of restraint is authorized by military usage.[15] Nor will mere error of judgment deprive the officer of the protection of his office. The case of *Dinsman v. Wilkes* [16] illustrates this proposition. If, at sea, a sailor should claim that the time of his enlistment had expired, and that he should thenceforth be carried as a passenger or put ashore, it is for the commander to judge this question. In the absence of bad faith, the decision of the commander is final and the sailor has no right of action against him for damages resulting from his continued detention. "If in his judgment the plaintiff was entitled to his discharge, it was his duty to give it, even if it was inconvenient to weaken the force he commanded. But if he believed he was not entitled, it was his duty to detain him in the service. Captain Wilkes might err in his decision. But that decision, for the time being, was final and conclusive; and it was the duty of

[13] Hall v. Howd, 1835, 10 Conn. 514, 27 Am. Dec. 696.
[14] Nixon v. Reeves, 1896, 65 Minn. 159, 67 N.W. 989, 33 L.R.A. 506; similarly, members of courts-martial have been held liable in civil actions, where the court-martial acted without jurisdiction, see *supra*, note 11.
[15] Schuneman v. Diblee, 1817, 14 Johns. (N.Y.) 235.
[16] 1851, 12 How. 390, 13 L. Ed. 1036; cf. the earlier case of Wilkes v. Dinsman, 1849, 7 How. 89, 12 L. Ed. 618.

the plaintiff to submit to it, as the judgment of the tribunal which he was bound by law to obey; and for any error of judgment in this respect, no action would lie against the defendant." Similarly, in an earlier English case,[17] where a commanding officer had arrested and imprisoned a sergeant in order to bring him before a general court-martial upon the charges of uttering words amounting to disorderly conduct to the prejudice of good order and military discipline, such action was held justifiable even though the words uttered referred to an order made by the commanding officer which he was not competent to make and although the sergeant was acquitted by the court-martial. Consequently, the sergeant failed in an action for damages against the commanding officer.[18] Whether the plaintiff was guilty of the acts charged before the court-martial was immaterial; the question was whether these acts, if shown, were such as constituted an offense justiceable before the court-martial; and the officer acted within the scope of his powers when, in the reasonable belief that such acts had been committed, he ordered the arrest of his subordinate for the action of the court-martial.[19]

Only one thing may deprive the superior of the protection which he derives from his office, and this is express malice.

[17] Bailey v. Warden, 1815, 4 M. & S. 400, 105 Eng. Rep. 882.
[18] The earlier case of Warden v. Bailey, 1811, 4 Taunt. 67, 128 Eng. Rep. 253, where the verdict of the lower court for the defendant commanding officer was set aside and a new trial ordered, relates primarily to the general question of the right of an inferior to maintain a civil action against his superior for acts done under the color of military authority; this subject is dealt with in the following paragraphs.
[19] To a similar effect is the case of Ferris v. Armstrong, 1813, 10 Johns. (N.Y.) 100, and the charge of Dillon, J., in Holmes v. Sheridan, 1870, C.C. Kan., Fed. Cas. No. 6644.

ARMY'S RIGHT OF SELF-REGULATION 63

The question has been before American courts only infrequently, and since it has received considerable attention at the hands of English judges, which cases in turn have formed the basis of the few American decisions, it is well to summarize briefly the somewhat erratic course of this phase of an officer's liability to his inferior.[20] In *Wall v. Macnamara*,[21] an action for damages by reason of illegal imprisonment, evidence was introduced to show that imprisonment of the plaintiff authorized by reason of disobedience of orders, was illegally prolonged and aggravated by several circumstances of cruelty. In summing up, Lord Mansfield said: "The principal inquiry to be made by a court of justice is, how the heart stood; and if there appears to be nothing wrong there great latitude will be allowed for misapprehension or mistake. But, on the other hand, if the heart is wrong, if cruelty, malice, and oppression appear to have occasioned or aggravated the imprisonment or other injury complained of, they shall not cover themselves with the thin veil of legal forms, nor escape, under the cover of a justification the most technically regular, from that punishment which it is your province and your duty to inflict on so scandalous an abuse of public trust." [22] The jury found a verdict for the plaintiff, with an award of £1000 damages. The case suggests that if military authority is exercised within legal limits, yet with excessive severity or cruelty, the abuse may amount to "excess" of jurisdiction. Cases in the years immediately following are in accord.[23]

[20] Cf. War Office, *Manual of Military Law 1929*, pp. 150 ff.; O'Sullivan, *Military Law and the Supremacy of the Civil Courts* (1921).
[21] 1779, cited in 1 T.R. 536, 99 Eng. Rep. 1239, and 172 Eng. Rep. 72 note *.
[22] Cited in Johnstone v. Sutton, 1 T.R. 510, 536, 99 Eng. Rep. 1225.
[23] Grant v. Shard, cited in 4 Taunt. 85, 128 Eng. Rep. 260; Swinton v. Malloy,

But then came the famous case of *Sutton v. Johnstone*.[24] The plaintiff was captain of a ship forming part of a squadron commanded by the defendant, in action with the enemy. The defendant ordered the plaintiff to slip his cable in order to engage the enemy, which the plaintiff failed to do. The defendant suspended the plaintiff from command, put him under arrest, and kept him thus until his trial by court-martial on the charge of disobedience of orders and the "delay of the public service." The court-martial acquitted the plaintiff, and he thereupon sued for damages from the defendant, for having maliciously and without probable cause imprisoned him, charged him with crime, and held him for court-martial. The case was twice tried, with verdicts for the plaintiff in both cases. On motion, the Court of Exchequer upheld the lower court, affirming the absence of probable cause for the defendant's action, and categorically denied the validity of defendant's argument, which was that "no action for a malicious prosecution will lie for a subordinate officer against the commander of a squadron for improper conduct while under his command; or, as put by one of the counsel, no action lies for a subordinate officer against

---

1783, cited in 1 T.R. 537, 99 Eng. Rep. 1239. In the earlier case of Barwis v. Keppel, 1766, 2 Wils. K.B. 314, 95 Eng. Rep. 831, where a verdict for damages against a commander for maliciously reducing a sergeant to the rank of private—the court-martial had thought suspension for a month sufficient—for neglect of duty during active service abroad, was not allowed to stand, the court said, p. 318: "By the Act of Parliament to punish mutiny and desertion the King's power to make Articles of War is confined to his own dominions; when the army is out of his dominions, he acts by virtue of his prerogative, and without the statute or Articles of War; and therefore you cannot argue upon either of them, for they are both to be laid out of this case, and flagrante bello, the common law has never interfered with the army: inter arma silent leges. We think (as at present advised) we have no jurisdiction at all in this case."

[24] Exch. 1786, 1 T.R. 493, 99 Eng. Rep. 1215.

ARMY'S RIGHT OF SELF-REGULATION

his superior officer, for an act done in the course of discipline, and under powers incident to his situation." [25] On appeal, however, the Court of Exchequer Chamber held that the plaintiff could not recover,[26] and this was affirmed by the House of Lords.[27] The Exchequer Chamber decided that there was no question but that the defendant had probable cause for his action, and that therefore the plaintiff must fail, but went on, wholly unnecessarily to the decision of the case, to point out that an undue delay (if any) in bringing Sutton to court-martial was a mere military offense, and further that even in the absence of probable cause an action would not lie, on the ground that if commanding officers abused their discretionary powers, the persons aggrieved had their proper remedy under military law and before a military tribunal.[28]

Whatever the hesitation of the higher courts in the case of *Sutton v. Johnstone*,[29] the dictum so broadly expressed therein became the guiding rule through the whole of the nineteenth century and well into the twentieth, namely, no civil action will lie against a superior officer for an act done in the ordinary course of duty, even if done maliciously and without reasonable and probable cause.[30] Not until the case of *Heddon v.*

[25] Eyre, B., at 1 T.R. 502.
[26] Johnstone v. Sutton, Exch. Ch. 1785, 1 T.R. 510, 99 Eng. Rep. 1225.
[27] Sutton v. Johnstone, Dom. Proc. 1787, 1 T.R. 784, 99 Eng. Rep. 1377.
[28] Lord Mansfield, who delivered the opinion in Wall v. Macnamara, *supra*, was here of the opinion that Sutton could in no case succeed; it is difficult to see the distinction between "cruelty in exercising jurisdiction" and "malice in exercising jurisdiction."
[29] The Lords in the Exchequer Chamber were doubtful as to the validity of their dictum, 1 T.R. 550, and Lawrence, J. states, 4 Taunt. 75, that the reasons assigned by the Exchequer Chamber were not adopted by the House of Lords.
[30] In re Mansergh, 1861, 1 Best & Smith, 121 Eng. Rep. 764; Dawkins v. Lord Rokeby, 1866, 4 F. & F. 806, 841, 176 Eng. Rep. 800; Dawkins v. Lord Paulet,

Evans [31] was the problem re-examined, and it was there decided that the doctrine was not intended to infringe fundamental common law rights. Mr. Justice McCardie did not believe that the "famous" words of Chief Baron Kelly, in *Dawkins v. Lord Rokeby:* "With reference to questions which are purely of a military character . . . all authorities show that a case involving questions of military duty alone are cognizable only by a military tribunal and not by a court of law," meant that in no case did an officer or soldier have recourse to a court of law; rather, he summarized the principles which should be guiding as follows: "First. A military tribunal or officer will be liable to an action for damages if when acting in excess of, or without, jurisdiction, it or he does, or directs to be done, to a military man, whether officer or private, an act which amounts to assault, false imprisonment, or other common law wrong, even though the injury purports to be done in the course of actual military discipline. Secondly, if the act causing the injury to person or liberty be within jurisdiction and in the course of military discipline no action will lie upon the ground only that such act has been done maliciously and without reasonable and probable cause." [32] Such is the law of England today, for only the House of Lords is free to hold that an action would lie solely on the ground of mali-

---

1869, L.R. 5 Q.B. 94, 107, 118; Dawkins v. Lord Rokeby, 1873, L.R. 8 Q.B. 255, 271, affirmed 1875, L.R. 7 H.L. 744, 749; Marks v. Frogley, [1898] 1 Q.B. 396, 888; Rex v. Army Council ex parte Ravenscourt, [1917] 2 K.B. 504, 513. In Fraser v. Balfour, 1918, 34 T.L.R. 502, the House of Lords did not affirm the wider proposition laid down by the Exchequer Chamber, and ruled that the point was still open to argument in the House of Lords.

[31] 1919, 35 T.L.R. 642.

[32] The dictum of Baron Kelly is quoted, *loc. cit.*, at p. 642, and the conclusions of Justice McCardie at p. 645.

ARMY'S RIGHT OF SELF-REGULATION 67

cious abuse of military authority without reasonable and probable cause, and it has not changed the principles enunciated in *Heddon v. Evans.*

As indicated earlier, civil suits for malicious prosecution against superior officers have been exceedingly infrequent in American courts. In *Holmes v. Sheridan* [33] Circuit Judge Dillon was careful to point out that recovery could be had if there had been malice, while in other cases, actions for assault and false imprisonment, the doctrine of *Sutton v. Johnstone* was carefully distinguished, and held not to be extended to this situation.[34] The question, however, has directly arisen in the recent case of *Wright v. White.*[35] The plaintiff, a warrant officer in the National Guard, was charged with violation of certain of the Articles of War by the defendant adjutant general and another and was held for court-martial. Upon a directed judgment of acquittal on all charges, the plaintiff brought a suit for malicious prosecution. Unfortunately the court was only referred to *Sutton v. Johnstone* and the cases following the doctrine there laid down.[36] The Oregon court permits of no inquiry, in civil suit, into the motive of superior

---

[33] 1870, 1 Dill. 351, 357, Fed. Cas. No. 6644.
[34] In Wilson v. Mackenzie, 1845, 7 Hill (N.Y.) 95, 42 Am. Dec. 51, Sutton v. Johnstone was distinguished, and Wall v. Macnamara followed, in allowing plaintiff to recover for a personal wrong committed by his commander under color of naval discipline; In Dinsman v. Wilkes, 1851, 12 How. 390, 402, 13 L. Ed. 1036, Sutton v. Johnstone was not to be extended, and it was held a question for the jury to determine that if, from malice, the commander inflicted punishment beyond that which in his sober judgment he would have thought necessary, he would be liable in an action for assault and false imprisonment.
[35] 1941, 166 Ore. 136, 110 P. 2d 948, 135 A.L.R. 1.
[36] Particularly Dawkins v. Lord Rokeby, 4 F. & F. 406, and Dawkins v. Lord Paulet, L.R. 5 Q.B. 94.

officers in exercising their authority to order courts-martial [37] and states, categorically but erroneously, "The rule first announced by Lord Mansfield as dictum and later adopted as judicial decision has stood undisturbed for more than one hundred and fifty years in this country and England; and apparently, to refer again to Lord Mansfield's language, it has never entered the head of any one in the United States to bring such an action, or, at any rate, to test in an appellate court the right to maintain it. . . . And we are of the opinion that it is quite as essential to the fearless and independent exercise of the authority conferred upon officers of the army and navy to enforce military discipline that they be free from the apprehension of vexatious suits grounded upon their official acts, as it is that a like immunity should be enjoyed by the judges of our civil courts." [38] The court further points out that a remedy is afforded by the Articles of War themselves,[39] and then proceeding to show that the complaint discloses that the defendants acted in the line of duty and within the scope of their authority, affirms the lower court's judgment for the defendants on the pleadings.

The other phase of the common law's interference with the army's right of self-regulation is evidenced by the well-

[37] Citing 2 Cooley on Torts, 4th ed., 426, § 312. If this privilege is intended to be extended only to officers of a court-martial, there seems to be no authority for such a rule, cf. Winthrop, *Military Law*, p. 880 f., citing Frye v. Ogle, 1743, 1 McArthur on Courts-Martial 406, but cf. note, 1941, 55 Harv. L. Rev. 651 n. 2.
[38] Wright v. White, 166 Ore. 136, 148, 110 Pac. 2d 948.
[39] A.W. 121, 10 U.S.C.A. § 1593, which dates back to provisions in the Code of James II (1688) is both antiquated and inadequate, see Winthrop, *Military Law*, pp. 600 ff., and very infrequently resorted to, cf. 1912–40 Dig. Op. J.A.G. § 479.

established but strictly limited judicial review of the proceedings and determinations of military tribunals.[40] The common law court asks only one question, Did the court-martial have jurisdiction?—and guides its own conduct accordingly. If it did not, then the court must, on a habeas corpus proceeding, discharge the petitioner from custody, or in an action for damages proceed to judgment. "If a court martial," says the Supreme Court, "has no jurisdiction over the subject matter of the charge it has been convened to try, or shall inflict a punishment forbidden by the law, though its sentence shall be approved by the officers having a revisory power of it, civil courts may, on an action by a party aggrieved by it, inquire into the want of the court's jurisdiction, and give him redress." [41] It follows then that there is one issue of fact or of law which the court-martial cannot conclusively determine, and that is the question of jurisdiction. This is clearly shown by such cases as *Wise v. Withers* [42] and *Martin v. Mott*.[43]

In both these cases the plaintiff brought suit against the officer who executed the judgment of a court-martial, the judgment taking the form of a fine. The officer, to satisfy the fine, levied upon the plaintiff's goods. In *Martin v. Mott* the plaintiff brought replevin for the goods, and in *Wise v. Withers* the plaintiff brought an action of trespass for damages. The plaintiff failed to recover in *Martin v. Mott* because the Supreme Court held that he, being a member of the New York militia, was subject to the jurisdiction of the court-martial from the

---

[40] Two recent studies of the judicial review of courts-martial, Covington, 1939, 7 Geo. Wash. L. Rev. 503–13, and Stein, 1941, 11 Brooklyn L. Rev. 30–62, afford reference to the cases dealing with this subject.
[41] Dynes v. Hoover, 1857, 20 How. 65, 82, 15 L. Ed. 838.
[42] 1806, 3 Cranch 331, 2 L. Ed. 457.   [43] 1827, 12 Wheat. 19, 6 L. Ed. 537.

moment when the order was issued drafting the New York militia into the national service. The court therefore having jurisdiction, the sole question involved in the replevin action was determined against the plaintiff. In *Wise v. Withers,* on the contrary, the plaintiff was a justice of the peace of the District of Columbia, and the question was whether or not he was such a judicial officer as to be exempt from militia duty in the District under the Militia Act, relating to the District, of March 3, 1803. The Supreme Court held that a justice of the peace was a judicial officer, and hence the court-martial had no jurisdiction to impose the fine; the court saying: "It follows, from this opinion, that a court martial has no jurisdiction over a justice of the peace, as a militiaman; he could never be legally enrolled; and it is a principle, that a decision of such a tribunal, in a case clearly without its jurisdiction, cannot protect the officer who executes it. The court and the officer are all trespassers." [44]

More frequently habeas corpus proceedings are utilized to test the validity of the jurisdiction of a court-martial. If the court has been legally constituted,[45] if it has jurisdiction of the person [46] and of the offense,[47] if it has proceeded in ac-

[44] Wise v. Withers, 1806, 3 Cranch 331, 337.
[45] Martin v. Mott, *supra*, note 43; Swaim v. United States, 1897, 165 U.S. 553, 17 S. Ct. 448, 41 L. Ed. 823; Deming v. McClaughry, 1902, C.C.A. Kan., 113 F. 639, affirmed McClaughry v. Deming, 1902, 186 U.S. 49, 22 S. Ct. 786, 46 L. Ed. 1049; Ex parte Givins, 1920, D.C. Ga., 262 F. 702, affirmed Givens v. Zerbst, 1921, 255 U.S. 11, 18, 41 S. Ct. 227, 65 L. Ed. 475. Cf. Winthrop, *Military Law*, pp. 57 ff., 70 ff.
[46] Runkle v. United States, 1884, 19 Ct. Cls. 396, 407, reversed on other grounds, 1886, 122 U.S. 543, 7 S. Ct. 1141, 30 L. Ed. 1167; In re Craig, 1895, C.C. Kan., 70 F. 969; Ex parte Gerlach, 1917, D.C. N.Y., 247 F. 616; Kahn v. Anderson, 1921, 255 U.S. 1, 7, 41 S. Ct. 224, 65 L. Ed. 469.
[47] Dynes v. Hoover, cit. *supra* note 41, at p. 82; Ex parte Mason, 1881, 105

ARMY'S RIGHT OF SELF-REGULATION

cordance with statutory regulations,[48] and if it has imposed no sentence beyond its legal powers,[49] then the collateral attack afforded at the hearing on the writ will be of no avail. Absolute want of power, not defective exercise thereof, is the determining factor.[50] If jurisdiction is found to be lacking, the sentence is void and the petitioner is released from custody.[51] But the general rule, repeatedly recognized, is well expressed by the Supreme Court, that "the acts of a court-martial, within the scope of its jurisdiction and duty, cannot be controlled or reviewed in the civil courts, by writ of prohibition or otherwise." [52]

A court-martial may err in matters of evidence, but no common law court can say that its judgment was void for that.[53] It may err in its conception of the elements of the crime charged, yet if it has jurisdiction to try the accused, its error,

---

U.S. 696, 699, 26 L. Ed. 1213; In re McVey, 1885, D.C. Cal., 23 F. 878; Carter v. McClaughry, 1902, 183 U.S. 365, 381, 22 S. Ct. 181, 46 L. Ed. 236.

[48] Ex parte Dickey, 1913, D.C. Me., 204 F. 322, 325; Johnson v. Biddle, 1926, C.C.A. Kan., 12 F. 2d 366, 369; Carter v. Woodring, 1937, App. D.C., 92 F. 2d 544, 546.

[49] Swaim v. United States, 1893, 28 Ct. Cls. 173, 233; Rose ex rel. Carter v. Roberts, 1900, C.C.A. N.Y., 99 F. 948; Sanford v. Robbins, 1940, C.C.A. Ga., 115 F. 2d 435.

[50] Carter v. McClaughry, cit. *supra* note 47, at p. 401.

[51] Dynes v. Hoover, cit. *supra* note 41, at p. 81; Keyes v. United States, 1883, 109 U.S. 336, 3 S. Ct. 202, 27 L. Ed. 954; United States ex rel. Harris v. Daniels, 1922, C.C.A. N.Y., 279 F. 844.

[52] Smith v. Whitney, 1886, 116 U.S. 167, 177, 6 S. Ct. 570, 29 L. Ed. 601. Thus, neither mandamus, United States ex rel. French v. Weeks, 1922, 259 U.S. 326, 335, 42 S. Ct. 505, 66 L. Ed. 965; nor certiorari, In re Vidal, 1900, 179 U.S. 126, 21 S. Ct. 48, 45 L. Ed. 118. On the use of the extraordinary remedies in England, see War Office, *Manual of Military Law 1929*, pp. 137 ff. Note the single case where prohibition was granted, Ex parte Webster, 1889, 10 New South Wales Rep. 79.

[53] Swaim v. United States, 1897, 165 U.S. 553, 561, 17 S. Ct. 448, 41 L. Ed. 823.

even in such a substantive matter, cannot be reviewed in a common law court.[54] Such errors, as any lawyer knows, are reviewable only by way of appeal; but there must be some machinery of appellate procedure provided, before the rulings of a court-martial, of the class described, can get before the common law court. Appeal is not a matter of common law, but always of statute, and therefore the common law court must look to a statute giving it appellate powers concerning actions of courts-martial. There are no such statutes in this country or England.[55] "Civil courts are not courts of error to review the proceedings and sentence of a court-martial, where such court-martial has jurisdiction of the offense and of the person of the accused, has complied with the statutory requirements governing the proceedings of the court, and acts within the scope of its lawful powers." [56]

A discussion of the extent of the judicial review of the decisions of military tribunals leads naturally enough to a consideration of the same subject with respect to the determinations of draft boards.[57] Under the conscription acts of 1917 and 1940 various administrative boards are set up to determine whether the person registered is or is not to be drafted, and the degree of exemption or deferment to be granted.[58] Such

[54] Collins v. McDonald, 1922, 258 U.S. 416, 42 S. Ct. 326, 66 L. Ed. 692.
[55] The statement to the contrary as regards England in the earlier edition appears to be erroneous, cf. War Office, *Manual of Military Law 1929*, p. 135.
[56] Ex parte Dickey, 1913, D.C. Me., 204 F. 322, 326.
[57] Cf. Gibbons, 1941, 9 Geo. Wash. L. Rev. 687, 691; Geraghty, 1941, 36 Ill. L. Rev. 310, 316; Carver, 1942, 30 Calif. L. Rev. 226; Bullock, 1942, 10 Geo. Wash. L. Rev. 827; Taintor & Butts, 1942, 14 Miss. L.J. 445, 463.
[58] Sec. 4, Selective Draft Act of 1917, as amended, 50 U.S.C.A. App. § 204; sec. 10 (a)(2), Selective Training and Service Act of 1940, 50 U.S.C.A. App. § 310.

ARMY'S RIGHT OF SELF-REGULATION

bodies are thus administrative agencies acting in a quasi-judicial manner.[59] Courts-martial, also, have long been recognized as "instrumentalities of the executive power . . . [with] only such [judicial] powers as are vested in it by express statute, or may be derived from military usage," [60] but there is considerable difference in the nature of draft boards and courts-martial with respect to the judicial review of the decisions thereof.

The statutes have expressly made the decisions of the draft boards final,[61] and yet there is no question but that, after the remedies provided by the acts have been exhausted,[62] recourse can be had to the courts. Since the boards are not judicial bodies in the strict sense of the term, certiorari is generally not available, although there have been instances where the writ has been granted.[63] Nor can a court of chancery enjoin a draft board from acting, for mere personal rights are not enforced

[59] "Inquiring briefly into these boards, they are administrative bodies created by the selective draft law, with powers, duties, and procedure conferred by the law and rules not inconsistent with the law and prescribed by the President. . . . Such bodies and persons are special tribunals vested by law with authority and duty to hear and determine such matters as the law directs. They are but quasi judicial, and of inferior and limited jurisdiction." Ex parte Beck, 1917, D.C. Mont., 245 F. 967, 969. Cf. United States v. Stephens, 1917, D.C. Del., 245 F. 956, 963.

[60] Winthrop, *Military Law and Precedents*, p. 49.

[61] Cit. *supra*, note 58. Cf. Boitano v. District Board, 1918, D.C. Calif., 250 F. 812, 813; United States ex rel. Pascher v. Kinkead, 1918, D.C. N.J., 248 F. 141, 143, affirmed 1918, C.C.A. N.J., 250 F. 692; reasserted in United States ex rel. Filomio v. Powell, 1941, D.C. N.J., 38 F. Supp. 183, 188.

[62] Napore v. Rowe, 1919, C.C.A. Mont., 256 F. 832, 834; cf. United States ex rel. Ursitti v. Baird, 1941, D.C. N.Y., 39 F. Supp. 872.

[63] Certiorari denied: In re Kitzerow, 1918, D.C. Wis., 252 F. 865; United States ex rel. Roman v. Rauch, 1918, D.C. N.Y., 253 F. 814; reasserted in Shimola v. Local Board, 1941, D.C. Ohio, 40 F. Supp. 808. Certiorari suggested as the proper remedy: Angelus v. Sullivan, 1917, C.C.A. N.Y., 246 F.

by equity, and such a court will not interfere in the exercise of functions by another department of government.[64] Direct appeal to the court has not been provided,[65] and actually habeas corpus is the only remedy available.[66] Thus the person who believes himself aggrieved must await induction into the armed forces and the restraint resultant therefrom before an application for the writ will be entertained.

A court will not hesitate to determine whether the board was acting within its jurisdiction, and in questions of statutory construction will substitute its own judgment for that of the board as to the correct interpretation of the act.[67] Indeed, "civil courts can afford relief from orders made by such boards in any case where it is shown that their proceedings have been

---

54, 63. Certiorari proper to bring up the record where the basis for a writ of habeas corpus is shown, Ex parte Platt, 1918, D.C. N.Y., 253 F. 413, 414.

[64] Angelus v. Sullivan, 1917, C.C.A. N.Y., 246 F. 54, 64; Bonifaci v. Thompson, 1917, D.C. Wash., 252 F. 878; reasserted in Stone v. Christensen, 1940, D.C. Ore., 36 F. Supp. 739, 741; Totus v. United States, 1941, D.C. Wash., 39 F. Supp. 7, 12. In Local Draft Board v. Connors, 1941, C.C.A. Mont., 124 F. 2d 388, the District Court was directed to dissolve a temporary restraining order against the Draft Board from enforcing its orders with respect to the induction of the registrant, but the higher court based its action on the broader ground that the trial court was without jurisdiction of the subject matter, rather than on the narrower point, "whether or not the District Court has any jurisdiction whatever in a case arising under the Selective Service Act other than by way of habeas corpus" (p. 391, with lengthy citation of cases arising under the Draft Act of World War I).

[65] "There is no provision in the act itself which gives the court jurisdiction to review the findings of the local board," Petition of Soberman, 1941, D.C. N.Y., 37 F. Supp. 522, 523; cf. Shimola v. Local Board, 1941, D.C. Ohio, 40 F. Supp. 808, 810.

[66] Neither mandamus nor prohibition are available, Brown v. Spelman, 1918, D.C. N.Y., 254 F. 215; Dick v. Tevlin, 1941, D.C. N.Y., 37 F. Supp. 836.

[67] Construction of the act to determine jurisdiction, Ex parte Fuston, 1918, D.C. Tenn., 253 F. 90; construction of regulations, United States ex rel. Filomio v. Powell, 1941, D.C. N.J., 38 F. Supp. 183, 185.

ARMY'S RIGHT OF SELF-REGULATION

without or in excess of their jurisdiction, or have been so manifestly unfair as to prevent a fair investigation, or that there has been a manifest abuse of the discretion with which they are invested under the act." [68] The extent of review is thus analogous to that afforded the decisions of other administrative bodies [69] and is clearly more extensive than that given the determinations of courts-martial. Although rare, cases exist where the court has held that sufficient evidence has not been presented to support the findings of the board.[70] The proceedings of the board, further, have been examined with a view to determining whether the petitioner has arbitrarily been denied a fair hearing or whether the officers of the board have manifestly abused the discretion committed to them.[71] The pure administrative process of the draft board, accordingly, is much more subject to judicial control than the proceedings of courts-martial, due perhaps to the fact that courts are loathe to interfere with practices largely established by usage in a sphere of law as old as the common law and wholly foreign to it.[72]

Only one thing more remains for notice, and that is the extent of the concurrent jurisdiction of courts-martial and com-

[68] Angelus v. Sullivan, 1917, C.C.A. N.Y., 246 F. 54, 67.
[69] E.g., immigration boards, and cf. Van Vleck, *Administrative Control of Aliens* (1932), chap. V: Judicial Review.
[70] Application of Greenberg, 1941, D.C. N.J., 39 F. Supp. 13; criticized in note, 1942, 30 Cal. L. Rev. 226. But if the registrant has not acted in good faith or where the evidence is self-contradictory, the courts have upheld the board's refusal to believe the testimony, United States ex rel. Pasciuto v. Baird, 1941, D.C. N.Y., 39 F. Supp. 411, 415; United States ex rel. Errichetti v. Baird, 1941, D.C. N.Y., 39 F. Supp. 388, 392.
[71] The decisions are collected and in part quoted in United States ex rel. Filomio v. Powell, 1941, D.C. N.J., 38 F. Supp. 183, 188.
[72] Cf. the oft-quoted remarks of Perry, J., reproduced in Smith v. Whitney, 1886, 116 U.S. 167, 178, 6 S. Ct. 570, 29 L. Ed. 601.

mon law courts. Many of the Articles of War treat as offenses against military discipline acts which also constitute crimes within the civil law; murder and rape alone are excepted from the jurisdiction of courts-martial in time of peace when such acts are committed within the geographical limits of the United States.[73] Now, if a soldier's wrongful act constitutes at the same time an offense against military discipline, punishable by a court-martial, and a crime forming the subject for prosecution in a civil court, it is obvious that neither tribunal can say that the other has no jurisdiction. The only thing that can be said is that the jurisdictions are concurrent, meaning thereby that the two jurisdictions shall settle between themselves which should proceed first,[74] and that if one does not act the other may.[75] When the accused is put upon his trial in either of two courts having jurisdiction, the fact that the other court could have tried him, had a proceeding to that effect been seasonably instituted, constitutes no defense in substance or in form, and this indifferently, whether the court to which objection is made be the military [76] or the civil court.[77]

"We do not mean to intimate," the Supreme Court has said, "that it was not within the competency of Congress to confer exclusive jurisdiction upon military courts over offenses committed by persons in the military service of the United States."[78] But the fact is that Congress has never expressly taken such action. Some few cases early in the nineteenth cen-

---

[73] A.W. 92 and 93, 10 U.S.C.A. §§ 1564–65.
[74] Ex parte Dunn, 1918, D.C. Mass., 250 F. 871, 873; Op. J.A.G. of Nov. 11, 1911, 1912–40 Dig. Op. J.A.G. § 432(2).
[75] Ex parte Mason, 1881, 105 U.S. 696, 699, 26 L. Ed. 1213.
[76] Ex parte Mason, cit. note *supra*.
[77] Franklin v. United States, 1910, 216 U.S. 559, 30 S. Ct. 434, 54 L. Ed. 615.
[78] Coleman v. Tennessee, 1878, 97 U.S. 509, 514, 24 L. Ed. 1118.

ARMY'S RIGHT OF SELF-REGULATION

tury suggested that the crimes acts of 1790 and 1825,[79] which reserved to courts-martial the right to punish offenses by members of the armed forces according to Articles of War already in existence, show that the acts "had no paramount operation over the land forces" and were "not intended to apply to the land forces." [80] The great weight of authority, however, insisted that civil and military courts had concurrent jurisdiction of crimes punishable by the laws of the land.[81] Then, in 1917, it was argued that the revision of the Articles of War in 1916 indicated Congress's intention to give exclusive jurisdiction to courts-martial over crimes committed by soldiers in time of war. In a District Court a writ of habeas corpus was granted to the military authority to remove a soldier accused of a murder on the streets of a Kentucky town from the jurisdiction of the state court.[82] The court based its holding upon the priority of military jurisdiction in time of war; "the civil authorities in time of war had no right to withhold a soldier accused of a crime from the military authorities, or to demand him from them in order to try him for an offense against the criminal laws of the land." [83] But the court went on to say: "It

---

[79] 1 Stat. 112, §§ 3, 8, and 4 Stat. 115, § 11, 18 U.S.C.A. §§ 454, 465 note, 481 note.
[80] United States v. Bevans, 1818, 3 Wheat. 336, 4 L. Ed. 404; United States v. Mackenzie, 1843, D.C. N.Y., Fed. Cas. No. 15,690; United States v. Mackenzie, 1843, D.C. N.Y., Fed. Cas. No. 18,313. These cases are treated and disposed of in Neall v. United States, 1902, C.C.A. Calif., 118 F. 699.
[81] United States v. Cornell, 1820, C.C. R.I., 2 Mason 60, 91, Fed. Cas. Nos. 14867–68; 1854, 6 Op. Atty. Gen. 413, 419; United States v. Cashiel, 1863, D.C. Md., 1 Hughes 552, Fed. Cas. No. 14744; United States v. Carr, 1872, C.C. Ga., 1 Woods, 480, Fed. Cas. No. 14732; United States v. Clark, 1887, C.C. Mich., 31 F. 710; Neall v. United States, 1902, C.C.A. Calif., 118 F. 699.
[82] Ex parte King, 1917, D.C. Ky., 246 F. 868; cf. notes on this case in 1918, 27 Yale L.J. 837, and 1918, 18 Col. L. Rev. 497.
[83] Case cited, at p. 872; so provided under the old A.W. 58 and 59, with no change in this respect by the new A.W. 74, 92 and 93.

is therefore a question under the existing articles of war whether the military authorities do not in time of war have exclusive jurisdiction of the crime of murder, when committed by a person subject to military law, no matter where he may be when committed. It is not necessary that I take any position on this question." [84]

The District Court's reasoning lacks cogency, because it is based on *Coleman v. Tennessee*,[85] whereas that case, dealing as it did with a crime committed in a hostile district, under military occupation, contains no dictum that is applicable to a crime committed in an American town in which no conditions of military control exist. Decisions of lower federal and state courts subsequent to *Ex parte King* emphatically deny that the revision of the Articles of War indicates any attempt by Congress to give courts-martial exclusive jurisdiction in time of war. Where the military waives its right and the civil authorities are permitted to proceed with the trial of the accused soldier, or where no demand of his custody is made by the military, the civil court is free to exercise its concurrent power to try the accused.[86] The Supreme Court has upheld this view in *Caldwell v. Parker*,[87] confirming the refusal of a lower court to grant a writ of habeas corpus to discharge a prisoner, a soldier convicted in a state court of the murder of a civilian at a

---

[84] Case cited, at p. 873; in the first edition of this work, Professor Glenn indicated that this was the basis of decision, exception to which was taken by Wilgus in his review, 1918, 17 Mich. L. Rev. 199.

[85] Cit. *supra*, note 78.

[86] United States v. Hirsch, 1918, D.C. N.Y., 254 F. 109; People v. Denman, 1918, 179 Cal. 497, 177 P. 461; Funk v. State, 1919, 84 Tex. Cr. 402, 208 S.W. 509; Ex parte Koester, 1922, 56 Cal. App. 621, 206 P. 116; Ex parte Sumner, 1942, Tex. Crim. App., 158 S.W. 2d 310.

[87] 1920, 252 U.S. 376, 40 S. Ct. 388, 64 L. Ed. 621.

ARMY'S RIGHT OF SELF-REGULATION

place within the state not subject in any way to military control. The revised Articles of War, the Supreme Court says: "contain no direct and clear expression of a purpose on the part of Congress, conceding for the sake of argument that authority existed under the Constitution to do so, to bring about, as the mere result of a declaration of war, the complete destruction of state authority and the extraordinary extension of military power." A proviso "except in time of war" in the Article of War which makes it the duty of a commanding officer to surrender soldiers accused of crimes to the civil authorities,[88] is not an indication of Congressional intention to confer exclusive jurisdiction, but probably nothing more than a recognition of the military's right, in time of war, to deal with crimes in areas affected by military operations or where the civil authority has been suspended.[89] Though expressly refusing to decide

---

[88] A.W. 74, 10 U.S.C.A. § 1546: "When any person subject to military law, except one who is held by the military authorities to answer, or who is awaiting trial or result of trial, or who is undergoing sentence for a crime or offense punishable under these articles, is accused of a crime or offense committed with the geographical limits of the States of the Union and the District of Columbia, and punishable by the laws of the land, the commanding officer is required, except in time of war, upon application duly made, to use his utmost endeavor to deliver over such accused person to the civil authorities, or to aid the officers of justice in apprehending and securing him, in order that he may be brought to trial. . . ."

[89] The court indicates that the introduction of this proviso in the 1874 A.W. was to deal with a condition resulting from the state of war interfering with the discharge of duties by the courts. But note that in World War I the War Department interpreted A.W. 74 to mean that the commanding officer was not to turn over offenders to the civil authorities in time of war unless the crime charged was a most serious one, primarily against the civil community, which would disqualify the soldier for military service, and where the commanding officer reasonably believed that the charge had some foundation and that the accused would be afforded a fair trial, letter of the Adjutant General, Dec. 3, 1917, Mil. Laws § 74 note, and 1918 Op. J.A.G. 723,

the question, it appears that the Supreme Court would view the state courts as having been given paramount jurisdiction, save in exceptional circumstances.

The question arose again in *Ex parte McKittrick v. Brown*,[90] this time a conflict between a state civil and a state military tribunal, in time of peace. A National Guardsman, called out under the governor's order, shot at an automobile disregarding his order to halt and killed the occupant. Held as a prisoner awaiting trial before a court-martial for homicide, the Attorney General brings habeas corpus to obtain custody of the prisoner to try him in a civil court for second-degree murder. The court held that by reason of another proviso introduced in 1916 into the same A.W. 74 referred to above [91]—surrender to civil authorities, except a soldier held to answer or awaiting court-martial or undergoing sentence thereunder—Congress had explicitly made clear that it was "unwilling to permit the civil courts to interfere with a criminal proceeding first started by military authorities, save with the consent of the latter." [92] The Missouri court refused to follow the dictum of the Supreme Court in *Caldwell v. Parker*, and remanded the prisoner to the state military authorities.[93]

1912–40 Dig. Op. J.A.G. § 432(3). The same policy is being followed in World War II, see 1 Bull. J.A.G., pp. 10, 274.

[90] 1935, 337 Mo. 281, 85 S.W. 2d 385. The case is criticized by Wiener, *Practical Manual of Martial Law* (1940), pp. 151 ff.

[91] *Supra*, note 89. [92] Case cit., at p. 290.

[93] It has been pointed out, in a note, 1935, 84 U. Pa. L. Rev. 259, that inasmuch as the court-martial can at most charge manslaughter in time of peace, the accused could successfully plead double jeopardy if subsequently prosecuted for murder by the civil authorities, since but one sovereignty is concerned; this may well be a direct threat to the doctrine of predominance of civil authority. However, the Supreme Court of New York, People v. Wendel, 1908, 59 Misc. (N.Y.) 354, 112 N.Y.S. 301, refused to consider a conviction

ARMY'S RIGHT OF SELF-REGULATION

In this connection we must not be confused by questions of jurisdiction as between state courts and federal courts. It is well settled that the plea of previous conviction or acquittal by court-martial (federal) will be swept aside in a state court, on the principle that the same act of misconduct may constitute two different offenses, one against the United States and one against the state; [94] "subjecting a party to double punishment for the same act, making two offenses, cannot be said to be in violation of the Constitution of the United States, by placing the party twice in jeopardy for the same offense." [95] Nor, in a reverse situation, will conviction or acquittal of a crime in a state court bar responsibility for the military offense based on the same facts.[96] It is to be noted, however, that in spite of apparent concurrent jurisdiction between state and federal courts, when a soldier commits a crime while acting in accordance with his orders and therefore within the duties imposed upon him by the United States, the federal court by writ of habeas corpus may assume jurisdiction over the matter and prevent further action by the state.[97] Since the granting of the writ is within the discretion of the judge, it is perfectly proper for the

---

by state court-martial for conduct unbecoming an officer and conduct to the prejudice of good order and military discipline a bar to an indictment for grand larceny founded upon the same transaction.

[94] United States v. Cashiel, 1863, D.C. Md., 1 Hughes 552, Fed. Cas. No. 14744; State v. Rankin, 1867, 4 Cold. (Tenn.) 145, writ of error dismissed, Rankin v. Tennessee, 1870, 78 U.S. 380, 20 L. Ed. 175; Coleman v. Tennessee, 1878, 97 U.S. 509, 513, 24 L. Ed. 1118. See also note 16 A.L.R. 1247, and Colby, 1926, 14 Geo. L.J. 169.

[95] State v. Rankin, *loc. cit.* at p. 160.

[96] Howe's Case, 1854, 6 Op. Atty. Gen. 506; In re Stubbs, 1905, C.C. Wash., 133 F. 1012.

[97] In re Fair, 1900, C.C. Nebr., 100 F. 149; United States v. Lipsett, ex parte Gillette, 1907, D.C. Mich., 156 F. 65; In re Wulzen, 1916, D.C. Ohio, 235 F. 362.

writ to be denied where the federal judge is not entirely satisfied that the act was done under the authority of the United States and to permit the state court to determine the guilt or the innocence of the accused.[98]

One question had been, rather willfully, left open by the Supreme Court in its decision in *Ex parte Mason*,[99] namely, the effect of a trial before a court-martial upon subsequent proceedings in a federal civil court. The reverse of the situation, also, had seen but little determination by the courts and that little not conclusive one way or the other.[100] The case of *Grafton v. United States* [101] has settled these situations once and for all. The appellant, a soldier of our army, while on sentry duty shot a Filipino. The civil court not acting promptly, Grafton was tried by court-martial on a charge of homicide, but not murder, because, since it was in time of peace, the court-martial could not try him for murder. He was acquitted. Thereafter the local civil court put him on trial for murder, to which he pleaded his previous acquittal in the court-martial. This plea was held bad, and thereupon Grafton was tried on the general issue and convicted. On appeal, the Supreme Court held the plea good, and therefore reversed the judgment of conviction.

[98] United States ex rel. Drury v. Lewis, 1904, C.C. Pa., 129 F. 823, affirmed 1906, 200 U.S. 1, 26 S. Ct. 229, 50 L. Ed. 343.
[99] 105 U.S. 696, 699, 26 L. Ed. 1213: "Whether, after trial by the court-martial, he can be again tried in the civil courts is a question we need not now consider." Cf., however, the language in Wilkes v. Dinsman, 1849, 7 How. 89, 123, 12 L. Ed. 618; and United States v. Clark, 1887, C.C. Mich., 31 F. 710, 713.
[100] In both In re Esmond, 1886, Sup. Ct. D.C., 5 Mackay (D.C.) 64, and In re Stubbs, 1905, C.C. Wash., 133 F. 1012, acquittal in a civil court was held not to bar action by a court-martial for a different offense based on the same acts. Cf. also Steiner's Case, 1854, 6 Op. Atty. Gen. 413, 419, 424.
[101] 1907, 206 U.S. 333, 27 S. Ct. 749, 51 L. Ed. 1084, 11 Ann. Cas. 640.

ARMY'S RIGHT OF SELF-REGULATION

The grounds for this decision were (1) "the prohibition of double jeopardy is applicable to all criminal prosecutions in the Philippines," (2) as the court-martial had jurisdiction to try Grafton, "its judgment will be accorded the finality and conclusiveness, as to all the issues involved, which attend the judgments of a civil court in a case of which it may legally take cognizance," and (3) the acquittal on a charge of homicide is essentially a bar to a prosecution on a charge of murder, on principles familiar to all common law practitioners. The doctrine laid down in the Grafton case has been steadfastly followed in the federal courts.[102]

The judgment of a court-martial is accorded the same finality and conclusiveness with respect to the issues involved as the judgments of a civil court.[103] But if the court-martial has not been legally composed or if it lacks jurisdiction, a record of its findings will not be accorded recognition in a subsequent common law proceeding.[104] In *Commonwealth v. McClean* [105] the defendant, a recruiting officer, and others were indicted for conspiracy to arrest the prosecutor as a pretended deserter, for the purpose of obtaining a reward granted for the arrest of deserters. The defense relied upon was the supposed conclusiveness of the decision of a court-martial that the prosecutor

[102] United States v. Block, 1920, D.C. Ind., 262 F. 205; Simmons v. United States, 1926, D.C. Ohio, not reported, but quoted in 1926 Dig. Op. J.A.G. 69. Cf. also Gavieres v. United States, 1911, 220 U.S. 338, 344, 31 S. Ct. 421, 55 L. Ed. 489; Puerto Rico v. Shell Co., 1937, 302 U.S. 253, 264, 58 S. Ct. 167, 82 L. Ed. 235.
[103] Ex parte Reed, 1879, 100 U.S. 13, 23, 25 L. Ed. 538; Grafton v. United States, cit. *supra* note 101, at p. 345.
[104] Brooks v. Adams, 1831, 28 Mass. 441; United States ex rel. Harris v. Daniels, 1922, C.C.A. N.Y., 279 F. 844, 846; but cf. Weirman v. United States, 1901, 36 Ct. Cls. 236.
[105] 1850, 2 Pars. Eq. Cas. (Pa.) 367.

was guilty of desertion, as a complete answer to evidence offered to show that the prosecutor never was a soldier. In upholding a verdict of guilty, the Court stated that to give the court-martial jurisdiction over the prosecutor, "it was necessary as a preliminary fact that he should have been a soldier in the service of the United States. Nor could the decision of a military tribunal, however exalted, conclude that fact. . . . A Court Martial can, and must of necessity, decide whether a party charged before it as a deserter is a soldier in the army of the United States; but their decision on *that question* does not conclude the civil tribunals of the country." [106] Naturally the judgment of a court-martial can have no higher value than the judgment of a common law court. As between the parties to it, a judgment is conclusive as to the matters litigated, but as between other parties it has no value, by way either of res judicata or evidence. In *United States v. Clark* [107] two soldiers had stolen government funds from the custody of an assistant paymaster, and the latter, under the statute, was liable absolutely for their loss to the government. The two thieves were afterwards convicted of the larceny by court-martial, largely on the claimant's testimony. Then the claimant filed in the Court of Claims, which had jurisdiction to determine his liability, a petition for relief. It was held that the petition should have been dismissed because the claimant did not testify, and the only evidence in support of his petition was afforded by the record of the court-martial, which involved parties different from those in the instant suit. Such evidence was incompetent.

Finally, it should be mentioned that the care with which the common law courts scrutinize the boundaries of a court-

---

[106] Case cit., at p. 376.   [107] 1877, 96 U.S. 37, 24 L. Ed. 696.

ARMY'S RIGHT OF SELF-REGULATION

martial's jurisdiction, has in it nothing of jealousy or of distrust.[108] A court-martial is composed of our own fellow citizens actuated by the same desire to administer justice as impels to his duty the judge of any common law court in the land. The guilty need fear its process to no greater or less degree than he need fear the vindicatory power of a common law judge. Nor need the public fear its favoring men of the service. Indeed, we may find in history, judicial and otherwise, instances to show that the guilty officer or soldier much prefers the civil jurisdiction. We need only mention the case of Captain Oberlin Carter from our own records,[109] or one from the records of a country which, although different in its system of law and language, has always been close to us—France. Marshal Ney, when punishment hung over his head for his undoubted act of treason in going over to Napoleon in desertion of the sovereign to whom he had taken the oath of allegiance, stated that he infinitely preferred to be tried by the Chamber of Peers rather than by a court-martial composed of his old comrades. The latter, to use his expression, undoubtedly would have shot him "like a rabbit," [110] but they would have done so only because of his clear guilt as it would have appeared to them on his trial.[111]

---

[108] E.g., In re Bogart, 1873, C.C. Calif., Fed. Cas. No. 1596, at p. 801; In re Davison, 1884, C.C. N.Y., 21 F. 618, 621; cf. Covington, 1939, 7 Geo. Wash. L. Rev. 503, 513.

[109] Carter v. Woodring, 1937, App. D.C., 92 F. 2d 544, with citation of earlier litigation at the close of the case. As indication of an attempt to create an American Dreyfus, see *I Also Accuse*, press release of Oct. 10, 1938, Justice for Carter Committee, 1008 Peoples Gas Bldg., Chicago, Ill.

[110] "Me fusilleraient comme un lapin."

[111] Houssaye, *1815—La Seconde Abdication et la terreur blanche*, pp. 570 f.

5. THE ARMY IN ITS RELATIONS WITH THE ENEMY

AS AGAINST the public enemy, using that term to denote a sovereign state *de jure* or *de facto*, other than our own nation, the army may be used only in time of war. So far as the common law is concerned, war, as to commencement, duration, and termination, is a matter of state. The war commences when government officially says it has commenced, and it ends when government says it has ceased to exist.[1] Nothing short of state-recognized belligerency, therefore, is war in the view of our courts; strained relations, however prophetic of hostilities, do not constitute flagrancy of war.[2]

As we have seen, the Constitution places with Congress the power of declaring war. It follows that, although the conduct of the war, once its state is created by Congressional action, is with the President, yet the latter has no power to direct the armed forces of this country against any nation with whom, for the lack of action by the legislative branch of our government, we are at peace.[3]

---

[1] Thus, so far as the courts were concerned, the Civil War terminated when the President proclaimed its cessation, as of April 2, 1866; The Protector, 1871, 12 Wall. 700, 20 L. Ed. 463. On the termination of the Spanish-American War and World War I, see, respectively, Ribas y Hijo v. United States, 1901, 1 Porto Rico Fed. 71, affirmed 1904, 194 U.S. 315, 323, 24 S. Ct. 727, 48 L. Ed. 994, and Hamilton v. Kentucky Distilleries and Warehouse Co., 1919, 251 U.S. 146, 158, 40 S. Ct. 106, 64 L. Ed. 194.

[2] Gray v. United States, 1886, 21 Ct. Cls. 340, 374; cf. Janson v. Dreifontein Consolidated Mines, Ltd., [1902] A.C. 484, 493.

[3] United States v. Smith, 1806, Fed. Cas. No. 16342, at p. 1230; Perkins v. Rogers, 1871, 35 Ind. 124, 135, 9 Am. Rep. 639.

THE ARMY AND THE ENEMY

But such executive acts, however unauthorized, may be ratified by later Congressional action. "I am perfectly satisfied," says Mr. Justice Story, "that no subject can commence hostilities or capture property of an enemy, when the Sovereign has prohibited it. But suppose he did, I would ask if the Sovereign may not ratify his proceedings, and thus by a retroactive operation give validity to them?"[4] The Supreme Court, in the time of our Civil War, repeated this proposition in the *Prize Cases*.[5] The court there referred to the fact that the battles of Palo Alto and Resaca de la Palma had been fought before the passage of the Act of Congress recognizing a state of war with Mexico, and said that "this act not only provided for the future prosecution of the war, but was itself a vindication and ratification of the act of the President in accepting the challenge without a previous formal declaration of war by Congress." In the same way the court refers to the fact that in the Civil War, Congress, at its first session after the attack on Fort Sumter, enacted a law ratifying all intervening acts of the executive authority. It follows that the only interest of our courts in such a matter is in whether, originally or by ratification, Congress has authorized the state of war; if so, the army may lawfully operate against the enemy.[6] But as the enemy state consists of subjects of all grades and classes, as well as a government and armed forces of its own, it is now in order to define more closely the term enemy, so far as our army's efforts in war may be concerned.

---

[4] Brown v. United States, 1814, 8 Cranch 110, 133, 3 L. Ed. 504.
[5] 1862, 2 Black 635, 17 L. Ed. 459.
[6] The requirement of a declaration of war prior to hostilities is one of those matters of international law with which common law cannot deal. On the fluctuation of this doctrine during recent centuries see Bordwell, *Law of War between Belligerents* (1908), pp. 36 ff., 186, 198; for the most recent years see Oppenheim, *International Law*, II (6th ed. 1940), 234 ff.

88 THE ARMY AND THE LAW

Within the term enemy is included not merely the opposing government, but human beings as well. That proposition, of course, conflicts with the Rousseau theory which has been previously discussed.[7] And it must be granted that the vogue which that theory obtained in the eighteenth century found small opposition in the common law doctrines then in force concerning trading with the enemy.

Up to the middle of the eighteenth century common law justices refused to interfere with transactions made with the enemy,[8] indeed, it was a distinct belief of Lord Mansfield that trading with the enemy should be encouraged.[9] But with the opening of the nineteenth century the contrary position was taken by the prize court, that court whose law derives from "the course of the admiralty and the law of nations," [10] in *The Hoop*, where Lord Stowell held that an insurance contract made with the enemy is void.[11] This view was followed in common law courts and the courts of chancery,[12] and by the time of the Crimean War, when the English courts came to consider the matter again, they took it that the doctrine was then clearly settled, the reason of it being, as stated by Mr. Justice Willes, that "the proximate object of war is to curtail the enemy's commerce as well as to capture his property." [13]

When the First World War broke out the English Crown

---

[7] *Supra*, chap. 2.
[8] Henkle v. Royal Exchange Assurance Co., 1749, 1 Ves. Sr. 317, 320, 27 Eng. Rep. 1055.
[9] Bell v. Gilson, 1798, 1 B. & P. 345, 354, 126 Eng. Rep. 942.
[10] Lord Mansfield, quoted in The Zamora, [1916] 2 A.C. 77, 91.
[11] 1799, 1 Ch. Rob. 196, 165 Eng. Rep. 146.
[12] See Potts v. Bell, 1800, 8 T.R. 548, 101 Eng. Rep. 1540; Evans v. Richardson, 1817, 3 Mer. 469, 36 Eng. Rep. 181.
[13] Exposito v. Bowden, 1857, 7 E. & B. 763, 779, 119 Eng. Rep. 1430.

THE ARMY AND THE ENEMY

issued two proclamations relating to trading, which were followed by the Trading with the Enemy Act, 1914.[14] Both proclamations recited that "it is contrary to law for any person resident, carrying on business, or being in our dominions, to trade or have any commercial intercourse with any person resident, carrying on business, or being in the German Empire without our permission." The view of the courts is well expressed by Lord Parker, in one of the leading cases construing the Act: "The rule against trading with the enemy is a belligerent's weapon of self-protection . . . Though it has been said by high authority to aim at curtailing the commercial resources of the enemy, it has, according to other and older authorities, the wider object of preventing unregulated intercourse with the enemy altogether. Through the Royal license, which validates such intercourse and such trade, they are brought under necessary control. Without such control, they are forbidden."[15] Profiting from the experience under the earlier Act, the Trading with the Enemy Act, 1939, was enacted upon the outbreak of the war.[16] In one important aspect, however, the new Act goes far beyond the old: whereas formerly only such acts and transactions were prohibited as were specified in particular proclamations, or as the courts construed as existing in the common law,[17] the new Act prohibits any intercourse with the enemy, no matter whether such deal-

---

[14] The proclamations and the Act (4 & 5 Geo. V, c. 87) are reproduced and discussed by Bentwich, 1915, 9 Am. J. Int. Law 352–71; cf. also Phillimore, 1915, 15 J. Soc. Comp. Leg., n.s., 17, 29.
[15] Daimler Co. v. Continental Tyre & Rubber Co., [1916] 2 A.C. 307, 344.
[16] 2 & 3 Geo. VI, c. 89; amendments, related acts, orders and decisions are to be found in Krusin-Rogers, *Solicitors' Handbook of War Legislation*, I (1940), pp. 223 ff., II (1942), 369 ff., and III (1942), 89 ff.
[17] Robson v. Premier Oil & Pipe Line Co., Ltd., [1915] 2 Ch. 124, 136.

ings are to the detriment or to the advantage of Great Britain.[18]

In the United States non-intercourse acts were enacted during the Revolutionary War, at the close of the eighteenth century when relations with France were strained, during the War of 1812, and early in the Civil War.[19] The last, the Act of July 13, 1861,[20] provided that the President might license commercial intercourse with any part of that section, and that such intercourse should be conducted pursuant to regulation prescribed by the Treasury.[21] This statute the courts strictly applied. No one but the President could grant a license; hence "those given by military authorities were nullities. They conferred no rights whatever. No one could give them but the President. From any other source they were void."[22] But while no governmental department other than the Treasury, could issue these licenses, the Treasury in the sphere of action thus allotted it was supreme. The Treasury used its power, as might have been expected, largely for the purposes of national revenue, and the courts upheld it in this course.[23]

[18] Formerly every case had to be considered on its own merits, and if the transaction was found to be beneficial to England, it was held valid even though it necessitated intercourse with the enemy. Now it is otherwise: there is illicit intercourse when there is contact of any kind with an enemy, or where there is intercourse with any person, enemy or not, which is to the benefit of the enemy. See generally, Blum and Rosenbaum, *Law Relating to Trading with the Enemy* (1940), particularly pp. 23-36.
[19] See Huberich, *Law Relating to Trading with the Enemy* (1918), pp. 22 ff.; briefly Winthrop, *Military Law and Precedents*, pp. 776 ff.
[20] 12 Stat. 255.
[21] The validity of the act was upheld in Hamilton v. Dillin, 1874, 21 Wall. 73, 22 L. Ed. 528; cf. Miller v. United States, 1870, 11 Wall. 268, 313, 20 L. Ed. 135.
[22] The Ouachita Cotton, 1867, 6 Wall. 521, 531, 18 L. Ed. 935; see also Coppell v. Hall, 1868, 7 Wall. 542, 19 L. Ed. 244; McKee v. United States, 1868, 8 Wall. 163, 19 L. Ed. 329.
[23] The Reform, 1865, 3 Wall. 617, 18 L. Ed. 105, and Hamilton v. Dillin, cit. *supra* note 21.

THE ARMY AND THE ENEMY

An elaborate Trading with the Enemy Act was enacted October 6, 1917,[24] with the professed aims (1) of preventing aid or comfort to the enemy by the prohibition of intercourse, providing for a system of licenses to permit such trade as deemed desirable, and (2) of making enemy funds in this country available for war financing.[25] The first aim was in line with earlier efforts, but in view of the fact that no licenses were ever issued, this phase of the Act played a relatively minor role. The other phase of the Act, by reason of the extension of the powers of the Alien Property Custodian by amendment and regulation, soon became a vital part of the war effort; this field, however, lies outside the scope of this book.[26] In 1933 and again in 1940 the licensing provisions of the 1917 Act were utilized to empower the President to regulate foreign exchange transactions in time of national emergency,[27] but now with the virtual reenactment of the whole Act, as amended,[28] it is quite likely that the prevention of intercourse and the licensing of trade will again occupy a secondary role.[29] For the most part, trading with the enemy legislation has nothing to do with the army

---

[24] 40 Stat. 411; the act, with amendments and decisions thereunder, 50 U.S.C.A. App. §§ 1–31.

[25] Alien Property Custodian, *Bulletin of Information* (1918), p. 7; Potterf, 1927, 2 Ind. L.J. 453, 460.

[26] See generally Huberich, *Law Relating to Trading with the Enemy* (1918); note, 1926, 35 Yale L.J. 345; Gathings, *International Law and American Treatment of Alien Enemy Property* (1940).

[27] Sec. 5(b) of the Act as amended by the Act of March 9, 1933, Public Resolution of May 7, 1940; executive orders of Jan. 15, 1934 and April 10, 1940, as amended; regulations of Nov. 12, 1934 and April 10, 1940, as amended. For the acts and the executive orders see 50 U.S.C.A. App. § 5(b), Supp. Cf. also notes, 1941, 41 Col. L. Rev. 1039, and 1942, 42 Col. L. Rev. 105; Bloch-Rosenberg, 1942, 11 Fordham L. Rev. 71.

[28] Title III of the First War Powers Act of Dec. 18, 1941, 55 Stat. 838, 50 U.S.C.A. App. §§ 616–618.

[29] See further, 1942, 20 Tex. L. Rev. 746; 1942, 51 Yale L.J. 1388; 1942, 36 Amer. J. Int. Law 460.

directly, but inasmuch as the license to trade has exceptionally affected the military, a paragraph hereof may not be amiss.

The holder of a permit to trade marches within the protection of the common law, and for seizure of his goods a military commander is liable in trespass; whereas the absence of such a permit places the trader, as to so much of his goods as may be in enemy country, in the position of an owner of enemy goods, and he cannot sue the commander who destroys them. That is the very distinction between such a case as *Mitchell v. Harmony* [30] and *Dow v. Johnson*.[31] The first case we will hereafter discuss.[32] In *Dow v. Johnson*, the plaintiff, loyal to the North, owned a plantation in Louisiana, which the defendant, the military commanding officer, stripped. For that act, afterwards, the plaintiff sued him. In holding for the defendant the court said: "We do not controvert the doctrine of Mitchell *v.* Harmony; on the contrary, we approve of it. But it has no application to the case at bar. The trading for which the seizure was there made had been permitted by the Executive Department of our Government. The question here is, what is the law which governs an army invading an enemy's country?" [33]

The evolution of doctrine and practice thus outlined reflects the entire viewpoint of present-day common law. However irresponsible the enemy government may be, whether or no it rules its people like an old-time despot, still no nation, on going to war with such a government, can get far with the theory that the war is only waged against that government. From the lawyer's standpoint as well as that of the soldier, war, of necessity, is waged against the individuals and assets whose

---

[30] 1851, 13 How. 115, 14 L. Ed. 75.
[32] *Infra*, chap. 8.
[31] 1879, 100 U.S. 158, 25 L. Ed. 632.
[33] Cit. *supra*, note 31, at p. 169.

labor or productivity enables the enemy government to maintain its existence. Such a clear proposition must not be confused with the program which formed a basis for the wars of Allied Europe against Napoleonic France, that a change of government will be a signal for peace. That is quite another thing from saying, as all lawyers must say, that, so long as a state of war does exist, it is waged, not merely against a government, but against people; wherefore the necessity of defining the term enemy in more than words of government.

Obviously, the first classification must rest upon citizenship, as defined by the laws of the respective countries and recognized by international law. A German or Japanese citizen, as such, is *ex vi termini* an enemy, wherever he may be, at home, abroad, or here. The tie of allegiance to the hostile government is what fixes his status, and therefore, the location of either his domicile or his property is wholly immaterial.

In a situation like that presented by our Civil War, the question of allegiance takes us over a very delicate surface. Without discussing, on the one hand, the historical aspects of the subject, or its constitutional aspects, on the other, let us note that at an early date in the Civil War the Supreme Court attributed to the Confederacy all the qualities of a *de facto* belligerent; the result was that Southern ports could be declared in a state of blockade, and that a neutral ship attempting to run the blockade would be lawful prize.[34] Similar necessities, such as that of upholding the principles of military government in occupied parts of the South, led the United States government, as recognized by the Supreme Court, to take a certain well-

---

[34] Prize Cases, 1862, 2 Black 635, 17 L. Ed. 439; cf. Smith v. Stewart, 1869, 21 La. Ann. 67, 99 Am. Dec. 709.

defined position: First, the war, "though not between independent nations, but between different portions of the same nation, was accompanied by the general incidents of an international war"; [35] in short, it took "the proportions of a territorial war, the insurgents having become formidable enough to be recognized as belligerents." [36] Second, the Confederate government, though entitled to no recognition as to legislative powers, was at least recognized as "the military representative of the insurrection against the United States," and the Confederate armies had belligerent rights as to organization, officers and men.[37] Third, therefore "the people of the loyal States on the one hand, and the people of the Confederate States, on the other, thus became enemies to each other, and were liable to be dealt with as such without reference to their individual opinions or dispositions." [38] There was only this difference, that no one residing in the North could claim allegiance to the Confederacy. His allegiance was only to the United States government, and no hostile act of his could be considered as less than treason.[39]

For persons owing allegiance to an enemy government there exists the age-old distinction between the armed forces on the one hand, and the peaceful population, or civilians, on the other.[40] During and since World War I several developments

[35] Dow v. Johnson, 1879, 100 U.S. 158, 164, 25 L. Ed. 632.
[36] Coleman v. Tennessee, 1878, 97 U.S. 509, 517, 24 L. Ed. 1118; cf. the collection of excerpts from Supreme Court, federal and state cases in Hubbard v. Harnden Express Co., 1872, 10 R.I. 244.
[37] Ford v. Surget, 1878, 97 U.S. 594, 605, 24 L. Ed. 1018.
[38] Dow v. Johnson, cit. *supra*, note 35, at p. 164.
[39] United States v. Cathcart, 1864, C.C. Ohio, Fed. Cas. No. 14,756.
[40] War Dept., *Basic Field Manual: Rules of Land Warfare* (FM 27–10), chap. 2.

have vitally affected this classification.[41] The growth in the number of combatants, the growth in the number of civilians engaged in the war effort, the development of aerial warfare, the primary role played by economic measures, and finally, the control over the individual exercised by totalitarian governments, all have "tended to accentuate the artificiality of the distinction, for many purposes, between the fighting forces and the civilian population." [42] For our purposes, however, the line between the belligerent member of the land, sea, or air forces and the civilian is still clear; each has certain rights, and to each our forces owe certain duties.

The belligerent class may be dismissed with a word. The soldier is entitled to the rights and obligations that the common laws of war allow him. The civilian, on the other hand, rests under an entirely different set of rules, as to his person and property, of which more will be said later. One observation, however, may properly be made at this juncture: the civilian deprives himself of all the rights allowed him by military law if he abuses his status. The enemy citizen, in short, must choose between the status of soldier and that of civilian. An attempt to exercise the powers of the soldier, without previously assuming the corresponding status, is a violation of a long-standing rule of law. The severities practiced by the Germans in 1870 for violations of this rule by French civilians are notorious enough. But the Germans were correct in their propositions of law; the only trouble with them was that then, as again in 1914 and at present, they showed themselves unfit ministers of justice. Under color of law they exhibited a spirit

---

[41] Oppenheim, *International Law*, Vol. II (6th ed. 1940), § 57a.
[42] *Ibid.*, p. 172.

of cruelty incompatible with all theories of sanction. But the laws of war remain of force, however unworthy may be those who for the time being have the power of administering them; and no rule of this system is better established than the one under mention. When Wellington, with an auxiliary Spanish army moving with him, crossed the Bidassoa in 1813 and stood upon the invaded soil of France, he had to meet two difficulties; the Spanish army took to plundering, and this excited the French peasantry to acts of hostility. Wellington was equally firm on both points. The Spanish commanders he admonished that plundering must cease, or their forces could no longer march with him. "He had not lost thousands of men to enable the Spaniards to pillage and ill-treat the French peasantry; he preferred a small army obedient to a large army disobedient and undisciplined. . . . The question between them was whether they should or should not pillage the French peasants. His measures were taken to prevent it," etc.[43] On the other hand, when the Spanish plundering had made the peasants rise in arms, Wellington issued a proclamation requiring them either to join Soult's army or stay at home, otherwise he would burn villages and hang the inhabitants. "Thus," says Napier, "notwithstanding the outcries against the French for this system of repressing the *partida* warfare in Spain, it was considered by the English general justifiable and necessary." [44]

The whole subject finds excellent presentation in the remarks of the historian Ropes concerning one of several orders issued by General Pope, when he took command of the forces in Virginia.[45] In only two respects did the Hague Regulations

---

[43] Napier, *Peninsular War*, Book 23, chap. 2.   [44] Napier, *loc. cit.*
[45] Ropes, *The Army under Pope* (1881), at p. 10: "Another order provides

THE ARMY AND THE ENEMY

of 1907 modify the established principles of this phase of the laws of war: Article 1 provides that irregular forces are to enjoy the privileges due to members of the armed forces of the belligerents, even though they do not act under authorization, provided they comply with certain other conditions of the laws of war; [46] Article 2 provides that the members of a levy en masse of the whole population, upon the approach of the enemy, spontaneously taking up arms to resist the invading enemy, are to be accorded the privileges due members of the armed forces.[47] For the rest, the position taken today is identical with that professed in the nineteenth century: "persons who take up arms and commit hostilities without having complied with the conditions prescribed by the laws of war for recognition as belligerents are, when captured by the injured party, liable to punishment as war criminals." [48]

---

that non-combatants in the rear of the army shall be responsible in damages for injuries done to the track of railroads, attacks on trains, assaults on soldiers, committed by guerillas—that is, by individuals not enlisted among the organized military forces of the enemy. Any injuries to tracks, etc., are to be repaired by the neighbors, or an indemnity paid; so, where soldiers are fired on from a house, the house shall be razed to the ground, and the occupants of it treated as prisoners. Harsh as these measures may seem to those who believe themselves to be defending their homes from an invader, it is certain that they are clearly warranted by the laws of civilized warfare. The only safety for the non-combatant population of an invaded country consists in the rule by which they are forbidden acts of private hostilities."

[46] Such conditions as carrying arms openly, observing the laws of war, and the like, set forth in *Rules of Land Warfare* (FM 27–10), § 9a.

[47] Cf. generally Oppenheim, *op. cit. supra* note 41, §§ 80–81.

[48] *Rules of Land Warfare*, § 348. The nature of "war rebels" and the acts which constitute "war treason" are to be found in §§ 349–50 of the Rules cited, as well as in the English counterpart, War Office, *Manual of Military Law 1929*, chap. XIV (as amended Jan. 1936), §§ 444–45. See further Oppenheim, 1917, 33 L.Q.R. 266–86, and §§ 254–55 of the same author's *International Law*, Vol. II.

The definition of the enemy is not exhausted with the test of allegiance. We must now deal with another enemy class, of equal importance. With its definition, citizenship plays no part, but residence in one case and situs of property in another are determining features.

"In war," says our Supreme Court, "all residents of enemy country are enemies." [49] And in another case that Court has declared that "it is ever a presumption that inhabitants of an enemy's territory are enemies, even though they are not participants in the war, though they are subjects of neutral states, or even subjects or citizens of the government prosecuting the war against the state within which they reside." [50] There can be no question of this proposition, which, originating many years ago, has again been affirmed by English and American courts in recent years.[51] In the same way of taking facts of residence rather than allegiance, it is clearly settled that the nature of enemy soil is to be determined not by matters of right or *status quo ante* but of physical possession. Any soil is enemy soil, no matter how forcible may be the manner of its occupation or how wrongful in inception, even though, prior to the enemy's invasion, it formed part of our own domain. This proposition, sustained nearly a century ago by our Supreme Court,[52] is admirably shown by the case of *United States v.*

---

[49] Lamar v. Browne, 1875, 92 U.S. 187, 194, 23 L. Ed. 650.

[50] Miller v. United States, 1870, 11 Wall. 268, 310, 20 L. Ed. 135.

[51] Porter v. Freudenberg, [1915] 1 K.B. 857; Daimler Co. v. Continental Fire Insurance Co., [1916] 2 A.C. 307, 319; Juragua Iron Co. v. United States, 1908, 212 U.S. 297, 29 S. Ct. 385, 53 L. Ed. 520; Faber v. United States, 1935, 81 Ct. Cl. 142, 148, 10 F. Supp. 602, certiorari denied, 296 U.S. 596, 56 S. Ct. 115, 80 L. Ed. 422.

[52] Thirty Hogsheads of Sugar v. Boyle, 1815, 9 Cranch 191, 195, 3 L. Ed. 701.

Rice.[53] In an action on a Custom House bond for goods imported into Castine, Maine, during its occupation by the British troops, was pleaded duress, arising from these facts: Previously the War of 1812 broke out, and the British troops captured Castine, and held it during the balance of the war. During their occupation, the British military authorities opened a custom house in the place, and appointed a collector. The goods in question were imported by residents of Castine, who, though United States citizens, continued to reside there, under the British occupation, and they paid the duties to the British military collector. After the treaty of peace, the British evacuated Castine, and the United States resumed possession, whereupon the United States collector seized the goods, and released them only upon the giving of the bond in suit. The Supreme Court considered that the bond was not enforceable and consequently upheld the plea on demurrer, saying,[54] through Mr. Justice Story: "By the conquest and military occupation of Castine, the enemy acquired that firm possession which enabled him to exercise the fullest rights of sovereignty over that place. The sovereignty of the United States over the territory was, of course, suspended, and the laws of the United States could no longer be rightfully enforced there, or be obligatory upon the inhabitants who remained and submitted to the conquerors. By the surrender the inhabitants passed under a temporary allegiance to the British government, and were bound by such laws, and such only, as it chose to recognize and impose. From the nature of the case, no other laws could be obligatory upon

---

[53] 1819, 4 Wheat. 246, 4 L. Ed. 562. Cf. also The Gutenfels, [1916] 2 A.C. 112.
[54] United States v. Rice, *loc. cit.* at p. 254.

them, for where there is no protection or allegiance or sovereignty, there can be no claim to obedience. Castine was, therefore, during this period, so far as respected our revenue laws, to be deemed a foreign port; and goods imported into it by the inhabitants, were subject to such duties only as the British government chose to require. Such goods were in no correct sense imported into the United States. The subsequent evacuation by the enemy, and resumption of authority by the United States, did not, and could not, change the character of the previous transactions."

But though such be the effect of occupation, yet the occupation is no less an act of *force majeure*, rather than one of state. Whether or not there was such occupation, therefore, is a question of fact, not one of state, and hence the courts can decide it like any other question of fact.[55]

In the same way may property become subject to treatment as though it belonged to an enemy, entirely irrespective of either the owner's allegiance or his residence. "Whether property be liable to capture as 'enemies' property' does not in any manner depend upon the personal allegiance of the owner. It is of no consequence whatever whether it belongs to an ally or a citizen. The owner, *pro hac vice*, is an enemy."[56] It follows that "for the purpose of capture, property found in enemy territory is enemy property, without regard to the status of the owner."[57]

[55] Clark v. United States, 1811, C.C. Pa., Fed. Cas. No. 2838; Fleming v. Page, 1850, 9 How. 603, 615, 13 L. Ed. 276; MacLeod v. United States, 1913, 229 U.S. 416, 33 S. Ct. 955, 57 L. Ed. 1260. Cf. generally Colby, 1925, 25 Col. L. Rev. 904, 907.
[56] Prize Cases, 1862, 2 Black 635, 674, 17 L. Ed. 459; cf. Young v. United States, 1877, 97 U.S. 39, 60, 24 L. Ed. 992.
[57] Lamar v. Browne, 1875, 92 U.S. 187, 194, 23 L. Ed. 650.

THE ARMY AND THE ENEMY

From this flows the duty of the loyal citizen to remove his assets from the hostile country as soon as possible, and delay puts him in the same state as an enemy. If such property, so left in the foe's domain, should be captured by our forces, no right of *jus postliminii* can require its delivery to the original owner. Once the property is impressed with the national character of the enemy nation, its subsequent capture by our forces does not change its status.[58] Nor is there any way to avoid this result by any act of the citizen, for it is equally unlawful for him, after war has started, to send a vessel to the enemy country to bring away his property.[59] Statutes alone can relieve such hardships, and our own history has furnished good examples of them.

In the War of 1812 Congress gave a six months' period of grace within which the President could allow safe conducts for the removal of property of British subjects within the United States.[60] And by the Act of March 12, 1863,[61] it was provided that property captured or found abandoned in the states composing the Confederacy was to be sold by the northern government, the proceeds to be held to satisfy claims by southern residents who remained loyal to the North, within two years after the cessation of the war.[62]

---

[58] The William Bagaley, 1867, 5 Wall. 377, 408, 18 L. Ed. 583.
[59] The Rapid, 1814, 8 Cranch 155, 163, 3 L. Ed. 520.
[60] Act of July 6, 1812, chap. 130, 2 Stat. 781; see dissenting opinion of Story, J., in Brown v. United States, 1814, 8 Cranch 110, 148, 3 L. Ed. 504.
[61] 12 Stat. 820.
[62] The privileges of the statute were extended to neutrals as well as those loyal to the North, United States v. O'Keefe, 1870, 11 Wall. 178, 20 L. Ed. 131; Carlisle v. United States, 1873, 16 Wall. 147, 21 L. Ed. 426. If the property of a non-resident alien had been used in aid of the Confederacy's military or other governmental operations, then *pro tanto*, its owner had been giving aid and comfort to the Confederacy and could not recover, Young v.

Within many of the treaties of the nineteenth century providing for the return of enemy subjects to their own countries within a limited time after the outbreak of a war are to be found provisions providing for the unrestrained withdrawal of the private property of these persons.[63] Several nations permitted enemy subjects to return to their native lands at the beginning of World War I, and Great Britain acted similarly in September, 1939.[64] The United States has acted otherwise, in spite of an act on the books providing for the enemy subject's "recovery, disposal, and removal of his goods and effects, and for his departure." [65] For, almost a month before the declaration of war with Japan, an executive proclamation and regulations purtenant thereto deprived the alien of permission to depart unless in possession of a valid permit from the Secretary of State,[66] and no permit to depart is granted if the departure of the alien is in any way prejudicial to the interest of the United States.[67] It would seem that the departure of an enemy

---

United States, 1877, 97 U.S. 39, 24 L. Ed. 992. A Presidential pardon operated as proof to the native born that the claimant gave no aid or comfort to the enemy, United States v. Padelford, 1869, 9 Wall. 531, 19 L. Ed. 788.

[63] E.g., art. xxiii of the Treaty with Prussia of July 11, 1799, Malloy, *Treaties between the United States and Other Powers*, II, p. 1494; art. xxv of the Treaty with Brazil of Dec. 12, 1828, Malloy, I, p. 141; art. xxi of the Treaty with Italy of Feb. 26, 1871, Malloy, I, p. 975.

[64] Oppenheim, *International Law*, p. 248.

[65] R.S. § 4068, 50 U.S.C.A. § 22; applied in Amory v. McGregor, 1818, 15 Johns. (N.Y.) 24, 8 Am. Dec. 205; Hughes v. Techt, 1919, 106 Misc. (N.Y.) 524, 176 N.Y.S. 356, affirmed 1919, 188 App. Div. (N.Y.) 743, 177 N.Y.S. 420, affirmed Techt v. Hughes, 1920, 229 N.Y. 222, 128 N.E. 185, 11 A.L.R. 166, certiorari denied 1920, 254 U.S. 643, 41 S. Ct. 14, 65 L. Ed. 454.

[66] Executive proclamation 2523 of Nov. 14, 1941, 6 Fed. Reg. 5821; Regulations of Nov. 19, 1941 [8 C.F.R. 175], 6 Fed. Reg. 5911.

[67] 8 C.F.R. § 175.24, 6 Fed. Reg. 5912.

subject, and certainly the removal of any property, would be of disadvantage to this country.[68]

With the enemy who comes to us with arms in his hands, or who, having borne arms, is sent back to us as a prisoner of war, the common law has little to do. His status is determined by the laws of war, and the common law courts will not entertain a writ of habeas corpus to test that determination.[69] By international convention, adopted by England and the United States, among others, he is "subject to the laws, regulations and orders in force in the armed forces of the detaining power." [70] Disciplinary measures and judicial proceedings are provided in case of insubordination, and general courts-martial now have jurisdiction over offenses committed,[71] although such was not

[68] Cf. control of transactions in foreign exchange and foreign-owned property pursuant to executive order No. 8389, of April 10, 1940, 5 Fed. Reg. 1400, as amended.

[69] Rex v. Schiever, 1759, 2 Burr. 765, 97 Eng. Rep. 551; The Three Spanish Sailors, 1779, 2 W. Black. 1324, 96 Eng. Rep. 775; Furly v. Newnham, 1780, 2 Doug. 419, 99 Eng. Rep. 269. These cases are cited with approval as the basis of the holding in Rex v. Vine Street Police Station Superintendent, [1916] 1 K.B. 268, 113 L.T. 971, which denied a resident enemy alien the right to sue out a writ of habeas corpus. The latter case has been criticized by McNair, *Legal Effects of War* (1920), p. 53, and the holding sharply limited and the dictum that an enemy alien be considered a prisoner of war disavowed in Schaffenius v. Goldberg, [1916] 1 K.B. 284, 113 L.T. 949. In this country alien enemies are differentiated from prisoners of war, Op. J.A.G. of July 20, 1918 and Aug. 5, 1918, 1918 Op. J.A.G. 581, 642. The position of resident enemy aliens is treated *infra*.

[70] Geneva Convention of July 27, 1929 [text in 47 Stat. 233] art. 45, incorporated as *Rules of Land Warfare*, § 118. Generally on the position of the prisoner of war according to international law, see Oppenheim, *International Law*, §§ 125 ff., and the references prefixed thereto; most recently Flory, *Prisoners of War* (1942).

[71] 1917 Op. J.A.G. 276 and 1918 Op. J.A.G. 783, digested in 1912–40 Dig. Op. J.A.G. § 369(7). Formerly military commissions had jurisdiction, Howland, Dig. Op. J.A.G., pp. 1066 ff.

always the case and instances of civil criminal trials are to be found in the books.[72] Whether the common law courts will afford the prisoner of war a remedy in the event that he suffers civil injury or loss while imprisoned or on parole, has not been settled, though the case of *Sparenburgh v. Bannatyne* [73] supports the affirmative. The plaintiff, a neutral serving as a sailor with the enemy fleet, was taken prisoner and later placed on board a merchantman returning to England; there being a scarcity of hands he was made a member of the crew, did his duty to the satisfaction of the captain, the defendant, and sued for his hire. Mr. Justice Heath, in affirming judgment for the plaintiff, says: "a prisoner of war is not adhering to the King's enemies, for he is here under protection from the King. If he conspires against the life of the King, it is high treason; if he is killed, it is murder; he does not therefore stand in the same situation as when in a state of actual hostility. It has been said, that a prisoner at war cannot contract; his case would be hard indeed if that were true." [74] And Mr. Justice Rooke adds: "An enemy under the King's protection may sue or be sued: that cannot be doubted. A prisoner at war is, to certain purposes, under the King's protection, and there are many cases where

---

[72] In Government v. M'Gregory, 1780, 14 Mass. 499, it was held that prisoners of war could be tried for murder in the ordinary tribunals; the fact that they might also be tried by court-martial "would not oust the courts of law of their general jurisdiction." Foster, *Crown Law* (1776), p. 185, who is referred to as presenting the English view, would seem to limit civil criminal trial to cases of high treason, cf. Lord Atkinson, in Johnstone v. Pedlar, [1921] 2 A.C. 262, 284, and Brereton, 1 Proc. Australian & N.Z. Soc. of Intern. Law, 1935, 143, 147. Other instances of concurrent civil criminal jurisdiction of prisoners of war during the Civil War, see Howland, Dig. Op. J.A.G., p. 1075; in England during World War I, Belfield, 9 Grotius Society, 1924, 131, 142.

[73] 1797, 1 Bos. & P. 163, 126 Eng. Rep. 837. [74] Case *cit.*, at p. 171.

THE ARMY AND THE ENEMY 105

he can maintain an action. . . . Under the licence of the King's officer he [plaintiff] pledged his labour at St. Helena, in order to procure a more comfortable subsistence. Accordingly he worked his way over, and earned a reasonable compensation. That being the case, I see no reason why he should not recover, even if he were alien enemy born." [75] There has been no decision on this point in the United States, yet the intimation in opinions of the military authorities is that a prisoner of war is entitled to civil protection.[76]

A slightly different question arises when the captured enemy turns out to be a traitor in arms. To which jurisdiction is it committed to try him for treason, he being thus apprehended in arms? When Perkin Warbeck was thus taken, having landed on English soil with armed forces bent on the dethronement of Henry VII, "it was resolved by the justices, that he could not be punished by the common law, but before the constable and marshal (who had special commission under the Great Seal to hear and determine the same according to martial law)." [77]

---

[75] The case was thoroughly considered and the doctrine approved in Schaffenius v. Goldberg, [1916] 1 K.B. 284, 301, 305, 113 L.T. 949. Cf. also Maria v. Hall, 1800, 2 Bos. & P. 236, 126 Eng. Rep. 1256; Maria v. Hall, 1807, 1 Taunt. 33, 127 Eng. Rep. 741. The contrary seems to be implied from the discussion of Sir M. Foster, *Crown Law* (1776), pp. 183 ff., see Baty and Morgan, *War: Its Conduct and Legal Results* (1915), pp. 251 f., and Brereton, *loc. cit. supra*, note 73.

[76] Sparenburgh v. Bannatyne is cited, without name, in Taylor v. Carpenter, 1846, C.C. Mass., Fed. Cas. No. 13,785, at p. 749, to the point that pleas of alienage are to be discouraged. The closest approach to adjudication of the point in the United States is the holding of the Judge Advocate General that the government is not liable for injuries suffered by a prisoner of war due to the negligent operation of a motor truck by a civilian employee of the government, Opinion of July 31, 1919, 1919 Op. J.A.G. 671.

[77] Summarized by Coke, in Calvin's Case, 1609, 7 Co. Rep. 1a, 6b, 77 Eng. Rep. 377; cf. Hale, *Pleas of the Crown*, I (1736), p. 59. In such a case as this the

But Warbeck was an alien, and the fact that he could not be indicted is no authority as regards a disloyal citizen; indeed, it has long been settled, both by common law and statute, that a citizen who joins the enemy's forces is by that very act guilty of the crime of high treason.[78] This is nowhere more forcefully demonstrated than in the more or less celebrated case of Wolfe Tone.

During the Irish Rebellion of 1798, Wolfe Tone was captured in Ireland, wearing the uniform of a French officer, having indeed but recently been landed from a French warship. The prisoner was put on trial before a court-martial in Dublin, convicted, and sentenced to execution; but his counsel, the eloquent Curran, appeared before the Irish King's Bench, and applied for a writ of habeas corpus on the morning of the day set for the execution. It was granted, and the court, according to the reporter, waited in a state of utmost agitation for its return. The jailor refused to deliver the prisoner, but before the court could put further measures into effect, the announce-

---

Court of the High Constable and Marshal, and in later centuries courts-martial (for the historical development see Winthrop, *Military Law and Precedents*, p. 46 f.; Great Britain, *Manual of Military Law 1929*, pp. 7 ff.) was authorized to sentence to the penalty of death, corporal punishment, or otherwise, "as by the rules and methods of war and the military laws of nations on that behalf ought to be inflicted," quoting from the court-martial of Tobias le Roy, alias Bourke, in 1695, cited by Clode, *Military Forces of the Crown*, I (1869), p. 188. The more humane treatment accorded the captured enemy soldier since the eighteenth century precludes the death penalty or corporal punishment, Oppenheim, *International Law*, Vol. II, § 125.

[78] Generally Hale, *Pleas of the Crown*, Vol. I, chaps. xi ff. Particularly on the citizen in enemy uniform, see Rex v. Vaughan, 1696, Holt K.B. 689, 90 Eng. Rep. 1280, 13 How. St. Tr. 485; Townley's Case, 1746, Foster 7, 18 How. St. Tr. 329; Rex v. Lynch, [1903] 1 K.B. 444, 88 L.T. 26. And in this country Respublica v. M'Carty, 1781, Pa. Sup. Ct., 2 Dallas 86, 1 L. Ed. 300; United States v. Greiner, 1861, D.C. Pa., 4 Phila. 396, Fed. Cas. No. 15,262.

ment was made that the prisoner had committed suicide. The entire proceeding was *ex parte;* counsel for the army was never heard, and the only "decision" lay in the action of the court in granting the writ on application of the prisoner's counsel.[79]

The point which is implicit in Curran's action is as true today as it was at the close of the eighteenth century: a court-martial has no jurisdiction to try a disloyal citizen for treason, even though he be captured while serving in the enemy's forces. If the traitor had been a member of the armed forces before his adherence to the enemy, he might be court-martialed for desertion,[80] or if in any way he had aided the enemy, he might be guilty of treasonable conduct punishable under the Articles of War,[81] but whenever and wherever civil courts function, military tribunals cannot try a citizen for the crime of treason, as such.[82]

---

[79] Wolfe Tone's Case, 1798, 27 How. St. Tr. 613. In the first edition of this book Professor Glenn took issue with Dicey, *Law of the Constitution* (9th ed. 1939), p. 293 f., for considering the case as "holding that there can be no state of martial law so long as the civil courts are open." Certainly, Curran's statements lend themselves to this interpretation, and the case has generally been taken as a milepost in the history of British martial law, cf. Clode, *Military Forces of the Crown*, II (1869), p. 169 f.; Fairman, *Law of Martial Rule* (1930), pp. 106 ff.; Rankin, *When Civil Law Fails* (1939), p. 181; Wiener, *Practical Manual of Martial Law* (1940), p. 132 n. 4.

[80] Opinions of the Judge Advocates General, see Howland, Dig. Op. J.A.G., pp. 1076 (IC11d3), 400 (IC2), and cf. Flory, *Prisoners of War* (1942), pp. 144 ff.

[81] A.W. 81, 10 U.S.C.A. § 1553: Relieving, corresponding with, or aiding the enemy. On the distinction between the offenses encompassed herein, and the civil offense of treason, see Winthrop, *Military Law and Precedents*, pp. 629 ff.

[82] In the United States treason has never been one of the civil offenses within the jurisdiction of courts-martial (A.W. 92, 93), so that trial thereof by military tribunals can occur only in the event of military government or martial rule, wherein military commissions and provost courts take the place of civil tribunals, see chap. VI, *infra*. But British statutory law accords to courts-

THE ARMY AND THE LAW

Outside of the question as to jurisdiction over armed traitors, the dealings between our army and that of the enemy are wholly beyond the pale of the common law. The rules of warfare, of truces, of bombardments and the like, are wholly matters of customary military law, as modified by international conventions. Violations of these rules constitute "war crimes" punishable in our military courts.[83] One of the most famous instances in our history of the exercise of this jurisdiction is to be found in the case of Major André. Major André, to repeat briefly what is with us a twice-told tale, was a commissioned officer of the British Army during our Revolutionary war. In plain clothes, he came within our lines to negotiate with the traitorous Arnold—commanding our strong place of West Point—for the delivery of that fortress to the British commander. Returning from this mission, Major André was apprehended near Tarrytown and delivered to General Washington. He was brought to trial at Tappan before a military commission or "board of general officers," composed of six major generals, and eight brigadiers, convened by order of the commander in chief. He was convicted of the charge of espionage and sentenced to be hanged, and the sentence was duly executed.[84] Protest regarding this judgment has been confined to English civilians, as distinct from military men.

martial jurisdiction over treason (along with murder, manslaughter, rape, and other civil offenses) by a person subject to military law, provided the offense is committed outside the United Kingdom, and, in addition, that the person was on active service or the locale was more than a hundred miles distant from the site of a competent civil court. Army Act § 41, Great Britain, *Manual of Military Law 1929*, p. 459 f.

[83] Oppenheim, *International Law*, II, pp. 328 ff., 450 ff.; Colby, 1925, 23 Mich. L. Rev. 482 ff., 606 ff.

[84] 2 Chandler's Criminal Cases, 157; further on Major André's trial see Hyde, *International Law*, II, p. 347 n. 3, and Oppenheim, *op. cit.*, p. 330 n. 5, and references there cited.

Obviously such matters are not actionable civilly. Civil litigation between enemy combatants is impossible in our courts, because the foreign alien enemy cannot sue one of our citizens.[85] Nor can the foreigner sue to recover damages after the war, based on an alleged breach of the laws of war governing the conduct of hostilities.[86] International convention has provided that a belligerent nation violating the 1907 Regulations respecting the laws of war shall be liable to pay compensation and in addition be responsible for all acts committed by persons forming part of its armed forces.[87] Treaties of peace often provide that the vanquished nation shall compensate for damage done the civilian population of the victor,[88] but an individual cannot found a claim on such a treaty, even though it appears he was intended to benefit from it, unless the state concluded the treaty as agent or trustee of the individual in question.[89]

The dealings between our army and the civilian inhabitants of occupied enemy territory are matters reserved for the next chapter. It remains then to notice the alien enemy who chooses to dwell within this country.

This sort of enemy occupies, in the present conflict, a most

---

[85] The common law rule, reiterated in sec. 7b of the Trading with the Enemy Act of Oct. 6, 1917, 50 U.S.C.A. App. § 7(b); cf. Rothbarth v. Herzfeld, 1917, 179 App. Div. (N.Y.) 865, 167 N.Y.S. 199, affirmed 1918, 223 N.Y. 578, 119 N.E. 1075, and further cases in the annotations in 50 U.S.C.A., pp. 220 ff., and Huberich, *Trading with the Enemy* (1918), pp. 191 ff.; recently Ex parte Colonna, 1942, 314 U.S. 510, 62 S. Ct. 373, 86 L. Ed. 357, treated by Battle, 1942, 28 Va. L. Rev. 429. The leading English cases are discussed in Porter v. Freudenberg, [1915] 1 K.B. 857, 869 ff., and by McNair, *Legal Effects of War* (1920), pp. 26 ff.
[86] Cf. *infra*, p. 118; on the right of a citizen to sue for violation by the armed forces of his own country, see chap. 9, *infra*.
[87] Hague Convention IV of Oct. 18, 1907, 36 Stat. 2277, § 3; *Rules of Land Warfare*, § 345.
[88] Oppenheim, *International Law*, II, pp. 462 f.
[89] Civilian War Rights Association v. The King, [1932] A.C. 14.

interesting position, quite different from that which he held during earlier periods in the history of our country. Upon the outbreak of the war with Japan, acting within the scope of a Congressional act that dates from the close of the eighteenth century,[90] the President issued proclamations and regulations respecting the conduct to be observed by resident Japanese, Germans, and Italians;[91] supervision thereof within the United States, Puerto Rico, the Virgin Islands, and Alaska was delegated to the Attorney General, and in the Canal Zone, the Hawaiian Islands, and the Philippine Islands, to the Secretary of War.[92] To the officials named, and to officers of the Department of Justice and military commanders designated by them, authority was given to arrest and intern such alien enemies as attempted to enter or to leave or were found in restricted or prohibited areas, or such as might be considered dangerous to the public peace or safety, or in any way violated regulations prescribed for their conduct.[93] The extent of control exerted may be somewhat broader than in earlier times, but a more interesting factor is the interposition of the army into the affairs of civilian alien enemies.

Not only in the territories but in the continental United

[90] Act of July 6, 1798, 1 Stat. 577, as amended by Act of April 16, 1918, 40 Stat. 531, 50 U.S.C.A. §§ 21–24. The act is constitutional, De Lacey v. United States, 1918, C.C.A. Cal., 249 F. 625; aliens who become alien enemies upon the outbreak of war have rights and privileges only by sufferance, Techt v. Hughes, 1920, 229 N.Y. 222, 236, 128 N.E. 185, 11 A.L.R. 166; further judicial construction of the act in the annotations to the 50 U.S.C.A., *loc. cit.*
[91] Dec. 7–8, 1941, 6 Fed. Reg. 6321 ff. Cf. the proclamations of President Wilson, in 40 Stat. 1651, 1716, 1730, 1772.
[92] By proclamation of Dec. 29, 1941, 7 Fed. Reg. 55, jurisdiction over Alaska was transferred from the Attorney General to the Secretary of War.
[93] The Presidential regulations were supplemented by those of the Department of Justice, 28 C.F.R. 30, 7 Fed. Reg. 844. For the mechanics of alien enemy control see Hill, 1942, 10 Geo. Wash. L. Rev. 851.

THE ARMY AND THE ENEMY

States itself the military authorities have entered into the supervision of alien enemies. By executive order of February 19, 1942, the Secretary of War and military commanders he might designate were authorized—with a view to carrying out the aims of the Espionage and Sabotage Acts—[94] to prescribe military areas and zones, within which any or all persons could be excluded, or could only remain under such restrictions as might be imposed; such prescription was to supersede the prohibited and restricted areas previously designated by the Attorney General.[95] Various military areas and zones have been so named, and alien enemies—along with citizens of Japanese ancestry—have been excluded and evacuated from certain portions of the United States, and in others have had their activities severely curtailed.[96] Violations of orders and regulations promulgated for such areas constitute misdemeanors punishable by the civil courts; [97] the possible alternate step of subjecting the offenders to the jurisdiction of courts-martial has not been taken.[98] In sum, the army has much more concern with the

---

[94] Espionage Act of June 15, 1917, 40 Stat. 217, as amended by Act of Mar. 28, 1940, 54 Stat. 79, 50 U.S.C.A. §§ 31 ff.; Sabotage Act of April 20, 1918, 40 Stat. 533, as amended by Act of Nov. 30, 1940, 54 Stat. 1220, and Act of Aug. 21, 1941, 55 Stat. 655, 50 U.S.C.A. §§ 101 ff.

[95] Executive order 9066, 7 Fed. Reg. 1407.

[96] E.g., War Dept. Public Proc. Nos. 1–2, 7 Fed. Reg. 2320, 2405, establish military areas and zones in the western states with varied degrees of restriction, while W.D. Proc. No. 3, 7 Fed. Reg. 2543, sets forth regulations for the conduct of alien enemies and citizens of Japanese ancestry in the restricted zones. Cf. also Exclusion orders, e.g., 7 Fed. Reg. 2581, 2871.

[97] Act of March 21, 1942, 18 U.S.C.A. § 97a. The Act has been held valid in the case of an American-born Japanese who had been elected to become a Japanese citizen upon arriving at majority, United States v. Minoru Yasui, 1942, D.C. Ore., 40 F. Supp. 40. The conflict as to its constitutionality with regard to American citizens of Japanese ancestry is dealt with *infra*, chap. 10.

[98] If the military offenses of relieving, corresponding with, or aiding the enemy (A.W. 81) or spying (A.W. 82) are not broad enough to give courts-

resident alien enemy and—to anticipate a subject dealt with in a later chapter—with our own civilian citizens than ever before.

Yet it may still be said that, for the most part, the resident civilian enemy is in the bourne of the common law. If he is here by permission, he rests in the full protection of the law.[99] He can sue and be sued;[100] indeed, there is reason to believe that even the interned alien enemy is entitled to a cause of action.[101] Until his permit is revoked, his person and his property are safe.

---

martial jurisdiction, there seems to be no constitutional objection to appropriate legislation in that respect. Note that the military areas and zones designated fall within the "Western Defense Command," War Dept. Order of Dec. 11, 1941—likewise the "Eastern Defense Command"—and thus the requisites of territorial jurisdiction, "theater of operations," may be satisfied; cf. Ex parte Kanai, 1942, D.C. Wash., 46 F. Supp. 286, 288; but contra, United States v. Minoru Yasui, 1942, D.C. Ore., 48 F. Supp. 40, 52.

[99] Kent, J., in Clarke v. Morey, 1813, 10 Johns. (N.Y.) 69, 72: "By the law of nations, an alien who comes to reside in a foreign country, is entitled, so long as he conducts himself peaceable, to continue to reside there, under the public protection." A survey of the position of aliens in time of war, in the Anglo-American law, by Cardozo, J., in Techt v. Hughes, cit. *supra,* note 90. See also Baty and Morgan, *War: Its Conduct and Legal Results* (1915), pp. 251 ff.

[100] The American and English cases up to the last war are collected by Oakes, 1917, 23 Case & Comm. 985. Noteworthy, in the present conflict, are Petition of Bernheimer, 1942, C.C.A. Pa., 130 F. 2d 396; Ex parte Kawato, 1942,—U.S.—, 63 S. Ct. 115, 87 L. Ed. 94. See also Huberich, *Law Relating to Trading with the Enemy* (1918), pp. 191 ff.; McNair, *Legal Effects of War* (1920), pp. 31 ff., and 1942, 58 L.Q.R. 191 ff.; note, 1942, 30 Calif. L. Rev. 358; Battle, 1942, 28 Va. L. Rev. 429.

[101] In the leading case of Wells v. Williams, 1697, 1 Ld. Raym. 282, 283, 91 Eng. Rep. 1086, it is stated that a resident alien enemy who is "here by the King's leave and protection ever since, without molesting the Government or being molested by it, may be allowed to sue, for that is consequent to his being in protection." In Schaffenius v. Goldberg, [1916] 1 K.B. 284, 113 L.T. 949, an "innocent" internee was granted a cause of action; it would seem that "criminal" internment—because of hostile attitude—would preclude the right to sue, see McNair, 1942, 58 L.Q.R. 191, 209.

THE ARMY AND THE ENEMY

As to person, an order of interment will end the matter. As to property, affirmative action of the legislature is necessary before the common law will sanction any adverse claim resting on the question of his status. Whatever may once have been the practice of the government in confiscating his assets with the outbreak of war, giving him back at the conclusion of peace what might remain on hand,[102] our Supreme Court has made it clear that the declaration of war does not of itself sanction confiscation proceedings, but that it "vests only a right, the assertion of which depends on the will of the sovereign power." [103] But the court did not deny the existence of the right. It has been said that Congress intended, by the Trading with the Enemy Act of 1917 and its amendments,[104] to confiscate the enemy property taken possession of by the Alien Property Custodian, rather than merely to sequester and conserve it until the termination of hostilities.[105] Today the control exercised

---

[102] The early doctrine is set forth in the opening chapters of Gathings, *International Law and American Treatment of Alien Enemy Property* (1940); see also Porter v. Freudenberg, [1915] 1 K.B. 857, 869, 112 L.T. 313.

[103] Brown v. United States, 1814, 8 Cranch 110, 123, 3 L. Ed. 504; cf. Britton v. Butler, 1872, C.C. N.Y., Fed. Cas. No. 1903.

[104] By the amendment of March 28, 1918, 40 Stat. 459, the purpose and scope of the Act was broadened, and when the President determined that the public interest required it, the Alien Property Custodian was empowered to make such disposition of the property seized as he saw fit, United States v. Chemical Foundation, 1925, C.C.A. Del., 5 F. 2d 191. The present powers of the Alien Property Custodian are set forth in executive orders of March 11 and April 21, 1942, 7 Fed. Reg. 1971, 2985, and regulations of March 26, 1942, 7 Fed. Reg. 2290; instances of vesting orders thereunder, 7 Fed. Reg. 2417, 2698.

[105] Armstrong, 1923, 9 J. Am. Bar Assoc. 485; Cohen, 1921, 21 Col. L. Rev. 666; Potterf, 1927, 2 Ind. L.J. 453. In one case, at least, the court indicates that the 1918 amendment means confiscation, Munich Reinsurance Co. v. First Reinsurance Co., 1925, C.C.A. Conn., 6 F. 2d 742, appeal dismissed, 1927, 273 U.S. 666; 47 S. Ct. 458, 71 L. Ed. 830. The Supreme Court has taken different positions on this question, intimating recently that confiscation was not in-

over resident alien enemies by virtue of the Alien Enemies Act, the Trading with the Enemy Act and the many other acts and regulations respecting aliens [106] is intended to eradicate fifth-column activity and to permit of full participation in the war effort. Such control is primarily vested in civilian authorities, but in a few instances, as has been indicated above, the army enters into the picture.[107]

---

tended, Becker Steel Co. v. Cummings, 1935, 296 U.S. 74, 56 S. Ct. 15, 80 L. Ed. 54, yet granting compensation or restitution to the alien enemy only by grace of Congress, Cummings v. Deutsche Bank, 1937, 300 U.S. 115, 57 S. Ct. 359, 81 L. Ed. 545.

[106] E.g., Alien Registration Act of June 28, 1940, 54 Stat. 673, as amended by Act of Oct. 13, 1941, 8 U.S.C.A. §§ 451 ff.; Registration of Agents of Foreign Principals, Act of June 8, 1938, 52 Stat. 631, as amended 22 U.S.C.A. §§ 601 ff.; Registration of organizations subject to foreign control (Voorhis Act) of Oct. 17, 1940, 54 Stat. 1201, 18 U.S.C.A. §§ 14 ff.

[107] Even before our entry into the war, the army expected to participate in the enforcement of the laws and regulations governing alien enemies, particularly in "such theaters of operations or coastal frontiers as may be established in United States territory," Mobilization Regulations of April 1, 1940 (MR 1-11.16, 18).

6. MILITARY OCCUPATION IN MATTERS OF GOVERNMENT

IN THE last chapter we considered the position, at common law, of the enemy when within our gates, and the law with respect to the alien enemy so placed. Necessarily we were forced to treat somewhat of the loyal citizen's rights and obligations, as well as those of the loyal soldier. We now deal with the enemy when met abroad, within his own country.[1]

In such a connection we need consider only the rights and obligations of our army and its commanders. For reasons we have already examined, no civilian of ours can have any rights enforceable within the scope of our common law. Our civilian cannot trade or correspond with the enemy abroad, and, if one of our citizens chooses to live in the enemy country, or leave property there, he is, *quoad hoc*, an enemy himself, and in the same class with the enemy so far as the common law view is concerned. The civilian, therefore, as such, has no place in the enemy country, unless he goes there with a license permitting him to trade with the enemy, as in *Mitchell v. Harmony*.[2] Out-

---

[1] For further treatment of matters discussed in this and the following chapter, the reader is referred to Magoon, *Reports on the Law of Civil Government* (3d ed. 1903); Birkhimer, *Military Government and Martial Law* (3d ed. 1914); Winthrop, *Military Law and Precedents* (2d ed. rev. 1920), pp. 798 ff.; H. A. Smith, *Military Government* (1920); Dowell, *Military Aid to the Civil Power* (1925), pp. 54 ff.; Betts, 1940, 4 Fed. B.A.J. 27 ff.; McNair, 1941, 57 L.Q.R. 33 ff.

[2] 1851, 13 How. 115, 14 L. Ed. 75, discussed *supra*, p. 92.

side that limited class we need consider only the army, and its entourage as prescribed by the Articles of War.

All members of this organization, as we have already seen, are subject to the jurisdiction of courts-martial, administering the body of military law, codified and uncodified, which is applicable to the soldier;[3] while the army is at home the criminal courts have a certain concurrent jurisdiction.[4] But the jurisdiction of military courts becomes exclusive the instant the army leaves our national boundaries. For the most part such jurisdiction is exercised by courts-martial.[5] As early as the Civil War, however, it was provided that "acts commonly recognized as crimes against society" committed by "soldiers, officers or other persons connected with the army" were "punishable by a court or military commission."[6] During World War I General Pershing specifically forbade that members of the armed forces in the area of occupation be tried by military commissions and provost courts,[7] but subsequently the intention appears to have been to give these tribunals jurisdiction over certain offenses, even if committed by soldiers.[8] However, the manual on *Military Government* issued in 1940 definitely provides that "persons subject to the military law of the United States charged

---

[3] *Supra*, pp. 32 ff.   [4] *Supra*, pp. 75 ff.
[5] See Colby, 1923, 17 Amer. Jour. Inter. Law 109 ff., and 1925, 25 Col. L. Rev. 904, 918 ff.
[6] Army of the Potomac, G.O. No. 2 of April 7, 1862, cited in 1861, 9 Rebellion Record, pt. 3, p. 77. Cf. Miller, 1941, 7 Ohio State L.J. 188, 203 ff., and note his definition of "military commission," 193 n. 10.
[7] Smith, *Military Government*, p. 103.
[8] *Manual for Courts-Martial* (1921), p. 2. According to the British *Manual of Military Law 1929*, pp. 67 ff., 476 ff., a special kind of court-martial, the field general court-martial, is convened for the trial of offenses committed abroad; Amendment 11 of August, 1935, substitutes "out of the United Kingdom" for "abroad."

MILITARY GOVERNMENT

with offenses will be tried by court-martial."[9] In any event, military tribunals alone have jurisdiction over our forces abroad. While marching through a friendly country or stationed therein, the courts have declared that our army is "exempt from the civil or criminal jurisdiction of the place."[10] The consent of the friendly government is either assumed as a matter of course,[11] or specifically procured. Thus, an article in the agreement leasing us bases in British territory reserves jurisdiction over members of the armed forces to the American military authorities,[12] while English legislation grants exclusive criminal

---

[9] *Basic Field Manual* (FM 27-5) § 25. This section has specific reference to the military government of occupied territory, but the language may apply to forces wherever abroad.

[10] Coleman v. Tennessee, 1878, 97 U.S. 509, 515, 24 L. Ed. 1118. The leading case upon this subject is The Exchange, 1812, 7 Cranch 116, 137, 3 L. Ed. 287. A thorough treatment of this topic by King, *Jurisdiction over Friendly Foreign Armed Forces*, 1942, 36 Am. J. Int. Law 539–67.

[11] "It is well settled that a foreign army permitted to march through a friendly country, or to be stationed in it, by permission of its government or sovereign, is exempt from the civil and criminal jurisdiction of the place. The sovereign is understood, said this court in the celebrated case of The Exchange (*supra*) to cede a portion of his territorial jurisdiction when he allows the troops of a foreign prince to pass through his dominions. In such a case, without any express declaration waiving jurisdiction over the army to which this right of passage has been granted, the sovereign who should attempt to exercise it would certainly be considered as violating his faith. By exercising it, the purpose for which the free passage was granted would be defeated, and a portion of the military forces of a foreign independent nation would be diverted from those national objects and duties to which it was applicable, and would be withdrawn from the control of the sovereign whose power and whose safety might greatly depend on retaining the exclusive command and disposition of this force. The grant of a free passage, therefore, implies a waiver of all jurisdiction over the troops during their passage, and permits the foreign general to use that discipline and to inflict those punishments which the government of his army may require." Coleman v. Tennessee, 1878, 97 U.S. 509, 515, 24 L. Ed. 1118.

[12] Agreement of March 27, 1941, Art. IV (Executive Agreement, ser. 235).

jurisdiction over American soldiers in the British Isles to the United States authorities.[13]

Such being the case with a friendly ally, it follows *a fortiori*, as the Supreme Court has said,[14] that our army, when within the enemy's country, is wholly exempt from the jurisdiction of his courts. "The fact that war is waged between two countries negatives the possibility of jurisdiction being exercised by the tribunals of the one country over persons engaged in the military service of the other for offenses committed while in such service. Aside from this want of jurisdiction, there would be something incongruous and absurd in permitting an officer or soldier of an invading army to be tried by his enemy, whose country he had invaded." [15]

If, then, a criminal court in the enemy country should, during the war, or after it, be asked to countenance the prosecution of an offense committed by a soldier of our army while the latter was within the enemy country, the common law view of the matter is that the court, being wholly without jurisdiction, should refuse to act. That was the decision in *Coleman v. Tennessee*.[16] The appellant, a soldier of the United States forces in hostile occupation of Tennessee during the Civil War, was tried by court-martial for murder, and acquitted. The war end-

---

[13] United States of America (Visiting Forces) Act, 5 & 6 Geo. 6, c. 61. Cf. also the arrangement by which Australian federal and state authorities have agreed to relinquish American soldiers arrested for civil offenses to the army authorities, King, *loc. cit.*, pp. 555 ff.

[14] Coleman v. Tennessee, cit. *supra* note 11, at p. 516.

[15] In accord Mitchell v. Clark, 1883, 110 U.S. 633, 648, 28 L. Ed. 279, 4 S. Ct. 170; Freeland v. Williams, 1889, 131 U.S. 405, 416, 33 L. Ed. 193, 9 S. Ct. 763. Cf. Birkhimer, *Military Government and Martial Law* (3d 1914), pp. 157 ff.; Colby, 1925, 23 Mich. L. Rev. 482, 484.

[16] 1878, 97 U.S. 509, 24 L. Ed. 1118.

ing, and Tennessee being restored as a state of the union, the appellant was indicted in a court of that state for the same murder. He pleaded, in bar, his former acquittal by the court-martial. If Tennessee had not been, at the time of the court-martial, enemy territory, that plea should have been sufficient.[17] But the Tennessee court held the plea bad even as a plea of *autre fois acquit*, and the appellant was then convicted. The Supreme Court held that the plea should not have been *autre fois acquit*, for that implied a concurrent jurisdiction in the Tennessee court, whereas really, Tennessee having been then enemy country, its courts had no jurisdiction at all of any military offense; the court-martial's jurisdiction being exclusive. The court, however, treated the plea as though it had properly stated this contention, and reversed the state court's judgment accordingly.

There is, however, in such a state of affairs, one tribunal of the enemy that can be said to have concurrent jurisdiction. If the culprit's act constitutes a "war crime" of the sort previously mentioned, then, should he be taken prisoner by the enemy's army, the latter's commander could put him to trial before a court-martial of the enemy's own choosing.[18]

So much, then, for criminal jurisdiction over the soldier when in the enemy's country; it is exclusively vested in military tribunals, normally the court-martial. Criminal laws of the enemy state "are continued in force, if such be the case, only for the protection and benefit of its own people. As respects them, the same acts which constituted offenses before the military

---

[17] Grafton v. United States, 1907, 206 U.S. 333, 51 L. Ed. 1084, 27 S. Ct. 749, 11 Ann. Cas. 640; discussed *supra*, chap. 4.
[18] *Supra*, chap. 5.

occupation constitute offenses afterwards; and the same tribunals, unless superseded by order of the military commanders, continue to exercise their ordinary jurisdiction." [19]

As the invading soldier remains under the jurisdiction of military tribunals as to criminal offenses, the same rule, by the very reason of the thing, applies to his torts or even his matters of contract. Clearly our soldier is not answerable civilly to an enemy court, because he has not come within the sanction of the enemy nation's municipal law. That law is "not for the protection or control of the army, or its officers or soldiers. These remain subject to the laws of war and are responsible for their conduct only to their own government, and the tribunals by which those laws are administered. If guilty of wanton cruelty to persons, or of unnecessary spoliation of property, or of other acts not authorized by the laws of war, they may be tried and punished by the military tribunals. They are amenable to no other tribunal, except that of public opinion, which, it is to be hoped, will always brand with infamy all who authorize or sanction acts of cruelty and oppression." [20]

In *Dow v. Johnson*, from which quotation has just been made, the defendant, in command of forces operating within the occupied portions of Louisiana during the Civil War, seized for the use of his force certain supplies belonging to the plaintiff. For this the plaintiff sued in the provisional court in New Orleans (of which more hereafter), and recovered judgment by default. After the war the plaintiff sued the defendant, on this judgment, in the federal court sitting in Maine. The Supreme Court held that a plea of *nul tiel record* was good because the

---

[19] Coleman v. Tennessee, cit. *supra*, note 16, at p. 517.
[20] Dow v. Johnson, 1879, 100 U.S. 158, 166, 25 L. Ed. 632.

provisional court had no jurisdiction. The court declared that "when our armies marched into the country which acknowledged the authority of the Confederate government, that is, into the enemy's country, their officers and soldiers were not subject to its laws, nor amenable to its tribunals for their acts. They were subject only to their own government, and only by its laws, administered by its authority, could they be called to account."

Nor, as a general proposition, has the enemy a right of action with respect to property seized, in any of the courts ordinarily having jurisdiction.[21] If anybody can be considered as liable for the tort, it is the United States government, not the military government of the occupied territory,[22] and for such a tort no action will lie against the United States.[23] The reason is simple. When our army operates in the enemy country, every act is an act of war, against one not in the peace of our state. No member of the forces can conceivably be liable in our courts for an act committed in the flagrancy of war and done to one who, at the time of the offense, had no right of action in our courts.[24] To say that, with the conclusion of peace, the injured

[21] Coolidge v. Guthrie, 1868, C.C. Ohio, Fed. Cas. No. 3185; Ford v. Surget, 1878, 97 U.S. 594, 24 L. Ed. 1018; Elphinstone v. Bedreechund, 1830, 1 Knapp P.C. 316, 12 Eng. Rep. 340.
[22] Wallace v. Alford, 1869, 39 Ga. 609.
[23] 28 U.S.C.A. §§ 41(20), 141; Ribas y Hijo v. United States, 1904, 194 U.S. 315, 24 S. Ct. 727, 48 L. Ed. 994; Herrara v. United States, 1912, 222 U.S. 558, 32 S. Ct. 179, 56 L. Ed. 316. In Juragua Iron Co. v. United States, 1909, 212 U.S. 297, 29 S. Ct. 385, 53 L. Ed. 520, it was held that a claim for confiscation for unlawful destruction of property during a war, under the order of an officer, is one sounding in tort and thus not recoverable; cf. Gallego, Messa & Co. v. United States, 1908, 43 Ct. Cl. 444. Whether compensation be granted or not is a matter for Congress and not the courts, United States v. Chemical Foundation, 1924, D.C. Del., 294 F. 300.
[24] Winthrop, *Military Law and Precedents*, p. 889.

enemy may sue in our courts, is to create an actionable tort *ex post facto;* and that, too, as of a time when it would have been against public policy even to have suggested that an action lay. This the common law courts will not do. When an act is done "*flagrante,* yet *non dum cessante bello,*" to paraphrase the words of Lord Tenterden, speaking for the Privy Council, "the municipal court has no jurisdiction to adjudge upon the subject, but if anything was done amiss, resort could only be had to the Government for redress." [25]

Along these lines our Supreme Court describes the United States government as the only source to which the plaintiff can look for redress, for violation of the laws of war; and that as a matter of grace, not right. In *Lamar v. Browne* [26] the plaintiff, after the close of the Civil War, sued the defendant in the federal court, sitting in Massachusetts, for the conversion of cotton. The defendant showed that he, as a government agent, seized this cotton in a Southern state under military occupation, under color of the Captured and Abandoned Property Act. The Supreme Court held this defense sufficient, because (*a*) being found in enemy territory, the cotton was enemy property, for reasons heretofore discussed, and (*b*) the cotton was a legitimate subject of capture, for reasons hereafter assigned. In *Ford v. Surget* [27] the same beneficent rule was applied in behalf of a Confederate officer who had burned cotton belonging to the plaintiff, the latter being a resident of and a sympathizer with the Confederacy. The destruction of the cotton, said the Court, "under the orders of the Confederate military authorities, for the purpose of preventing it from falling into the hands

[25] Elphinstone v. Bedreechund, cit. *supra* note 21, at p. 360.
[26] 1876, 92 U.S. 187, 23 L. Ed. 650.   [27] Cit. *supra,* note 21.

MILITARY GOVERNMENT

of the Federal army, was, under the circumstances alleged in the special pleas, an act of war upon the part of the military forces of the rebellion, for which the person executing such orders was relieved from civil responsibility at the suit of the owner voluntarily residing at the time within the lines of the insurrection." And in *Elphinstone v. Bedreechund* [28] the plaintiff's property had been seized under the defendant's order; the defendant mistakenly supposing it to be the property of the hostile sovereign or public moneys. No active hostilities were then being carried on in the immediate neighborhood of the seizure, though the war was not at an end. The Privy Council held that this was an act of war, within the protection of the rule we have mentioned, and that the defendant was not liable.

It is different in the case of controversies between enemy subjects. They are not necessarily bound to resort to the courts established by the conqueror; on the contrary, their original courts may remain open for all ordinary civil business, and, within limits of the nature above and hereafter outlined, for criminal business as well. But this is entirely at the will of the commander. What does that mean?

Military government, of which we are now to speak, is a thing familiar to our courts.[29] During the War of 1812, a portion of Maine was taken and occupied by the British. In the Mexican War, not merely were parts of Mexico occupied by our forces, but the territory afterwards ceded to us was first subject to our armed occupation. From a strategic point of

---

[28] Cit. *supra*, note 21.
[29] Cases respecting military government are cited in Winthrop, *Military Law*, pp. 800 f.; Birkhimer, *Military Government and Martial Law*, pp. 53 ff., 80 ff., 89 ff., and *passim;* Wigmore, *Guide to American International Law*, Part II (1942), §§ 80 ff.

view the history of our Civil War was one of slow constriction of the South; from a legal point of view it was a broadening drama of military occupation, successive governments being established as the Confederacy gave ground. The Confederates, on the other hand, established but one military government, in Arizona,[30] Lee's occupation of southern Pennsylvania producing no such result. Cuba, Puerto Rico, and the Philippines were for a time under military government, while the American forces acted with their allies in the occupation of the Rhineland at the close of World War I.[31]

Military occupation means, in this connection, several things: *First:* The very fact of the occupation severs the political relation between the people of the hostile country and the former sovereign, and the inhabitants owe the commander the duty of obeying his regulations and none other.[32] This, however, does not effect a change of allegiance. The commander has no right to require the inhabitants to take an oath of allegiance; at best he can only ask for an oath of obedience to his orders. That was the mistake made by General Pope in the Civil War, when he included, among his famous orders, a requirement that all inhabitants of the occupied districts must either take an oath of allegiance or depart to the enemy lines. The trouble with such an order was that it confounded military occupation with annexation.[33]

Never should that mistake be made. A country remains

---

[30] Birkhimer, *op. cit.*, p. 93.
[31] War Dept., *Military Aid to the Civil Power* (1925), pp. 75 ff., 89 ff., 105 ff.
[32] *Basic Field Manual: Military Government* (FM 27–5), sec. 4; *Basic Field Manual: Rules of Land Warfare* (FM 27–10), secs. 271 ff.; Colby, 1926, 26 Col. L. Rev. 146 ff.; Betts, 1940, 4 Fed. B.A.J. 27 ff.
[33] Ropes, *The Army under Pope*, pp. 9 ff.; see also Spaight, *War Rights on Land*, p. 332.

MILITARY GOVERNMENT

foreign soil to us, although completely within our military control. To make that soil ours, within the purview of our constitution and laws, it must be ceded to us; nought else will suffice. Cuba, though completely under our military control, was never a part of our domain,[34] and Puerto Rico only when ceded to us ceased to be a foreign country.[35]

Nevertheless, the enemy subject does owe the duty of obedience above mentioned. The rationale of this duty may be the subject of dispute; but that the commander has the right to enforce such obedience cannot be denied.[36] "The right to govern the territory of the enemy during its military occupation is one of the incidents of war, being a consequence of its acquisition," says our Supreme Court,[37] and the English authorities are to the same effect.[38]

Second: The Executive, as commander in chief, can form a temporary civil government for the occupied territory, to operate under the direction of the military commander. To support such a government, taxes can be collected from the

---

[34] Neely v. Henckel, 1900, 180 U.S. 109, 120, 21 S. Ct. 302, 45 L. Ed. 448.
[35] De Lima v. Bidwell, 1901, 182 U.S. 1, 194, 21 S. Ct. 743, 45 L. Ed. 1041.
[36] See Bordwell, *Laws of War*, p. 300; Oppenheim, *Legal Relation between Occupying Power and Inhabitants*, 1917, 33 L.Q.R. 363. Discussion of the nature of this "war allegiance" and the resulting crime of "war rebellion," punishable by the commander, gets nowhere, and frequently ends in the realm of nominalism (see Birkhimer, *op. cit.*, p. 69). The fact is that this temporary allegiance is a part of the laws of war, and breaches of it are, therefore, punishable by the military authority; see generally Colby, *loc. cit. supra*, note 32.
[37] Coleman v. Tennessee, 1878, 97 U.S. 509, 517, 24 L. Ed. 1118.
[38] "When His Majesty's forces are in armed occupation of hostile territory, it is competent to His Majesty's commanders to declare that martial law shall prevail in such territory, and to lay down rules which they deem essential for the preservation of His Majesty's forces and military stores." 8 Halsbury's Laws of England (2d ed. 1933), § 1403, citing opinions of Crown Law officers. Cf. most recently, McNair, 1941, 57 L.Q.R. 34, 40 f.

inhabitants, and tariff duties imposed upon imports. All such directions are valid until Congress sees fit to supersede them; wherefore one who has paid taxes to such a government, although under protest, cannot maintain an action to recover them back. Such was the holding in *Cross v. Harrison* as to customs duties paid to the provisional government of California,[39] and to the same effect is *Fleming v. Page* relating to the provisional government of Tampico.[40]

With the cessation of the military occupation this government of necessity ends. Such interesting questions as might otherwise arise in connection with outstanding contracts and obligations of the provisional government are usually settled by treaty when the war is between independent states. The common law so far has not conclusively spoken on the subject, for we do not consider *New Orleans v. New York Mail Steamship Co.*[41] as an actual pronouncement on this point. There the military government, ruling the occupied city of New Orleans, leased certain water-front property, which belonged to the city, for a ten-year term. A year later the control of the city was handed back to the city authorities. They tried to repudiate the lease, but the decision which the court rendered, upholding the lease, is not of much help. The city undoubtedly could elect to adopt the lease and thus succeed to all the former government rights under the contract; and its election to do this was shown in the fact that it had collected one installment

---

[39] 1853, 16 How. 164, 14 L. Ed. 889.
[40] 1850, 9 How. 603, 13 L. Ed. 276. See also Dooley v. United States, 1900, 182 U.S. 222, 21 S. Ct. 762, 45 L. Ed. 1074; MacLeod v. United States, 1913, 229 U.S. 416, 33 S. Ct. 955, 57 L. Ed. 1260.
[41] 1874, 20 Wall. 387, 22 L. Ed. 354. Cf. Isbell v. Farris, 1868, 5 Cold. (Tenn.) 426.

MILITARY GOVERNMENT

of rent prior to its attempted repudiation of the lease. Mr. Justice Hunt rests his special concurring opinion on this ground alone; but the majority opinion, while admitting "the general principle that the contracts of the conqueror touching things in conquered territory lose their efficacy when his dominion ceases," yet considered that the peculiar necessities of the city at the time this lease was made gave implied authority to the military government to bind itself and all future governments for a period of years. This is especially hard to understand when we recall that the Supreme Court has placed itself clearly on record as repudiating any doctrine, of the *postliminii* variety, that conquest alone can give title.[42]

Third: The military, as to all controversies with civilians, are normally subject only to the jurisdiction of their own court-martial, as we have seen. And it is customary to leave the courts of the country in operation for all civil litigation between the inhabitants, and, for their governance, to leave the municipal laws of the country in force.[43] In fact, the com-

[42] De Lima v. Bidwell, cit. *supra,* note 35. In Fleming v. Page, cit. *supra,* note 40, is a dictum that mere conquest gives title. If Cross v. Harrison, cit. *supra* note 39, did not overrule this dictum, as the court later said it did, the case of De Lima v. Bidwell certainly had that effect.

[43] "By such occupation the political relations between the people of the hostile country and their former government or sovereign are for the time severed; but the municipal laws—that is, the laws which regulate private rights, enforce contracts, punish crime and regulate the transfer of property, remain in full force, so far as they affect the inhabitants of the country among themselves, unless suspended or superseded by the conqueror. And the tribunals by which the laws are enforced continue as before, unless thus changed. In other words, the municipal laws of the State and their administration remain in full force so far as the inhabitants of the country are concerned, unless changed by the occupying belligerent. Halleck, Int. Law, c. 33." Coleman v. Tennessee, 1878, 97 U.S. 509, 517. Cf. further Winthrop, *Military Law,* p. 800 n. 75; Birkhimer, *Military Government and Martial Law,*

mander's affirmative action is required to change the municipal law; until he acts, it is presumed that he intends to leave it of full force.[44] Sometimes, however, the military authorities may set up, in the place of an old local court, a new and provisional court with the same jurisdiction. Such was the course followed during the Civil War, strikingly evidenced in the case of New Orleans, after the Federal forces completed their military hold upon that city.[45]

Such courts can only exercise the jurisdiction thus allowed them. The commander may reserve for his own jurisdiction, exercised through a provost court or military commission or separate military tribunal, any cases he may choose, and his directions must be obeyed.[46] Likewise, he may determine to try before provost court or military commission breaches of his proclamations and orders, violations of the laws of war, or even crimes which would ordinarily be cognizable by state or federal courts.

---

pp. 91 ff., 134 ff.; *Basic Field Manual: Military Government* (FM 27–5), sec. 10d.

[44] Wingfield v. Crosby, 1867, 5 Cold. (Tenn.) 241, 246; United States v. Caparros, 1900, 1 Porto Rico Fed. 59.

[45] Birkhimer, *op. cit.*, pp. 146 ff.; an interesting account of these courts in Moore, *Rebellion Record*, X, pp. 341–46.

[46] "The national military authorities took the place of all ordinary civil jurisdiction or controlled its exercise. All courts, whether state or national, were subordinated to military supremacy, and acted, when they acted at all, under such limitations and in such cases as the commanding general, under the directions of the President, thought fit to describe. Their process might be disregarded and their judgments and decrees set aside by military orders. . . . The military tribunals, at that time, and under the existing circumstances, were competent to the exercise of all jurisdiction, criminal and civil, which belongs under ordinary circumstances to civil courts." Chief Justice Chase, speaking of the courts established during the occupation of Confederate territory, in his address to the bar, at Raleigh, N.C., in June 1867, Chase's Decisions, p. 133.

MILITARY GOVERNMENT

Neither the provisional court nor the military tribunal, as above outlined, is a court-martial in the sense wherein we have previously used that term; for the court-martial is a tribunal that deals with the crimes of the soldier and has long been recognized by statute, whereas courts of the type now under discussion derive their authority from the laws and usages of war and only function during time of war, military occupation or martial law.[47] But these various courts are all alike in the respect that the sentence of each requires the confirmation of the appointing power before it can be effective as a judgment; the court, in short, is an advisory committee, to advise the commander as to the facts, and likewise inform his conscience as to the punishment.[48]

Although war courts are met with in our history since the time of the Revolutionary war,[49] it was not until 1847 that a military commission, so designated, was established by General Scott in the Mexican War.[50] Civil offenses and violations against military orders were tried before this tribunal, while specific offenses against the laws of war were handled by a "council of war." [51] Subsequently, the jurisdictions of the two were united into one, the military commission, and this tribunal has been extensively employed from the time of the Civil War to the present.[52] Three kinds of extraordinary military tribu-

---

[47] Ex parte Jones, 1913, 71 W.Va. 567, 581 ff., 77 S.E. 1029, 45 L.R.A. n.s. 1030; cf. Davis, *Military Law*, pp. 307 ff.
[48] See Colby, 1926, 26 Col. L. Rev. 158 f.
[49] The early history of American war courts in Birkhimer, *op. cit.*, pp. 351 ff.
[50] G.O. 20 of Feb. 19, 1847 (as amended by G.O. 287) is set forth in full in Birkhimer, *op. cit.*, Appendix 1.
[51] Winthrop, *Military Law*, pp. 832 f.
[52] An extensive treatment of the nature and functions of the military commission in our history, with elaborate annotations, is to be found in the recent

nals, other than the court-martial, are now utilized by our armed forces: the military commission, the superior provost court, and the inferior provost court.[53] Normally these courts "have jurisdiction over all acts or omissions made crimes or offenses by the laws of the country occupied, over offenses against the laws of war, and over violations of the proclamations, ordinances, regulations, or orders promulgated by the commanding general, theater of operations, or by any of his subordinates within the scope of his authority";[54] but provision is made that the commanding officer may confer jurisdiction over civil cases to these tribunals.[55] The composition of the courts and the procedure thereof is governed, or as near as may be, by that of general, special, and summary courts-martial; and the jurisdiction is just as exclusive.[56]

If, then, the commander chooses to send a certain criminal case to the military court, the civil court cannot release the prisoners by way of habeas corpus. Such was the holding in the courts of Mississippi, during the Reconstruction period, while that state, according to the theory finally adopted,[57]

German spy case, Ex parte Quirin, 1942,—U.S.—, 63 S. Ct. 2, 87 L. Ed. 1. See also, of recent date, King, 1942, 30 Calif. L. Rev. 612 ff.; Note, 1942, 29 Va. L. Rev. 317–38.

[53] *Basic Field Manual: Military Government* (FM 27–5), § 22. Cf. Navy Department, *Naval Courts and Boards*, Appendix D, § 12 ff.

[54] FM 27–5, § 25b.

[55] There is some old authority to the effect that military commissions have no jurisdiction over civil cases, Vance v. United States, 1895, 30 Ct. Cl. 252; Walt v. Thomasson, 1872, 10 Heisk. (Tenn.) 151. But present-day practice indicates that this is no longer true, FM 27–5, § 32.

[56] Winthrop, *Military Law*, pp. 835 ff.; Birkhimer, *Military Government*, pp. 356 ff.; FM 27–5, §§ 23 ff.

[57] Prior to the settling of that question, Nelson, J., sitting in New York, discharged from the Albany penitentiary a prisoner sent there under the judgment of a military commission sitting in South Carolina in September,

MILITARY GOVERNMENT

remained under the control of the military authorities.[58]

The judgments of provisional courts and military commissions, in all cases whereof they have jurisdiction, are entitled to receive from our courts the same measure of faith and credit as would be due the judgment of the court of any foreign country. In *Dow v. Johnson* [59] the judgment of the New Orleans provisional court was given no effect because, for reasons already detailed, it lacked jurisdiction of the subject matter; but in all cases not involving such a question as that presented by *Dow v. Johnson* full faith and credit was given to the judgments of these courts, not merely by other courts on collateral attack, but by the succeeding regular courts of the states in which such judgments had been rendered.[60] Likewise, the judgments of provost courts and military commissions have been declared valid by the courts and are not subject, as such, to be appealed to, or revised by, any civil tribunal.[61]

1865; his reasoning being that military control ceases with the termination of actual hostilities. In re Egan, 1866, C.C. N.Y., Fed. Cas. No. 4304. Accord, that the jurisdiction of a military commission ceases with the termination of military government, Ex parte Ortiz, 1900, C.C. Minn., 100 F. 955, 962.

[58] In re McCardle, 1867, D.C. Miss., 2 Amer. L. Rev. 355; Ex parte Hewitt, 1868, D.C. Miss., 3 Amer. L. Rev. 382. Generally on military authority and jurisdiction under the Reconstruction Acts, see Winthrop, *Military Law*, pp. 846–62.

[59] 1879, 100 U.S. 158, 25 L. Ed. 632.

[60] The Grapeshot, 1869, 9 Wall. 129, 19 L. Ed. 651; Pennywit v. Eaton, 1872, 15 Wall. 382, 21 L. Ed. 114; Pepin v. Lachenmeyer, 1871, 45 N.Y. 27; and particularly Hefferman v. Porter, 1869, 6 Cold. (Tenn.) 391. According to Colby, 1926, 26 Col. L. Rev. 156 note 190, little weight should be attached to the approval granted by the Supreme Court in Leitensdorfer v. Webb, 1857, 20 How. 176, 15 L. Ed. 891, to the validity of the judgments of the provisional courts established in New Mexico, for this government was far too complete prior to the legal transfer of sovereignty.

[61] Ex parte Vallandigham, 1864, 1 Wall. 243, 17 L. Ed. 589; cf. generally, Miller, 1941, 7 Ohio State L.J. 400 ff.

Fourth: These concessions are but concessions; and in the end the power of the commander is supreme. Concessions granted may be withdrawn; they need not be granted in the first place. As stated both by Lord Halsbury [62] and by Oppenheim,[63] the law administered, by whatever pattern the commander may choose to model it, is martial law. In Napoleon's words, "the laws of war confer on the Commander *la grande police* over the country which is the theatre of war." [64] "The question here," says the Supreme Court, "is, what is the law which governs an army invading an enemy's country. It is not the civil law of the invaded country; it is not the civil law of the conquering country; it is military law—the law of war—and its supremacy for the protection of the officers and soldiers of the army, when in service in the field in the enemy's country, is as essential to the efficiency of the army as the supremacy of the civil law at home, and in time of peace, is essential to the preservation of liberty." [65] And when, from one point of view, we ask for a definition of this sort of martial law, the oft-quoted definition given by Wellington is as good as any. "Martial law," said the Duke, "is the will of the commanding officer of an armed force or of a geographical military department, expressed in time of war, within the limits of his military jurisdiction, as necessity demands and prudence dictates, restrained or

[62] Laws of England, *loc. cit. supra*, note 38.
[63] *International Law*, Vol. II, § 170.
[64] Picard, *Préceptes et jugements de Napoleon*, p. 97.
[65] Dow v. Johnson, 1879, 100 U.S. 158, 170, 25 L. Ed. 632. Cf. the language in New Orleans v. New York Mail Steamship Co., 1874, 20 Wall. 387, 394: "There is no limit to the powers that may be exerted in such cases save those which are found in the laws and usages of war. . . . In such cases the laws of war take the place of the Constitution and laws of the United States as applied in time of peace." This language is cited with approval in Daniel v. Hutcheson, 1893, 86 Tex. 51, 61, 22 S.W. 933.

enlarged by the orders of his military or supreme executive chief." [66]

Nevertheless, the enforcement of martial law is hedged about with requirements of a sort no civilized conqueror can ignore. "The commander of any city where martial law (*état de siège*) [67] prevails," says Napoleon, "is, after all, a magistrate, and he should conduct himself with such moderation and decency as circumstances will permit." [68] While the soldiers in occupation are answerable only to court-martial, yet they are also answerable, says our Supreme Court, to the tribunal of public opinion, "which, it is to be hoped, will always brand with infamy all who authorize or sanction acts of cruelty and oppression." [69] As the Army Field Manual puts it: "Military government should be just, humane, and as mild as practicable, and the welfare of the people governed should always be the aim of every person engaged therein. As military government is executed by force, it is incumbent upon those who administer it to be strictly guided by the principles of justice, honor and humanity—virtues adorning a soldier even more than other men for the very reason that he possesses the power of his arms against the unarmed. Not only religion and the honor of the Army of the United States require this course but also policy." [70]

Thus, while it is for the commander to prescribe the extent to which the local courts shall exercise jurisdiction, our Su-

---

[66] 115 Hansard, Parliamentary Debates (3d ser. 1891), p. 879; cf. Sutherland, *Constitutional Power and World Affairs* (1919), p. 80.
[67] On the nature of the French *état de siège* see Radin, 1942, 30 Calif. L. Rev. 634 ff.
[68] Picard, *op. cit.*, p. 101.
[69] Dow v. Johnson, 1879, 100 U.S. 158, 166, 25 L. Ed. 632.
[70] *Military Government* (FM 27–5), sec. 9b.

preme Court got a chance, in the instance of a state under reconstruction, to decide that a commander could not arbitrarily upset the judgment rendered in a case of which he had allowed the local court to take jurisdiction.[71]

Whenever the common law has the opportunity, as it did in the case just mentioned, it expresses what it conceives to be a principle of the laws of war; that, even in a conquered country, the commander's power, next to securing the welfare of the army and sternly repressing all forms of war treason, should work for just treatment of the civil population.[72] The best evidence that the common law has correctly interpreted the rule of the laws of war is to be found in the professions of our enemy, made during World War I and in the course of the present struggle.[73] As to his actual practices, and those of his allies, mankind has already found the facts and rendered judgment in the first case, and will do so again at the termination of the present hostilities.

[71] "We have looked carefully through the acts of March 2, 1867, and July 19, 1867. They give very large governmental powers to the military commanders designated, within the States committed respectively to their jurisdiction; but we have found nothing to warrant the order here in question. It was not an order for mere delay. It did not prescribe that the proceeding should stop until credit and confidence were restored, and business should resume its wonted channels. It wholly annulled a decree in equity regularly made by a competent judicial officer in a plain case clearly within his jurisdiction, and where there was no pretense of any unfairness, of any purpose to wrong or oppress, or of any indirection whatsoever . . . It was an arbitrary stretch of authority, needful to no good end that can be imagined. Whether Congress could have conferred the power to do such an act is a question we are not called upon to consider. It is an unbending rule of law, that the exercise of military power, where the rights of the citizen are concerned, shall never be pushed beyond what the exigency requires," Raymond v. Thomas, 1876, 91 U.S. 712, 715, 28 L.Ed. 434.

[72] Such, indeed, is the view of international law, see Hague Regulations, art. 43, and generally, Oppenheim, *International Law*, II, 342 ff.

[73] See, for example, Solansky, *German Administration in Belgium* (1928), and

MILITARY GOVERNMENT

To the credit of this country's arms, an occurrence of the kind described in *Raymond v. Thomas* [74] is very much the exception. Military control of occupied territory is generally accompanied by friction, for high-spirited people are chafed by the very sight of their conquerors. It was so during the occupation of our coast cities by the British during the Revolution; [75] it was so during the Reconstruction period through which the Southern States were compelled to pass after the close of the Civil War.[76] Yet the following tribute may well be quoted from a brochure concerning the latter era, as indicative of the spirit that pervades our armed forces, now as well as then: "In investigating this whole subject it has been necessary to read many pages of the correspondence between the commanding officers of the Federal armies and the civil departments, and especially between them and Judge Advocate General Holt, and it gives pleasure and speaks well for human nature, to note that whenever a gallant Union soldier had to deal with the matter of the treatment of a Confederate soldier or citizen, his tone was one of mercy, of justice, and of respect, without insult or harsh expression, and with the utmost consideration for the defenseless, the weak, and the unfortunate. Everyone knows this was characteristic of Grant, but the same may well be said of Sheridan, of Sherman, of Thomas and of many others." [77]

Poland, Ministry of Foreign Affairs, *German Occupation of Poland* (1941), pp. 62 ff.
[74] Cit. *supra*, note 71.   [75] E.g., see Jones, *History of New York*, II, p. 186.
[76] E.g., see Reynolds, *History of Reconstruction in South Carolina*, pp. 40 ff.; Pendleton, *Life of Alexander H. Stephens*, pp. 343 ff.
[77] Blackford, *The Trials and Trial of Jefferson Davis*, p. 39. The only exception noted is in the case of the officer to whose charge Mr. Davis was committed, and his behavior is ascribed to the tone of the instructions given him by the Secretary of War.

7. MILITARY OCCUPATION IN MATTERS OF PROPERTY

SINCE, as we have seen in the last chapter, the common law view is that conquest confers no sovereignty over occupied regions, it naturally follows that no portion of enemy territory can pass to the conqueror. Both public and private titles in land, therefore, remain unaffected by invasion. To real estate the conqueror may not acquire title, although in many instances the usufruct thereof may be enjoyed.[1] It is only personal property and choses in action—movables—that may be seized, and then only such as may directly or indirectly be used in connection with military operations.[2] Statutes of confiscation would be necessary to affect the title to land; during the foreign wars of the United States, Congress has never attempted to so legislate. Such statutes, however, were a feature of the Civil War on both sides.

The Confederate legislation is described in *Dewing v. Perdicaries*,[3] although the Supreme Court declined to recognize its

---

[1] The present rules respecting the treatment of enemy property in occupied territory by the armed forces of the United States are set forth in *Basic Field Manual: Rules of Land Warfare* (FM 27–10), §§ 313–44. These incorporate numerous articles of the 1907 Hague Regulations respecting the laws and customs of war. The international law aspects of the subject are outside the scope of this work, so for further discussion, the reader need be referred only to Oppenheim, *International Law*, Vol. II, §§ 133–54, and Hyde, *International Law*, Vol. II, §§ 657, 692 ff., and the bibliographies therein.

[2] FM 27–10, §§ 320, 331.

[3] 1878, 96 U.S. 193, 24 L. Ed. 654, affirming Perdicaries v. Charleston Gaslight Co., 1877, C.C. S.C., Fed. Cas. No. 10973. See also Williams v. Bruffy, 1878, 96 U.S. 176, 24 L. Ed. 716.

MILITARY OCCUPATION AND PROPERTY 137

validity, since that would have involved recognition of the Confederate government as existing *de jure*.

The first Federal statute was that of August 6, 1861,[4] which confiscated all property used in aid of the rebellion. The second was the Act of July 17, 1862,[5] which confiscated the property of certain classes of persons in the Confederacy, whether or not such property was being used in aid of the rebellion; but, in view of the constitutional provision that no attainder of treason shall work a forfeiture except during the life of the person attained, a joint resolution amended the statute so as to make the forfeiture only for the life of the person in question.[6] The third Federal statute was the Captured and Abandoned Property Act of March 12, 1863,[7] whose effect we have heretofore considered.

These statutes had varying effects. The Act of 1861, which confiscated property used in aid of the rebellion, was upheld as an exercise of the government's war powers. It was purely impersonal, and acted *in rem*, directly on the offending and hostile property, wherefore a condemnation sale under this statute would pass a fee simple title to the purchaser.[8] The Act of 1862, on the contrary, had a very different object—"not to make the property a lawful subject of capture and prize, as in the Act of 1861, but to punish the owner for countenancing the rebellion. . . . In this way the condemnation of real property under the Act of 1862 was confined to the natural life of the offending owner; but nothing of the sort was done with the

---

[4] 12 Stat. 319.   [5] 12 Stat. 589.
[6] Miller v. United States, 1871, 11 Wall. 268, 20 L. Ed. 135; Jenkins v. Collard, 1892, 145 U.S. 546, 12 S. Ct. 868, 36 L. Ed. 812.
[7] 12 Stat. 820.
[8] Miller v. United States, cit. *supra*, note 6; Kirk v. Lynd, 1882, 106 U.S. 315, 1 S. Ct. 296, 27 L. Ed. 193.

Act of 1861, because that had reference only to the capture and condemnation of property for its unlawful use."[9] The Captured and Abandoned Property Act likewise had an impersonal nature. It swept into the Treasury the proceeds of all property which the Federal troops might pick up during their penetration into the South, leaving it to the owner to assert his claim, in the Court of Claims, on establishing his loyalty. For all three acts a pardon operated to purge the claimant of disloyalty.[10]

Now, while legislation of this sort is peculiar to civil war, and can form no precedent for a war between independent nations, two of these statutes, those of 1861 and 1863, serve as an indication of the common law's view of capture. The operation of each statute is wholly *in rem*. It is not necessary that the owner of the property be named; the property itself is the defendant, and the owner appears on the record only as a claimant.[11] That accords precisely with the common law's view of capture of enemy property during the operations of war, as stated in an opinion of the Supreme Court.

"Property captured during the war," said that court, "was not taken by way of punishment for the treason of the owner, any more than the life of a soldier slain in battle was taken to punish him. He was killed because engaged in war, and exposed to its dangers. So property was captured because it had become involved in the war, and its removal from the enemy was necessary in order to lessen their warlike power. It was not

---

[9] Kirk v. Lynd, cit. *supra*, note 8, at 319. Cf. United States v. Dunnington, 1892, 146 U.S. 338, 13 S. Ct. 79, 36 L. Ed. 996.
[10] United States v. Padelford, 1870, 9 Wall. 531, 19 L. Ed. 788; United States v. Klein, 1872, 13 Wall. 128, 20 L. Ed. 519.
[11] The Confiscation Cases, 1874, 20 Wall. 92, 22 L. Ed. 320.

MILITARY OCCUPATION AND PROPERTY

taken because of its ownership, but because of its character. But for the provisions of the Abandoned and Captured Property Act, the title to and the proceeds of all captured property would have passed absolutely to the United States. By that Act, however, the privilege of suing for the proceeds in the Treasury was granted to such owners as could show they had not given aid or comfort to the rebellion." [12]

A sharp contrast between capture at sea and seizure on land vitally affects the common law's treatment of enemy property. For, ever since medieval times, there has existed a tribunal known as a prize court with exclusive jurisdiction "to proceed upon all and all manner of captures, seizures, prizes and reprisals, of all ships and goods that are, or shall be, taken; and to hear and determine, according to the course of the admiralty and the law of nations." [13] Each maritime state has prize courts, which are national courts instituted by municipal law; but every state is bound by international law to enact only such statutes and regulations for its prize courts as are in conformity with international law.[14] Yet, despite the international and exclusive aspects of its jurisdiction, a prize court, when sitting in any common law country, really administers a body of law common to all such countries.[15]

[12] Young v. United States, 1878, 97 U.S. 39, 67, 24 L. Ed. 992.
[13] Lord Mansfield, in Lindo v. Rodney, 1782, 2 Doug. 612, quoted in The Zamora, [1916] 2 A.C. 77, 91. Generally on prize law, see Hyde, *International Law*. Vol. II, §§ 890 ff.; Oppenheim, *International Law*, Vol. II, §§ 192, 434 ff. See also *Prize Cases decided in the United States Supreme Court*, ed. by Scott (1918); Garner, *Prize Law during the World War* (1927).
[14] The Consul Corfitzon, [1917] A.C. 550. The constitution and procedure of prize courts in the United States is to be found in 34 U.S.C.A. §§ 1131 ff.
[15] "The United States having, at one time, formed a component part of the British empire, *their* prize law was our prize law. When we separated, it continued to be our prize law, so far as it was adapted to our circumstances

According to prize law, no title passes in sea capture until the captured thing has been brought into the prize court and condemned by its final judgment; wherefore, if an enemy vessel be taken by our ship *A*, rescued by an enemy war vessel, and then again captured by our ship *B*, who brings her into the custody of the prize court, she is lawful prize of the *B*, not the *A*.[16] But such is not the case with regard to movable property on land; there capture, if valid, changes the ownership without adjudication.[17]

Because the validity of a capture at sea depended on an adjudication, prize law became crystallized at an early date. With captures on land, on the contrary, there have been few opportunities, save in connection with the Civil War, for our common law courts to adjudicate questions in this field. A number of cases resulted from military operations during the Spanish-American War in which the Supreme Court recognized the right of commanders to seize or destroy enemy property, provided this be demanded by the necessities of war.[18] Further, in the first decade of this century, the Hague Regulations set forth in detail what was intended to be a fairly comprehensive statement of the treatment of enemy property according to international law.[19] The action of Germany during World War I

---

and was not varied by the power which was capable of changing it. . . . A case professing to be deciding on ancient principles will not be entirely disregarded, unless it be very unreasonable, or be founded on a construction rejected by other nations." Marshall, C.J., in Thirty Hogsheads of Sugar, 1815, 9 Cranch 191, 198, 3 L. Ed. 701.

[16] The Astrea, 1816, 1 Wheat. 125, 4 L. Ed. 52.

[17] Lamar v. Browne, 1876, 92 U.S. 187, 23 L. Ed. 650.

[18] Herrera v. United States, 1912, 222 U.S. 558, 572, 32 S. Ct. 176, 56 L. Ed. 316; cf. Juragua Iron Co. v. United States, 1908, 212 U.S. 297, 29 S. Ct. 385, 53 L. Ed. 520.

[19] Hague Regulations of 1907, arts. 23, 28, 46–56, adopted by the United

and the radical changes in the nature of military operations in World War II has brought the question to the fore again. On the basis of the cases, supplemented where necessary by provisions of international law, we may gather the common law view of capture on land.

At the outset of this inquiry we find two propositions accepted by the common law mind. One is that the mere fact of a state of war does not of itself transfer title to enemy property. Secondly, property situated in enemy country is lawfully subject to capture, subject, however, to certain considerations.

First: It must be taken into possession, for the Roman doctrine of *inter praesidia* is a guiding principle.[20]

Second: The title to all such public property as may be captured passes directly to the United States government.[21] There is no exception or limitation to this proposition.

Third: Private property constituting the subject matter of capture also passes directly to the government. The right of private pillage is not recognized by the laws of war as read by common law courts. Up through the Napoleonic wars pillage was recognized as lawful in the case of a town taken by storm,[22] but that rule has become obsolete; pillage indeed being made a

---

States and Great Britain, among others, and reproduced in *Basic Field Manual: Rules of Land Warfare* (FM 27-10), §§ 24, 61, 313-42; and in War Office (Great Britain), *Manual of Military Law 1929*, Amendment 12 of Jan. 1936, chap. XIV, §§ 405-34.

[20] United States v. Padelford, cit. *supra* note 10, at p. 541; Oakes v. United States, 1899, 174 U.S. 778, 787, 19 S. Ct. 864, 43 L. Ed. 1169. On inter praesidia see Bordwell, *Law of War*, pp. 9 ff.

[21] United States v. Huckabee, 1873, 16 Wall. 414, 434, 21 L. Ed. 457; Lamar v. Browne, cit. *supra* note 17, at p. 194. See also FM 27-10, § 327.

[22] This exception is recognized by Kent, 1 Comm. 92. Indeed, it goes far back of Grotius' time, Vattel, *Droit des gens*, iii, § 173.

special object of prohibition under all circumstances. The Hague Convention forbids pillage,[23] but long before that Lieber's Code forbade it "even after taking a place by main force." [24] Pillage, therefore, confers no title. Not only have we for this the high authority of the Supreme Court,[25] but we also have two decisions to that effect rendered in Georgia after the Civil War; each case being a possessory action for property of the plaintiff which had been taken by the pillagers, following in the wake of the Federal army.[26]

Finally arises the question whether there should be any distinction in classes of personal property subject to capture. We have on the one hand the theory of Clausewitz [27] that requisitions of enemy property should have no limit except as fixed by the final exhaustion of the country, and that in fact requisitioning should be used as a method of keeping the country down.

Opposed to that we have the theory that there must be some quality, appurtenant to the property itself, rather than the personality of its owner, which would justify the capture. And this quality must relate, in however direct or remote degree, to the welfare of the captor's government; it must subserve a war purpose of that government.[28] The necessary line of distinction regarding private property had been so clearly drawn prior to

[23] Art. 28; FM 27-10, § 61.   [24] G.O. 100, § 24.
[25] United States v. Klein, 1872, 13 Wall. 128, 20 L. Ed. 519.
[26] Worthy v. Kinomon, 1870, 44 Ga. 297; Huff v. Odum, 1872, 49 Ga. 395.
[27] *On War,* V, chap. 14, 3. The practice of Germany in World War I, see Ferrand, *De réquisitions en matière de droit international public* (1917), pp. 434-44, seems well on the way to being increased in the present conflict.
[28] Hyde, *International Law,* Vol. II, § 694; Oppenheim, *International Law,* Vol. II, § 141; FM 27-10, §§ 320, 331.

MILITARY OCCUPATION AND PROPERTY 143

our Civil War by many writers, including Halleck [29] and the common law man Kent,[30] that our Supreme Court, during that conflict, accepted Kent's dictum that capture of private property is restricted "to special cases dictated by the necessary operation of the war," and never includes "the seizure of the private property of pacific persons for the sake of gain." [31] This, indeed, left a broad field for the courts' operations.

In the first place, it gave the courts room to establish a contraband list for land captures; and the article first placed upon this list was, as might be imagined from the nature of the Confederacy's resources, cotton. It was, said the Supreme Court, well known that cotton constituted "the chief reliance of the rebels for means to purchase the munitions of war in Europe," and that "rather than permit it to come into the possession of the national troops, the rebel government had everywhere devoted it, however owned, to destruction." [32] Independently, therefore, of the legislation afforded by the Confiscation Act of August 6, 1861, already mentioned, the court considered cotton a fair subject of capture. It became, therefore, axiomatic during the Civil War "that cotton, though private property, was a legitimate subject of capture." [33] Not that it was treated as contraband in the modern sense, but rather as hostile property.[34] Accordingly, it is extremely doubtful whether such

---

[29] *International Law* (1861), p. 456.
[30] 1 Comm. 91–93.
[31] Mrs. Alexander's Cotton, 1865, 2 Wall. 404, 419, 17 L. Ed. 915; Briggs v. United States, 1892, 143 U.S. 346, 357, 12 S. Ct. 391, 36 L. Ed. 180.
[32] Mrs. Alexander's Cotton, cit. *supra*, note 31, at p. 420.
[33] Lamar v. Browne, 1876, 92 U.S. 187, 194, 23 L. Ed. 650.
[34] Brandon v. United States, 1911, 46 Ct. Cl. 559. Since raw cotton is now employed in the manufacture of high explosives, it may well be subject to

property would fall within the present requirements of international law.[35]

Second in our order of speaking was the principle that all property needful for the army was a legitimate subject of capture. Here we are at one of those many points of contact where the common law meets a principle originating in another body of law.

Among the laws of war was the system of requisitions which had grown up, as a substitute for pillage. This system finds codification in an oft-quoted passage from the memoirs of Marshal Saxe,[36] but it originated long prior to the Marshal's time.[37] In Napoleon's works may be found a valuable code of rules regarding a system which, as he said, had been used "time out of mind," and is based on the fundamental proposition that war

---

seizure and certainly is contraband, Oppenheim, *International Law*, Vol. II, pp. 666 f.

[35] Hyde, *International Law*, Vol. II, pp. 375 f. In those times cotton was neither "susceptible of direct military use" (FM 27–10, § 331) and thus liable to confiscation, nor could it serve "the needs of the army of occupation" (FM 27–10, § 335) and so be requisitioned.

[36] See Bordwell, *Law of War*, pp. 43 ff. In a letter to the Chief of Staff of the Army in Spain, Napoleon approves the Saxe regulations as standing out from "a collection of exceedingly mediocre reflections." Picard, *Préceptes et jugements de Napoléon*, p. 545.

[37] In Defoe's *Journal of the Plague Year*, he has a refugee from London assert that, despite a quarantine maintained in a village, he and his friend could take food and fire there, provided they first tendered money; to which his companion replied: "You talk your old soldier language, as if you were in the Low Countries now." Dugald Dalgetty, that lifelike figure which Scott gives us, in the *Legend of Montrose*, of a soldier of fortune fresh from the wars of Gustavus Adolphus, is full of the learning of requisitions. An excellent sketch of the historical development of the practices of requisition and contribution is to be found in Keller, *Requisition und Kontribution* (1898), pp. 5–26.

MILITARY OCCUPATION AND PROPERTY

should support war.[38] By the Hague Regulations requisitions in kind are recognized, but they may be made only so far as they are really required for the needs of the army.[39] Further, they must be paid for in cash, or if this be impossible, must be acknowledged by receipt, and payment must be made as soon as possible. Of similar character are contributions, the payment of money demanded from municipalities or enemy inhabitants, which by virtue of the Hague Regulations may not be extortionate and are to be devoted exclusively to the needs of the army, for example, to pay for requisitions or for the administration of the territory occupied.[40] Our armed forces afford numerous examples of both practices,[41] and our courts have occasionally had occasion to deal with the same, reflecting the contemporaneous views of the laws and usages of war.

[38] On the subject of requisitions, Picard, *op. cit. supra*, note 36, at pp. 228–30, has collected from Napoleon's writings over two pages of valuable reflections.
[39] Art. 52. See generally Oppenheim, *International Law*, Vol. II, §§ 146–47, and further references therein.
[40] Arts. 49, 51. Cf. Oppenheim, *op. cit.*, § 148.
[41] E.g., in the Civil War, one of General Pope's orders provided for a system of requisitions, and to it no exception can be taken, Ropes, *The Army under Pope*, p. 9. General Sherman excuses the system of foraging which he employed during the march to the sea, because "the country was sparsely settled, with no magistrates or civil authorities, who could respond to requisitions, as is the case in all the Wars of Europe." Sherman, *Memoirs*, Vol. II, p. 183. This, of course, has nothing to do with the destruction of property that occurred during the march. During the Confederate invasion of Pennsylvania, in the campaign of Gettysburg, General Early, commanding a division of the leading corps (Ewell's) imposed two contributions, one on Gettysburg, the other on York. The first contribution the General failed to collect, the second he collected in part. Gordon, *Reminiscences*, pp. 146–147; Doubleday, *Chancellorsville and Gettysburg*, p. 113; Beecham, *Gettysburg*, pp. 38–40. For General Lee's protest against the excessive assessments levied by General Milroy on Winchester, and General Halleck's disavowal of the same, see Freeman, *Robert E. Lee*, II (1934), p. 482.

Such is that branch of the common law of war. For acts done in conformity with such rules, no officer or soldier should be in anywise liable. The Supreme Court fully expressed that view in these words: "But there could be no doubt of the right of the army to appropriate any property there, although belonging to private individuals, which was necessary for its support or convenient for its use. This was a belligerent right, which was not extinguished by the occupation of the country, although the necessity for its exercise was thereby lessened. However exempt from seizure on other grounds private property there may have been, it was always subject to be appropriated, when required by the necessities or convenience of the army, though the owner of property taken in such case may have had a just claim against the government for indemnity." [42]

Nor can a collateral attack upon a requisition order be any more effective. If the subject of the requisition be a chose in action, not merely must the debtor obey the order of attachment, but his payment in obedience thereto constitutes a perfect defense to a subsequent action by the original creditor.[43]

But while the courts thus accepted the principle, its application is quite a different thing. It is easy to state the principle as a theory of law, while giving the defendant the favorable side of it; it is quite a different matter to hold, in a common law

[42] Dow v. Johnson, 1879, 100 U.S. 158, 167, 25 L. Ed. 632. And compare Freeland v. Williams, 1889, 131 U.S. 405, 9 S. Ct. 763, 33 L. Ed. 193, at p. 416: "Ever since the case of Dow v. Johnson, the doctrine has been settled in the courts, that in our late civil war each party was entitled to the benefit of belligerent rights, as in the case of public war, and that, for an act done in accordance with the usages of civilized warfare, under and by military authority of either party, no civil liability attached to the officers or soldiers who acted under such authority."

[43] Harrison v. Myer, 1876, 92 U.S. 111, 23 L. Ed. 606; Gates v. Goodloe, 1879, 101 U.S. 612, 25 L. Ed. 895.

court, that a commander's acts, committed in enemy country against the public enemy, were void in point of law. Outside of certain limits, narrow indeed as compared with the principle so readily accepted in the abstract, our courts have never even dreamed of holding any such acts to have been actionable or void.

During the flagrancy of the war, the commander's judgment as to the propriety of a contribution or requisition necessarily must be absolute, and so agree all the cases.[44] Consequently, an officer acting under the lawful orders of his superior, is not liable to civil action for property requisitioned.[45] The same proposition would apply to confiscation or destruction of property, as distinct from its consumption or use, during an active campaign. For any such act the commander and his subordinates are not liable, in a civil action, to the aggrieved owner,[46] nor is the government liable to suit in the Court of Claims because of the principle to which further attention will later be called, that no claim lies against the government for a tort.[47] The existence of war, however, will not justify wanton trespasses upon the property of civilians,[48] or other injuries not

[44] Elphinstone v. Bedreechund, 1830, 12 Eng. Rep. 340; Taylor v. Nashville & Chattanooga Ry., 1869, 6 Cold. (Tenn.) 646, 98 Am. Dec. 474; Herrera v. United States, 1912, cit. *supra* note 18; O'Neill v. Central Leather Co., 1915, 87 N.J. Law 552, 94 Atl. 789, L.R.A. 1917A, 276, affirmed Oetjen v. Central Leather Co., 1918, 246 U.S. 297, 38 S. Ct. 309, 62 L. Ed. 726.

[45] Sutton v. Tiller, 1869, 6 Cold. (Tenn.) 593, 98 Am. Dec. 471; Cummings v. Diggs, 1870, 1 Heisk. (Tenn.) 67.

[46] Smith v. Brazelton, 1870, 1 Heisk. (Tenn.) 44, 2 Am. Rep. 678; Thomasson v. Glisson, 1871, 4 Heisk. (Tenn.) 615; Koonce v. Davis, 1875, 72 N.C. 218.

[47] Ribas y Hijo v. United States, 1904, 194 U.S. 315, 24 S. Ct. 727, 48 L. Ed. 994; Herrera v. United States, cit. *supra* note 18.

[48] Christian County Court v. Rankin, 1866, 2 Duv. (Ky.) 502, 87 Am. Dec. 505; Beck v. Ingram, 1867, 1 Bush. (Ky.) 355; Price v. Poynter, 1867, 1 Bush. (Ky.) 387, 89 Am. Dec. 631.

sanctioned by the laws and usages of war,[49] nor will it justify wrongs by irresponsible unauthorized parties.[50]

The final conclusion to be derived from adjudged cases is that the act of a commander cannot be questioned, except when it occurs during a quiet occupation of territory as distinct from occupation in full campaign. In full campaign the commander's acts are non-justiciable.[51] But when the conquest has subsided into government, the common law power of review can intrude itself. Such a review was had in *Raymond v. Thomas* [52] and in *Planters Bank v. Union Bank;* [53] and such a review possibly would have been had in *O'Reilly v. Brooke*,[54] were it not for the circumstances of ratification to which we shall advert.

Since the government is in no way liable to a former enemy in any claim of tort, his suit of necessity must be brought against the officer making or authorizing the capture. If the capture was not in accordance with the laws of war as above outlined, then theoretically the plaintiff could recover, but it is always open to our government to ratify an act committed by an officer.[55] When that ratification has been made, the case is then

---

[49] Tyson v. Rogers, 1863, 33 Ga. 473; Terrill v. Rankin, 1867, 2 Bush. (Ky.) 453, 92 Am. Dec. 500; Bryan v. Walker, 1870, 64 N.C. 141. Particularly not after the cessation of hostilities, Wilson v. Franklin, 1869, 63 N.C. 259; McLaughlin v. Green, 1874, 50 Miss. 453; Lincoln v. United States, 1906, 202 U.S. 484, 26 S. Ct. 728, 50 L. Ed. 1117.

[50] Taylor v. Jenkins, 1866, 24 Ark. 337, 88 Am. Dec. 773; Lewis v. McGuire, 1867, 3 Bush. (Ky.) 202; Branner v. Felkner, 1870, 1 Heisk. (Tenn.) 228.

[51] The common law "will not undertake to rejudge acts done flagrante bello in the face of the enemy," Tyler v. Pomeroy, 1864, 8 Allen (Mass.) 480, 484. Cf. Bell v. Louisville & N. R. Co., 1867, 1 Bush. (Ky.) 404, 89 Am. Dec. 632; Broadway v. Rhem, 1874, 71 N.C. 195.

[52] 1876, 91 U.S. 712, 23 L. Ed. 434, see *supra*, p. 134, note.

[53] 1873, 16 Wall. 483, 21 L. Ed. 473.

[54] 1908, 209 U.S. 45, 28 S. Ct. 439, 52 L. Ed. 676.

[55] Both federal and state enactments have relieved persons in the military

MILITARY OCCUPATION AND PROPERTY

within the principle whose existence in the abstract remains, however modified by pledge or practice, that whatever "shall be the subject of capture, as against his enemy, is always within the control of every belligerent. Whatever he orders is a justification to his followers." [56] The case then passes from the domain of the common law into affairs of state, of which the common law courts can take no cognizance. In *O'Reilly v. Brooke*, General Brooke, during the military occupation of Cuba, issued an order abolishing the office of Hereditary Slaughterer of Cattle in Havana, and the concessionaire, a Spanish countess, sued him for damages. On the defendant showing that after his order had been issued it was ratified by the indemnity provision contained in the Platt amendment,[57] the Supreme Court held that the defendant was not liable. The court said that, whatever might be the modern rule as to the protective effect of a master's ratification of his servant's tort, the old doctrine of full protection "still is applied, to a greater or less extent, when the master is the sovereign." Therefore, "where, as here, the jurisdiction of the case depends upon the establishment of a 'tort only in violation of the law of nations, or of a treaty of the United States,' it is impossible for the courts to declare an act a tort of that kind when the Executive, Congress, and the treaty-making power all have adopted the act." [58]

In this connection let us again return to the Civil War stat-

---

service from civil liability for acts done under military orders, as evidenced by Crosby v. Cadwalader, 1870, C.C. Pa., Fed. Cas. No. 3419; Clark v. Dick, 1870, C.C. Mo., Fed. Cas. No. 2818; Franklin v. Vannoy, 1872, 66 N.C. 145; Ochoa v. Hernandez, 1913, 230 U.S. 139, 33 S. Ct. 1033, 57 L. Ed. 1427.

[56] Lamar v. Browne, cit. *supra* note 17, at p. 195.
[57] Act of March 2, 1901, 31 Stat. 897.
[58] O'Reilly v. Brooke, cit. *supra* note 54, at p. 52.

utes. The confiscation acts of 1861 and 1862 might have been considered as merely defining classes of enemy property fit for capture, leaving it for the courts to devise a method of condemnation proceedings *in rem* similar to the proceedings of a prize court.[59] But the Captured and Abandoned Property Act went even further in language. Despite the "humane maxims" of the modern law of nations, which exempt private property of non-combatant enemies from capture as booty of war, this statute failed to define the classes of property suitable for capture. As no claimant could succeed in a suit for the property's proceeds unless he could show that he had been either loyal or pardoned, it would result that, on the face of the statute, all property belonging to real enemies was the subject of lawful capture.[60] The Supreme Court, however, never gave the statute such a broad meaning, but rather, in the cases actually before it, was careful to point out that cotton, which was the subject matter of each decided case, was, for the reasons already given, lawful spoil. It was also careful to say that, while statutes like the confiscation acts might enlarge the classes of property subject to capture, the government might equally well, by a public pledge, limit such classes. The whole tenor of the legislation and proclamations during the Civil War constituted such a pledge; a pledge that districts brought under complete and permanent control by the United States troops were not to be treated as theaters of war or as subject to requisitions.[61] The law then stood practically that in the absence of a

[59] Miller v. United States, cit. *supra* note 6; Tyler v. Defrees, 1871, 11 Wall. 331, 20 L. Ed. 161.
[60] Lamar v. Browne, cit. *supra* note 17.
[61] The Venice, 1865, 2 Wall. 258, 17 L. Ed. 866; Planters Bank v. Union Bank, cit. *supra* note 53. In Gates v. Goodloe, 1879, 101 U.S. 612, 25 L. Ed. 895, the

MILITARY OCCUPATION AND PROPERTY

pledge restricting, or a statute extending, the classifications of private property for purposes of capture, the courts will, in theory, allow the doctrines of the common laws of war.

And those doctrines, as we have seen, whatever they may be, can be applied by common law courts only in the case of quiet government as distinct from full campaign; and even then only to the extent that the government has neither directed nor ratified the act in question. The Supreme Court was right, therefore, in saying that by none of the decisions already examined was it "intended to express a limitation upon the undoubted belligerent right to use and confiscate all property of an enemy and to dispose of it at will," and that, as for Kent's rule, "the question could be raised whether it presented a case for judicial cognizance, even if a court could share the indignation which the learned commentator says all mankind would feel (at a violation of it)." [62]

The subject thus discussed has, so far, presented itself to our courts only with respect to enemy property in the shape of goods and credits. Concerning the conqueror's alleged right to requisition the service or labor of the enemy citizen for non-military purposes, no common law court has as yet had occasion to make a suggestion. Consistency with the scheme of this book would, therefore, induce a like silence on the writer's part.[63]

---
court noted, as a distinguishing feature, that the military occupation was neither complete nor substantial.
[62] Herrera v. United States, cit. *supra* note 18, at p. 571.
[63] For the international law aspects, see Hyde, *International Law*, Vol. II, § 699; Oppenheim, *International Law*, Vol. II, § 170; FM 27-10, sec. 302.

8. THE SOLDIER'S RELATION TO THE CIVILIAN IN TIME OF PEACE

AT AN earlier juncture we dealt with the soldier in relation to his fellow or superior in the army. We have just examined the relation which the army and its members bear to the enemy, armed and non-combatant, at home and abroad. It remains to consider the duties and obligations of the army and its members with respect to the civilian population of our own country. These duties and obligations vary with the circumstance of peace or war, and necessarily, because the uses of the army expand or contract according to whether its medium is the state of peace or the state of war.

When we commence our inquiry, as we naturally would, with the state of peace, we realize instantly that all questions as between the soldier and the civilian are within the jurisdiction of common law courts. Naturally the common law controls all the actions of all persons except those who, by virtue of particular status, have put themselves within the exclusive jurisdiction of some special court. The court-martial, as we have seen, has jurisdiction only of military offenses, and at best its jurisdiction is merely concurrent with that of a civilian criminal court in a case where a military offense may also constitute a crime.

SOLDIER AND CIVILIAN IN PEACETIME

Outside of military offenses, there is no question of status about the soldier. If he is interested in a proposition of property or contract, that question is determined in the civil courts. Usually it is a matter of accident that a party happens to be in the military service, the materiality of such a circumstance consisting mostly in questions of domicile.[1] For that reason, the demand for some sort of moratorium with respect to debts owing and necessary burdens, like life insurance premiums, borne by soldiers now in our service, had to be fulfilled by statute, for, in the absence of a statute, no common law court can refuse to enter judgment against a debtor simply because he is doing his duty for the government. Such a statute Congress gave us, during World War I, in the Act of March 8, 1918;[2] many of the states likewise enacted legislation to protect the soldier or the sailor serving his country,[3] and the courts, federal and state, repeatedly dealt with the numerous questions arising thereunder.[4] In the present conflict, Congress and the states have again sought to protect the interests of the members of the armed forces, or their suretors and guarantors, and, in certain

---

[1] "It appears that General Grant at the time of his death was an officer in the regular army of the United States. The domicile of military men is often more difficult for the courts to determine than is the domicile of those in civil life. The adjudications bearing on the principle of domicile, applicable to non-military persons, are not, I think, always relevant in cases involving the principle of domicile as it is applied to military or naval men." Surrogate Fowler, in Matter of Grant, 1913, 83 Misc. (N.Y.) 257, 260, 151 N.Y.S. 1119. Cases involving the domicile of military men collected in 129 A.L.R. 1383, 1387, 1390.

[2] 50 U.S.C.A., Appendix §§ 101 ff.

[3] E.g., Oregon Act of Feb. 19, 1917, Laws 1917, chap. 275, p. 515; Wisconsin Act of June 16, 1917, Laws 1917, chap. 409, § 423a.

[4] The cases are collected in the annotation to 50 U.S.C.A., pp. 178 ff.; cf. also the annotation, 130 A.L.R. 774-93. A selection of cases with further references in Schiller, *Military Law and Defense Legislation*, pp. 527-74.

respects, of their dependents.[5] The interpretation and construction of these statutes is a matter for the civil courts, but inasmuch as the subject is, indeed, outside the scope of this book and is adequately and extensively treated elsewhere, no further discussion is warranted herein.[6]

The only case in which the soldier's status can be of any substantive interest to a common law court, therefore, is where the issues involve the duties and obligations of the soldier in so far as they may impinge upon a civilian's rights. If a soldier shoots a civilian in the street and is sued for an assault, obviously the fact that the defendant is a soldier is of no importance. But if the soldier were a sentry and shot a civilian who was trying forcibly to enter a government reservation, then the fact that the defendant was a soldier requires the court to determine whether he had exerted such powers as the law allowed him, and no more, in committing the act.

In considering a case of this sort we must eliminate at once any circumstances which, apart from the particular questions in which we are interested, cannot be of decisive force. First of all, let us remember that no case of this sort can arise unless the defendant pleads that he committed the acts under the obligations which his official position, as recognized by law, imposed upon him. The defendant must plead an obligation resting upon

[5] The federal enactment is the Act of Oct. 17, 1940, 54 Stat. 1178, as amended Oct. 6, 1942, 56 Stat. 776, 50 U.S.C.A. App. §§ 501 ff. Among the state acts are those of New York, Laws 1941, chap. 686 [Military Law, Art. XIII]; Maryland Laws 1941, chap. 710; Massachusetts Laws 1941, chap. 708, §§ 19–21, 25.

[6] Cases construing the present act in 50 U.S.C.A., Appendix §§ 510 ff. Consult, further, the studies of Ferry, Rosenbaum and Wigmore, 1918, 12 Ill. L. Rev. 444; Bendetson, 1940, 2 Wash. & Lee L. Rev. 1; Taintor & Butts, 1941, 13 Miss. L.J. 467; Baldwin and Clark, *Legal Effects of Military Service* (3 ed. 1942); finally, the survey and bibliography of Schmehl, 1942, 35 L. Lib. J. 187.

him to do, as he conceived it, the acts which harm the plaintiff. The source of such an obligation is exterior to the defendant's will. The common law court cannot recognize any impulse other than one recognized by the law itself, and as the defendant, by the plea in question, admits that, outside of the special obligations of his position, his act would be a wrong, he must find a foundation for his obligation in a positive rule in the shape of a statute, or regulation enacted pursuant to statute, or the order of a superior given pursuant to regulation and statute. If he can find something of the sort, then he presents a case where, although the harm, to use Professor Burdick's terminology,[7] as distinct from the injury, was undoubtedly inflicted, the cause of the harm, the person responsible therefor, is not the defendant but the government.

Assuredly the court has jurisdiction to pass upon the soundness of such a plea, for if the defendant fails to make it good, then the case must proceed to judgment. "Where an individual is sued in tort for some act injurious to another in regard to person or property, to which his defense is that he had acted under the orders of the government . . . he is not sued as, or because he is, an officer of the government, but as an individual, and the court is not ousted of jurisdiction because he asserts authority as such officer. To make out his defense he must show that his authority was sufficient in law to protect him." [8]

The authority vested in military personnel may be general or express, according to which the defendant's field of volition is broad or narrow. The first situation is that of the officer who

---

[7] *Torts* (4th ed.), p. 76.
[8] Cunningham v. Macon, etc., R.R. Co., 1883, 109 U.S. 446, 452, 3 S. Ct. 292, 27 L. Ed. 992; cf. Stanley v. Schwalby, 1893, 147 U.S. 508, 13 S. Ct. 418, 37 L. Ed. 259.

acts under general authority involving a power of decision. So long as he can point to lawful authority outlining the field of jurisdiction, within which his decision is made, he is safe on any decision made in good faith, even though his decision on the facts presented to him may be wrong. Just as with the case of a court-martial or the action of a superior with respect to an inferior in the service, so it is with respect to the officer's decision in so far as it affects a civilian. The only question is whether the decision is made on a question which is within the defendant's jurisdiction to decide. In any such case as that he acts in a quasi-judicial capacity, and the common law then gives him the benefit of the same rule that it applies to anyone else who is rightfully vested with a power of decision. The officer in such a case is not liable in damages for the result of his decision, even though it might have been wrong, because with the power of decision goes, according to the common law, immunity from the consequences of the decision; the common law taking the homely view that, in the very nature of things, a power of decision must carry with it immunity from its consequences, so long as the quasi-judicial functionary uses his judgment in good faith. An officer vested with such a power of choice is, in the language of the Supreme Court, at least to be considered as "the expert on the spot," and while he may be called upon later in court to justify his conduct, still "great weight is to be given to his determination, and the matter is to be judged on the facts as they appeared then and not merely in the light of the event." [9]

Whether an officer is so vested is of course a question of law. Thus in *Dinsman v. Wilkes*,[10] which we previously consid-

[9] Moyer v. Peabody, 1909, 212 U.S. 78, 85, 29 S. Ct. 235, 53 L. Ed. 410.
[10] 1851, 12 How. 390, 13 L. Ed. 1036; see *supra*, chap. 4.

ered, it was held that the captain of a war vessel was vested with such quasi-judicial power in the case of a seaman who claimed that his term of enlistment had expired, the vessel being then in foreign parts. The seaman there had previously the special status of a member of the military force, and by his very assumption of that status had submitted himself to the judgment of just such a quasi-judicial tribunal.

But if the officer thus possessing a field of jurisdiction takes a course which is entirely outside of the jurisdiction conferred upon him by general orders or regulations, then he is not within the protection of the doctrine applicable to a quasi-judicial officer. It is on this point that such a case as *Bates v. Clark*,[11] and the more famous case of *Mitchell v. Harmony* [12] turn. In the first case the defendant, an army captain, seized some whiskey, supposing it to be destined for an Indian country, but as the Indians had recently been removed from the reservation in question, it was not, under the statute, Indian country. It was held that the defendant was liable in an action for the value of this whiskey, on the same basis as any other case of conversion.

In *Mitchell v. Harmony*, as subsequently stated by Mr. Justice Field [13] "the property of the plaintiff had been seized by an officer of the Army of the United States, upon the belief that he was unlawfully engaged in trading with the enemy. It turned out that he had been permitted by the Executive Department of the Government to trade with the inhabitants of neighboring Provinces of Mexico which were in possession of the military authorities of the United States. In an action for trespass for

[11] 1877, 95 U.S. 204, 24 L. Ed. 471.   [12] 1851, 13 How. 115, 14 L. Ed. 75.
[13] In Beckwith v. Bean, 1878, 98 U.S. 266, 303, 25 L. Ed. 124.

seizing the property, the defendant, among other reasons, justified the seizure on the ground that he acted in obedience to the order of his commanding officer, and therefore was not liable." The court, however, held him liable, adding "that the defendant did not stand in the situation of an officer who merely obeys the command of his superior, for it appeared that he advised the order and volunteered to execute it, when that duty more properly belonged to an officer of an inferior grade." The defendant assumed the right to decide in the matter. That being so, it was upon him to justify the jurisdiction which he thus assumed; and the fact of the Presidential license to the plaintiff depriving him of jurisdiction, he was left as utterly without defense as was the defendant in *Bates v. Clark*.[14]

With respect to the second situation mentioned, the liability of a subordinate who in good faith carries out the express—but unlawful—order of his superior, the Supreme Court early adopted a rule of strict accountability: that unlawful military orders will not excuse an obedient subordinate. Apt illustration is afforded by *Little v. Barreme*.[15] There an officer, acting under Presidential order, seized an American vessel sailing from a French port, and was cast in damages, because the court held that that order was not justified by any executive power confided by the Constitution. That case established the principle that illegal instructions cannot change the nature of the transaction or legalize an act which, without those instructions, would

---

[14] It is to be noted that the officer is liable when the unlawful acts are within the scope of his authority but are committed or ordered maliciously or in bad faith, Luther v. Borden, 1849, 7 How. 1, 12 L. Ed. 581; Tyler v. Pomeroy, 1864, 8 Allen (Mass.) 480; State ex rel. O'Connor v. District Court, 1935, 219 Iowa 1165, 260 N.W. 73, 99 A.L.R. 967.
[15] 1804, 2 Cranch 170, 2 L. Ed. 243.

have been a plain trespass. Chief Justice Marshall's first bias was, as he said "in favor of the opinion that though the instructions of the Executive could not give a right, they might yet excuse from damages," but he yielded that prepossession in favor of the rule above stated. On the authority of such a decision, the Supreme Court has said: "Whatever may be the rule in time of war and in the presence of actual hostilities, military officers can no more protect themselves than civilians in time of peace, by orders emanating from a source which is itself without authority." [16]

The Supreme Court has never departed from this view and it is reflected in the great majority of federal and state decisions of the first three quarters of the nineteenth century; [17] "an order which is in fact illegal—which commands the doing of an act which is unlawful or legally unauthorized—can, however regular, proper, or just it may appear on its face, protect no one concerned in the performance; that the superior who gives it and causes its execution, and the inferior who actually executes it as ordered, will both, or either, be liable in damages as for a trespass to any person aggrieved." [18]

It is of interest to note, however, that in cases such as these, the common law recognized the pressure of obligation which is the constant companion of the soldier. It did not withhold judgment against him, but, the substantive right being settled, it controlled the quantum of damages. For the existence of or-

[16] Bates v. Clark, cit. *supra* note 11, at p. 209.
[17] Clay v. United States, 1855, Ct. Cl., Devereux 25; Holmes v. Sheridan, 1870, C.C. Kan., Fed. Cas. No. 6644; Griffin v. Wilcox, 1863, 21 Ind. 370; Druecker v. Salomon, 1867, 21 Wis. 621, 94 Am. Dec. 571; Stanley v. Schwalby, 1892, 85 Tex. 348, 19 S.W. 264.
[18] Winthrop, *Military Law*, p. 887.

ders prevented the imposition of punitive damages upon a subordinate, since they evidenced his good faith.[19] Indeed, it has even been held that the existence of military orders might lead to the mitigation of damages.[20]

But the rule of the Supreme Court, the doctrine of strict accountability, has gradually given way to one of a more lenient nature. An early instance is afforded in the decision of *McCall v. McDowell*.[21] General McDowell, department commander at San Francisco, ordered the provost marshal to arrest all persons expressing sympathy with the assassination of President Lincoln, as "virtually accessories after the fact." Judge Deady held that General McDowell was liable since he had acted under his own will and volition, and not in pursuance of the special authority of the President, since there was no state of martial law; but that the provost marshal was not liable because he acted under the orders of General McDowell, his superior, and that the order was not "palpably illegal."

"Except in a plain case of excess of authority, where at first blush it is apparent and palpable to the commonest understanding that the order is illegal, I cannot but think that the law should excuse the military subordinate when acting in obedience to the orders of his commander. . . . If the law excuses the wife on the presumption of coercion, for what reason should it refuse a like protection to the subordinate and soldier when acting in obedience to the command of his lawful superior? . . . Between an order plainly legal and one palpably

---

[19] Beckwith v. Bean, 1878, 98 U.S. 266, 25 L.Ed. 124; McLaughlin v. Green, 1874, 50 Miss. 453.
[20] Carpenter v. Parker, 1867, 23 Iowa 450; Milligan v. Hovey, 1871, C.C. Ind., Fed. Cas. No. 9605.
[21] 1867, C.C. Calif., Deady 233, Fed. Cas. No. 8673.

otherwise there is a wide middle ground, where the ultimate legality and propriety of orders depends or may depend upon circumstances and conditions of which it cannot be expected that the inferior is informed or advised. In such cases, justice to the subordinate demands, and the necessities and efficiency of the public service require, that the order of the superior should protect the inferior; leaving the responsibility to rest where it properly belongs,—upon the officer who gave the command." [22]

The doctrine enunciated in *McCall v. McDowell* is the one that is widely accepted today, not only by the courts,[23] but by all of the text writers who have considered the topic in recent times.[24] The task before the court, then, is to decide whether the subordinate is reasonable in obeying the command of his superior; it must consider, among other things, whether there was an opportunity of determining the legality of the order, the rank of the officer who issued it, the existence of an emergency or not.[25] In spite of the fact that the "palpably illegal"

[22] Cit. *supra*, at 15 Fed. Cas. 1240, 1241.

[23] Despan v. Olney, 1852, C.C. R.I., Fed. Cas. No. 3822; O'Shee v. Stafford, 1908, 122 La. 444, 47 So. 764, 16 Ann. Cas. 1163; Franks v. Smith, 1911, 142 Ky. 232, 134 S.W. 484, L.R.A. 1915A, 1141; Hatfield v. Graham, 1914, 73 W.Va. 759, 81 S.E. 533, L.R.A. 1915A, 175; Herlihy v. Donohue, 1916, 52 Mont. 601, 161 Pac. 164, L.R.A. 1917B, 702; Neu v. McCarthy, 1941, 309 Mass. 17, 33 N.E. 2d 570, 133 A.L.R. 1298. There is no clear authority in England as to whether a subordinate can escape liability by proving that he acted under orders which were not manifestly illegal, see Dawkins v. Lord Rokeby, 1865, 4 Fost. & F. 806, 176 Eng. Rep. 800; Keighly v. Bell, 1866, 4 Fost. & F. 763, 176 Eng. Rep. 781; Marks v. Frogley, L.R. [1898] 1 Q.B. 404.

[24] Fairman, *Law of Martial Rule* (1930), p. 232; Restatement, *Torts* (1934), § 146; Wiener, *Practical Manual of Martial Law* (1940), p. 143; Glen, 1941, 135 A.L.R. 37; Note, 1942, 55 Harv. L. Rev. 653.

[25] See note, 55 Harv. L. Rev. 654, which adds: "With these factors in mind, it is possible to reconcile the Supreme Court cases to the doctrine of palpable illegality. In Little v. Barreme, since the subordinate, a naval captain, received a copy of the statute which the orders violated at the same time he received

rule may place a standard upon a subordinate that is higher than he is capable of observing,[26] nevertheless it appears so much fairer than the rule of absolute accountability, that it is to be hoped that the Supreme Court will confer its sanction upon it in the near future.

It is of course possible to have a case where the remedy which the plaintiff seeks does not involve holding an officer at all. If an officer remains in possession of property taken from the plaintiff, the plaintiff may bring a possessory action which, resulting in the restoration of the property, will terminate the matter. Such cases are *Meigs v. McClung* [27] and *Wilcox v. Jackson*,[28] in each of which the plaintiff brought ejectment for land which the government had occupied as an army post.

On the other hand, the plaintiff may seek against the officer relief which is highly improper in any action, other than one against the United States itself. Such a case arises where the officer, in behalf of the government, is using apparatus which infringes a patent owned by the plaintiff. The usual remedy which an injured patentee seeks is not damages against the infringer, but equitable relief in the shape of an injunction to prevent the continuance of the use, and an accounting for the profits which the wrong-doer, up to that time, might have derived from the use of the infringing apparatus. The courts long ago held that a suit should not succeed against an officer who has used the apparatus only in the government's behalf. Only

---

the orders and was told to consider it part of his instructions, the basis of his liability might well have been his failure to examine the statute. In Bates v. Clark and Mitchell v. Harmony there was no emergency, and so it might have been reasonable to require the subordinates to consider the facts upon which the validity of the orders turned."

[26] For the standards to be applied, see *loc. cit.*, 654 n. 24.

[27] 1815, 9 Cranch 11, 3 L. Ed. 639.   [28] 1839, 13 Peters 498, 10 L. Ed. 264.

the government has derived any profits, and it cannot be sued; nor should an injunction be granted whose effect impedes a government activity. The officer's possession being solely for governmental use, the suit in effect is against the government, and, therefore, it cannot be maintained. That proposition was finally decided by the Supreme Court, in *Belknap v. Schild*.[29] A decision similar in principle was rendered in England, where the principal for whom the subordinate was acting was a foreign sovereign,[30] and hence also immune from suit. The point of both decisions was the same, that an injunction would be of no avail because the real offender was the government, and an accounting for profits would be unavailing, because the governmental principal had received the profits, and not the officer actually using the apparatus. The whole question was rendered academic by legislation allowing the injured patentee to sue the government, not for an injunction it is true, but for profits, in the Court of Claims.[31] This gives the government a roundabout method, at once of appropriating the use of a patent by way of eminent domain, and of compensating the owner for such use. It follows that the officer or agent through whom the government acts is not liable to the owner even in an action for damages, to say nothing of an accounting.[32]

That leads us to the general question, if the officer acted under due authority of law, when, if ever, can the plaintiff turn for redress to the government which authorized the act?

In the absence of particular legislation such as that relating

---

[29] 1896, 161 U.S. 10, 16 S. Ct. 443, 40 L. Ed. 599.
[30] Vavasseur v. Krupp, 1878, L.R. 9 Ch. Div. 351.
[31] Act of June 25, 1910, 36 Stat. 851, as amended July 1, 1918, 35 U.S.C.A. § 68.
[32] Cramp v. Inter. Curtis Marine Turbine Co., 1918, 246 U.S. 28, 38 S. Ct. 271, 62 L. Ed. 560.

to patents, no citizen can obtain redress from the government merely because damage has been sustained, either by suit in the Court of Claims or in the District Courts.[33] In any such case the plaintiff must go remediless. It is only where an authorized act has resulted in the enrichment of the government by the taking of a plaintiff's property, or perhaps even its use, that the plaintiff can have any redress against the government.[34] In any other case of authorized damage, the plaintiff can sue neither the officer who acted under authority, nor the government.

A situation of more difficulty may arise where the government undertakes to ratify a wrong which in the beginning was unauthorized. Parenthetically, we must note that this intention to ratify should appear, because a mere subsequent authorization cannot operate as a ratification.[35] If the government were in like case with a human principal, its ratification of a tort could not terminate its servant's liability; it would simply add to the number of parties who would be liable for the tort. That, at least, seems to be the modern view, whatever might have been the original state of the law.[36] But the government's ratification, if it is to have any effect at all, must make the act no tort, because, if the ratification is valid, it goes back to the date of the act, and then it would have the effect of making the act legal which previously had been illegal.

Obviously, in a case of ratification it would be just as incumbent on the defendant to plead the ratification as it would be incumbent on a defendant, acting under prior authority, to

[33] Ribas y Hijo v. United States, 1904, 194 U.S. 315, 24 S. Ct. 727, 48 L. Ed. 994; Herrera v. United States, 1912, 222 U.S. 558, 32 S. Ct. 176, 56 L. Ed. 316.
[34] United States v. Russell, 1871, 13 Wall. 623, 20 L. Ed. 474.
[35] Ex parte Field, 1862, C.C. Vt., 5 Blatch. 63, Fed. Cas. No. 4761.
[36] See opinion of Holmes, J. in O'Reilly v. Brooke, cit. *supra*, p. 149.

SOLDIER AND CIVILIAN IN PEACETIME 165

show it. What the defendant should never overlook is that, outside the domain of authority, he has committed a tort. And it is for him to show authority, whether previously existing or flowing from ratification. If he does not show this, he cannot blame the court for proceeding to judgment against him. Viewed in this light the case of *Bean v. Beckwith*,[37] which some seem to have thought open to criticism as being one of those cases where the military officer "may be liable to be shot by a court-martial if he disobeys an order, and to be hanged by a judge and jury if he obeys it," [38] has no such bad effect. As the Supreme Court in a later case pointed out,[39] the defendant's plea was insufficient. In other words "whether there was in that case a special order of the President to the provost marshal, or whether he assumed to arrest and imprison the plaintiff under some proclamation or general order, did not appear by the plea, and as it was a case of arrest and imprisonment, this court held that the authority of the defendants to make it should be specifically set forth." [40] Even a verbal order in any such case would be sufficient.[41]

Instances of ratification are provided by indemnity acts of Civil War times, and to a greater extent by the statute which protected General Brooke.[42] At the time that he abolished the plaintiff's office of Hereditary Slaughterer of Cattle, General Brooke had not even color of authority, unless it was such authority as flowed from the law of military occupation. That

---

[37] 1874, 18 Wall. 510, 21 L. Ed. 849.
[38] Dicey, *Law of the Constitution* (9th ed.), p. 303.
[39] Mitchell v. Clark, 1884, 110 U.S. 633, 4 S. Ct. 170, 28 L. Ed. 279.
[40] *Loc. cit.*, at p. 646.   [41] Pollard v. Baldwin, 1867, 22 Iowa 328.
[42] O'Reilly v. Brooke, 1908, 209 U.S. 45, 28 S. Ct. 439, 52 L. Ed. 676, discussed *supra*, in chap. 7.

was either sufficient or it was not, but as the Supreme Court's decision did not turn on that at all, we may take it as though the general acted entirely without color of authority. He was thus left to the Platt Amendment, which ratified all acts done during the military occupation. The acts of the Civil War, on the contrary, ratified only such acts as were done under orders, leaving the officer who constituted the source of the order helpless in the absence of being able to point to some order or regulation ahead of him. This is illustrated by the decision in *McCall v. McDowell*,[43] which has already been discussed. The problem of indemnity, however, is more properly a question arising in connection with the soldier's relation to the civilian in time of war, to which we may now turn.

[43] Cit. *supra,* note 21.

9. RELATION OF SOLDIER TO CIVILIAN IN TIME OF WAR

THE army's primary function, as previously said, is the defense of the nation from the public enemy. That defense can be expressed only in terms of physical force; there is no other medium. The qualities of the great commander may reach the highest points of intellectual endeavor, but they are exerted in the assembly and direction of force. No war has ever been won by means of anything else; words have never been a substitute for armed endeavor, once resort is made to belligerency, from the days of Byzantium even to our own. When war is declared, the army stands ready to deliver the necessary blows; it is lawful for it to do so, and the common law recognizes the fact. The army's sphere of lawful action, therefore, automatically enlarges with the coming of the state of war.

As an immediate consequence—immediate in point of law, however delayed by circumstances it may be in application—the orb of the citizen's right contracts. Things that the soldier might not lawfully do in time of peace, he may conceivably do now with lawful immunity; and, conversely, things of which the citizen might rightfully complain in the days of peace will not serve as the subject matter of a suit when the nation is at war. Nor is this theorem limited to direct acts of the army and those of its instant direction. With a force equal in the abstract, but much more apparent to the average observer, it applies to the constitutional restraints of government. In support of the war, and, therefore, of the army, the government's constitutional powers take on a wider range. The "war powers" of the executive, the wider scope of permissible legislation given Congress, may properly reach far beyond the landmarks which the Constitution fixes for our journey through the days of peace.

Of this proposition in the abstract, there can be no doubt. Proofs of its acceptance, so far as governmental and legislative action is concerned, lie all about us at this writing. Among the war measures now in force we have the act respecting the restraint, regulation and removal of alien enemies,[1] together with the Trading with the Enemy Act of 1917, as amended, with the executive orders thereunder dealing with the Alien Property Custodian.[2] The Emergency Price Control Act of January 30, 1942 [3] and the Inflation Control Act of October 2, 1942 [4] concern our internal economy, while the resuscitated Espionage Act [5] enables the Government to combat subversive activities. Over all, the First and Second War Powers Acts and the executives orders thereunder are devoted to the all-out prosecution of the war.[6] No one has claimed that the Congressional war measures are unconstitutional, and the Presidential orders, though some of them have been challenged, appear to be authorized by Congress or to fall within the war powers of the Executive.[7] Indeed, all should approve them so far as they subserve their one object, the successful conduct of the war.

[1] 50 U.S.C.A. § 21, dating back to the Act of July 6, 1798, 1 Stat. 577.
[2] 50 U.S.C.A. Appendix §§ 1 ff.   [3] 56 Stat. 23, 50 U.S.C.A. App. §§ 901 ff.
[4] 56 Stat.—, 50 U.S.C.A. App. §§ 961 ff.   [5] 50 U.S.C.A. §§ 31 ff.
[6] Acts of Dec. 18, 1941, 55 Stat. 838, and March 27, 1942, 56 Stat. 176, 50 U.S.C.A. App. §§ 601 ff., 631 ff.
[7] Berdahl, *War Powers of the Executive* (1920); see *supra*, chap. 2, note 14.

Yet they outdo anything in our history; not even World War I was fought with such an array of enactments to further the war effort. England has proceeded to like extremes; England, the home of the individualist, has in some points outstripped us.[8]

The principle which justifies these things is as old as the common law; older than written constitutions, it, therefore, informs them. Indeed the principle is older than the common law; like the *jus naturae* of the medievalists, it pervades every system of law. That principle is that the rights of the individual must yield to those of the state in the time of the state's peril from the public enemy. This amounts to no deification of the state, and nothing of the Prussian is in it; for the state's right, in time of her peril, should be supreme, and the acts of her agents, in carrying out her commands, lawful; else we would have no state at all. "In these cases," says our Supreme Court, "the common law adopts the principle of the natural law, and finds the right and the justification in the same imperative necessity." [9]

This proposition finds ample room in Coke's reports—that fount of the common law. In the *Case of the King's Prerogative in Saltpetre* [10] it is said: "For the commonwealth a man shall suffer damage, as, for saving of a city or town, a house shall be plucked down if the next be on fire." It is therefore undoubted law today that no action lies for such an act as just described, when done by one acting under lawful authority.[11] In another

---

[8] Notably by the Personal Injuries (Emergency Provisions) Act, 1939, 2 & 3 Geo. 6, c. 82, and the War Damage Act, 1941, 4 & 5 Geo. 6. c. 12. These and further war measures collected and annotated in Krusin and Rogers, *The Solicitors Handbook of War Legislation*, 3 vols. (1940–42).
[9] Bowditch v. Boston, 1880, 101 U.S. 16, 19, 25 L. Ed. 980.
[10] 1606, 12 Co. Rep. 12, 77 Eng. Rep. 1294.
[11] Ralli v. Troop, 1894, 157 U.S. 386, 405, 15 S. Ct. 657, 39 L. Ed. 742.

case in the same volume of Coke's reports reference is made to the same doctrine.[12]

This principle, according to the same unquestioned authority, applies in time of war. "When enemies," says Coke, "come against the realm to the seacoast, it is lawful to come upon my land adjoining to the same coast, to make trenches or bulwarks for the defence of the realm, for every subject hath benefit by it. And, therefore, by the common law, every man may come upon my land for the defence of the realm, as appears 8 Edward IV 23. And in such case on such extremity they may dig for gravel, for the making of bulwarks; for this is for the public, and everyone hath benefit by it; but after the danger is over, the trenches and bulwarks ought to be removed, so that the owner shall not have prejudice in his inheritance." [13] At a later date this proposition was repeated as undoubtedly of sound law; [14] further, counsel for the defendant in the famous case of Ship-Money admitted that their contention did not invalidate this principle.[15]

The same right, in case of emergency, extends to the property of neutrals which may be found within the country. But the limits of this rule of angary, as extended by the United States government during the Civil War, overlap so much the bounds of international law as to place the whole subject outside the proper domain of this book; [16] the topic of domestic requisitioning, indeed, being brought into our present discus-

[12] Mouse's Case, 1608, 12 Co. Rep. 63, 77 Eng. Rep. 1341.
[13] Case of the King's Prerogative, cit. *supra*, note 10.
[14] Samborne v. Harilo, 1621, J. Bridg. 9, 123 Eng. Rep. 1162.
[15] Rex v. Hampden, 1637, 3 How. St. Tr. 826, 975, 1011 ff.
[16] See The Zamora, [1916] 2 A.C. 77, and the American authorities there discussed.

SOLDIER AND CIVILIAN IN WARTIME

sion more by way of illustration than as a principal objective.

For all such acts it was long thought, in England, that the state itself did not owe any duty of compensation. That view of the common law was most recently expressed in a case early in World War I, when the Crown seized a subject's land for purposes of an aviation camp.[17] But in the subsequent *De Keyser's Royal Hotel Ltd.* case, when the hotel premises were taken for the accommodation of the personnel of the Royal Flying Corps, that doctrine was most definitively overthrown.[18] Indeed, a careful study of the ancient records revealed to the Master of the Rolls "that it does not appear that the Crown has ever taken the subject's land for the defence of the realm without paying for it; and even in Stuart times I can trace no claim by the Crown to such a prerogative." [19] This view found full acceptance in the opinions of the Lords.[20] English law today, therefore, provides that compensation must be paid for property seized in time of war, under the Defence Act of 1842.[21] Since this act covers the whole ground of something which could be done under the prerogative, it is the statute that rules; [22] as declared by Lord Atkinson: "when a statute expressing the will and intention of the King and of the three Estates

---

[17] In re a Petition of Right, [1915] 3 K.B. 649.
[18] Attorney-General v. De Keyser's Royal Hotel, Ltd., [1920] A.C. 508; a most comprehensive study of this case, with full discussion of the nature of the Royal Prerogative and all earlier cases involving it, by Scott & Hildesley, *The Case of Requisition* (1920).
[19] Lord Swinfen, [1919] 2 Ch. 197, 221.
[20] Lord Dunedin, *loc. cit. supra*, note 18, at p. 524; Lord Atkinson, at p. 538; Lord Sumner, at p. 563; Lord Parmoor, at p. 573. Incidentally, the Lords perceived no basis for distinguishing the De Keyser case from In re a petition of Right, so that the latter must be considered as overruled, as far as the compensation point is concerned, Lord Dunedin, at p. 525.
[21] 5 & 6 Vict., c. 94.   [22] Lord Dunedin, *loc. cit. supra*, note 18, at p. 528.

of the Realm is passed, it abridges the Royal Prerogative while it is in force to this extent, that the Crown can only do the particular thing under and in accordance with the statutory provisions, and its prerogative power to do it is in abeyance." [23]

Whether the English view prevalent at the close of the eighteenth century was the reason or not, our national Constitution provided that private property shall not be taken for public use without compensation.[24] This makes our courts draw a distinction between the mere destruction of property in times of emergency, and its use or taking. In the one case there is no state obligation of payment; [25] but where the government has used or appropriated the thing in question, then an implied obligation, of compensating the owner, is imposed upon the government.[26]

But our government, however just the debt it may owe, is not suable by petition of right as is the English crown; [27] and hence, in any such case of a taking, the owner will go remediless unless Congress appropriates funds for his relief, or confers jurisdiction on the Court of Claims or local federal courts to hear the application.[28]

Our constitutional provision requires compensation for a taking, as we have seen. The government's implied contract to

---

[23] *Loc. cit. supra,* note 18, at p. 539.
[24] U.S. Constitution, Fifth Amendment.
[25] Bowditch v. Boston, cit. *supra,* note 9.
[26] United States v. Russell, 1871, 13 Wall. 623, 20 L. Ed. 474; United States v. Pacific R.R. Co., 1887, 120 U.S. 227, 239, 7 S. Ct. 490, 30 L. Ed. 634.
[27] United States v. Lee, 1882, 106 U.S. 196, 1 S. Ct. 240, 27 L. Ed. 171; Canterbury v. Attorney-General, 1843, 4 How. St. Tr. (n.s.) 767, 778; Commercial and Estates Co. of Egypt v. Board of Trade, [1925] 1 K.B. 271.
[28] It is noteworthy that Congress excluded such cases from the Court of Claims' jurisdiction during the Civil War, see United States v. Russell, cit. *supra,* note 26.

pay the owner for the property taken arises, says the Supreme Court, only when "an extraordinary and unforeseen emergency" requires the taking of the property at once by the commander.[29] That is the very distinction between such cases as *Mitchell v. Harmony*,[30] heretofore discussed, on the one hand, and *United States v. Russell*[31] on the other. In *Mitchell v. Harmony* the commander was not justified in what he did, because no situation of emergency existed; consequently there was no obligation on the government, and he remained liable as for a trespass. In *United States v. Russell*, on the contrary, where a commander during the Civil War used two vessels for a period, it was held that the government was under the obligation of payment, so of course the commander was not personally liable.

It is, then, a question of supreme emergency. Circumstances of that character justify the act of the soldier, for it is the act of the state. The nature and extent of the justifying exigency have never been entirely defined; we have only illustrations such as are afforded by the instances already mentioned. There are of course others.

If for example, the citizen's property or person should be situated within the theater of active military operations, there can be no doubt, in the common law mind, that they are subject to the control of the commander in charge. He could forcibly remove the citizen's person from the scene of arms; he could do the like with the citizen's property; the latter, indeed, he could destroy if in his judgment such a course would best subserve his purposes of combat. All of this Coke has told us in

[29] United States v. Russell, cit. *supra*, note 26, at p. 628.
[30] 1851, 13 How. 115, 14 L. Ed. 75.   [31] Cit. *supra*, note 26.

the passages already quoted; but if more were needed, it is to be found in *Ford v. Surget*.[32] The plaintiff, a resident of the Confederacy, owned cotton whose situation, as the Confederate lines fell back, was brought ever nearer to the presence of the hostile Federal troops. The defendant, the local Confederate commander, finally ordered the cotton to be burned, in order to prevent its falling into the hands of the Union troops. For this, after the close of the war, he was sued by the plaintiff. The Supreme Court held for the defendant. Considering that the Confederacy was *de facto* a belligerent, the court treated the suit exactly as if a resident of Gettysburg had sued an officer of General Meade's army for destroying a Pennsylvania homestead in order to prevent its military use by General Lee's men. The property in each case, being in the theater of operations, was at the commander's disposal, and for no act of his with respect thereto was he liable, so long as it was done in good faith.

In the same category should be placed the situation which arose from the battle of New Orleans. On December 15, 1814, General Jackson declared martial law over the territory ranging from four miles above the city to four miles south of it. The battle whose happy issue saved the city from capture was fought on the eighth of the next month, but the General refused to relax his control until official advices reached him. Matters being thus situated, one Lovallier was taken into military custody for seditious language, and the civil court issued a writ of habeas corpus for him. General Jackson's answer was to arrest the judge. Then official news of peace arrived, and martial law ceased. The judge, on being released, fined General Jackson for

[32] 1878, 97 U.S. 594, 24 L. Ed. 1018.

SOLDIER AND CIVILIAN IN WARTIME 175

contempt, and the fine was paid. Later, Congress passed an act to refund to the General the amount of the fine.[33]

Along the same lines, the decision of the Privy Council in *Ex parte Marais* is in point.[34] There the petitioner, residing within thirty-five miles of Cape Town, was arrested and held for a military court on a charge of sedition. He was taken to a place three hundred miles distant for trial; but martial law had been proclaimed over all this territory, the Boer War then being in progress. The Privy Council held that the prisoner was not entitled to release by way of habeas corpus, although the civil courts were open in the affected territory. The court considered that war was raging over the entire section and that, therefore, martial law necessarily prevailed, the civil courts being open only on the commander's sufferance.

To this extent then, the Supreme Court is justified in the exception which it makes when, speaking of the rules applicable in times of peace to the relation of soldier and civilian, it pushes to one side, as not within the scope of its remarks, the "rule in time of war"—"whatever" it may be.[35] In time of war, let us repeat, the relation of soldier and civilian takes on an entirely different color according to the exigency imposed by the pressure of the conflict. But, beyond the demand of the occasion, the old restraints of the common law remain; its self-abnegation goes just that far and no further. "It is an unbending rule of law that the exercise of military power, where the rights of the citizen are concerned, shall never be pushed beyond what the exigency requires." [36]

---

[33] A complete history of this case, with the surrounding circumstances, appears in Rankin, *When Civil Law Fails* (1939), pp. 5-25.
[34] [1902] A.C. 109.   [35] Bates v. Clark, 1877, 95 U.S. 204, 209, 24 L. Ed. 471.
[36] Raymond v. Thomas, 1876, 91 U.S. 712, 716, 23 L. Ed. 434.

Who is to judge of that? We had best answer that question with another. Who is to determine whether a case is within the jurisdiction of a court-martial? We have already gained, it is to be hoped, not merely the answer to that question, but the philosophy of it. The common law must determine such matters. It can never turn away a suitor unless a case is non-justiciable; and whether such a case, on its facts, is of that class, the common law court alone must determine, for no other court or power can do so. The question must be determined; other courts are of limited jurisdiction, and in an English speaking commonwealth, executive or administrative powers are non-judicial; and so the burden of this decision must fall on the common law court. Every act done to the person or property of the citizen in time of war, therefore, must ultimately be submitted to the arbitrament of the common law; the question in each such case being whether an emergency existed which justified the measure as one of salvation for the state. Once that is determined in the defendant's favor, he goes free unless a case of express malice be shown. In that event, of course, the case is turned into one of oppression under color of office, and is actionable, it is submitted, on the same basis as a case of abuse of lawful process.[37] In the absence of such malicious abuse of power as "Flogging Fitzgerald" furnished during the Irish rebellion of 1798, the defendant goes free. But always must he be prepared to show the existence and nature of the emergency constituting his impulse to action, and it is for the court to say whether its judgment, in that regard, coincides with his.

The commander, therefore, goes through his arduous duties with the possibility of civil actions to greet him at the close of

[37] See Wright v. Fitzgerald, 1799, 27 How. St. Tr. 759.

the war. It is a situation pregnant with injustice. If the defendant can show a situation of emergency of the nature above discussed, then he will be safe enough. But the soldier works under the double pressure proceeding from the duty of absolute obedience to orders, and, in war times, a feeling of responsibility for the national safety, that may well lead him to give orders not justified by any compelling emergency that later a common law court could fairly visualize. Yet the military man must act, although he knows that in the very decision he makes he is entailing litigation for himself upon the coming of peace. Hard indeed is his situation.

Recognizing this fact, legislative action in both England and America has taken a curious course, illogical in the extreme, but still so well established as to serve nowadays as a thing of precedent. This practice is to pass, at the close of a war whose effects have included collisions between the ordinary rights of citizens and the powers of the military, an act of indemnity. In England such statutes followed the Old Pretender's rebellion of 1715, the Young Pretender's invasion of England in 1745, and the Irish rebellion of 1798.[38] During the nineteenth century similar indemnity acts were passed in several of the colonies following disturbances in the suppression of which the military was employed.[39] Typical of the English indemnity acts was that enacted subsequent to World War I, the Indemnity Act, 1920,[40] which states well the extent of such legislation: "No

---

[38] These enactments are discussed by Clode, *Military Forces of the Crown*, II (1869), pp. 164 f., 172.
[39] So, in Jamaica, in 1865, the Local Act being set forth in Clode, *op. cit.*, II, p. 494; in Cape Colony and Natal following the Boer War, e.g., Cape of Good Hope Acts, No. 6 of 1900, No. 4 of 1902.
[40] 10 & 11 Geo. 5, c. 48.

action or other legal proceedings whatsoever, whether civil or criminal, shall be instituted in any court of law for or on account of or in respect of any act, matter or thing done, whether within or without His Majesty's Dominions, during the war before the passing of this Act, if done in good faith, and done or purported to be done in the execution of his duty or for the defence of the realm or the public safety, or for the enforcement of discipline, or otherwise in the public interest, by a person holding office under or employed in the service of the Crown in any capacity, whether naval, military, air-force or civil, or by any other person acting under the authority of a person so holding office or so employed." [41] Such enactments, in the view of an eminent English scholar,[42] illustrate the highest exertion of the sovereign power wielded by Parliament "to make legal transactions which when they took place were illegal, or to free individuals to whom the statute applies from liability for having broken the law." [43]

As we have seen, such statutes were not unknown to us prior to the Civil War; and the wane and close of that conflict were marked by two indemnity acts passed by the United States Congress.[44] Then, following the Spanish-American War, the Platt Amendment relieved military personnel of liability for their acts during the course of military operations in Cuba.[45] Some of these statutes merely provide indemnification to a particular

[41] Sec. 1(1); note that malicious acts will not be protected, Wright v. Fitzgerald, 1799, 27 How. St. Tr. 759, 765.
[42] Dicey, *Law of the Constitution* (9th ed.), pp. 49, 232–37, 413.
[43] *Ibid.*, p. 49.
[44] Act of March 3, 1863, c. 81, §§ 4, 7, 12 Stat. 755; Act of May 11, 1866, c. 80, §§ 1, 2, 14 Stat. 46.
[45] Act of March 2, 1901, c. 803, 31 Stat. 897; this act was concerned in the case of O'Reilly v. Brooke, *supra*, pp. 149 f.

officer for damages which he might have been compelled to pay for a tort committed by him. Such was the case with General Jackson, following his military control of New Orleans during the War of 1812.

The other form of statute is exemplified by the Civil War legislation just mentioned. There it was provided "that any order of the President, or under his authority, made at any time during the existence of the present rebellion, shall be a defence in all courts to any action or prosecution . . . for any acts done, or omitted to be done, under and by virtue of such order, or under color of any law of Congress." [46] A further provision limited to two years after the date of the enactment or after the commission of the act, any right of action arising out of acts done "by virtue or under color of any authority derived from or exercised by or under the President, or by or under any act of Congress." [47] Such legislation reflects that of the English Parliament, but in the United States a constitutional question is involved. Congress may ratify anything which it could have authorized in the first instance.[48] But can Congress ratify an act which could not have been authorized in the first place be-

---

[46] Act of March 3, 1863, c. 81, § 4; the failure to observe this provision led to the amendment of 1866 in which defense to an action was specifically afforded an officer or person acting under the orders of the President, Secretary of War or military commander of a department, district, etc.

[47] Act of March 3, 1863, c. 81, § 7.

[48] "That an act passed after the event, which in effect ratifies what has been done, and declares that no suit shall be sustained against the party acting under color of authority, is valid, so far as Congress could have conferred such authority before, admits of no reasonable doubt." Justice Miller, in Mitchell v. Clark, cit. *infra*, note 54, at p. 640. Thus, a defect in the authority of the governor of the Philippines to deport a person may be cured by subsequent adoption of the act, Tiaco v. Forbes, 1912, 228 U.S. 549, 556, 33 S. Ct. 585, 57 L. Ed. 960.

cause it was unconstitutional, for example, that an injured person would be deprived of a right of action and therefore of property without due process of law. Legal scholars are divided in their understanding of the cases which construed these statutes.[49]

The indemnity provision of the 1863 Act was upheld in the case of *McCall v. McDowell*, which we have already discussed.[50] Of the two defendants sued, one had given the order, and the other had obeyed it, the final result being injury to the plaintiff. The court held, as we have seen, that the plaintiff could not recover against the defendant who had executed the order, because he was protected, if not by the common law principles discussed in Chapters 4 and 8, then because the case came within the purview of the indemnity acts. But the plaintiff was allowed to recover against the defendant who gave the order, because he had gone off on his own and could point to nothing justifying his conduct, however meritorious it might have been.[51] But in *Milligan v. Hovey* [52] the indemnity provisions were declared to be unconstitutional since the Supreme Court had decided that Congress could not constitutionally have authorized the trial of Milligan,[53] and thus the members of the military commission were liable in spite of the fact that they were carrying out orders.

---

[49] See Lieber, 163 North American Rev. 549 ff.; Birkhimer, *Military Government*, pp. 575 ff.; Randall, 1922, 20 Mich. L. Rev. 589 ff.; Fairman, *Law of Martial Rule*, pp. 206 ff.; Willoughby, *Constitutional Law* (2d ed. 1929), Vol. III, § 1610; Wiener, *Practical Manual of Martial Law*, §§ 142 ff.

[50] 1867, C.C. Cal., Fed. Cas. No. 8673, *supra*, pp. 160 ff.

[51] The indemnity section was assumed to be valid in Crosby v. Cadwalader, 1870, C.C. Pa., Fed. Cas. No. 3419.

[52] 1871, C.C. Ind., Fed. Cas. No. 9605.

[53] Ex parte Milligan, 1866, 4 Wall. 2, 18 L. Ed. 281.

SOLDIER AND CIVILIAN IN WARTIME

The Supreme Court passed upon the acts in the case of *Mitchell v. Clark*.[54] That case was a suit for rent due, the tenant answering that payment had been made for and on account of the plaintiff to the provost-martial of the army, by order of General Schofield, as a necessary means of carrying on the war. Following decisions in the Supreme Court of Missouri, the case was brought to the Supreme Court on writ of error, where it was held that Congress could provide a statute of limitation for the state as well as federal courts, when a case was capable of being removed from one to the other. No impairment of the obligation of contracts was involved, for "it has been repeatedly held that a statute of limitation which reduced materially the time within which suit may be commenced, though passed after the contract was made, is not void if a reasonable time is left for the enforcement of the contract by suit before the statute bars that right." [55] According to one view, the Supreme Court has done no more than uphold the validity of the statute of limitations provision, since it was unnecessary to decide whether the section which denied all right of action was constitutional or not.[56] But there are other writers [57] who consider that the court approved of the statutes as a whole, just as had been done in the earlier decision of *Beard v. Burts*, where the question of constitutionality was not before the court.[58] "If these expressions of the supreme Federal tribunal did not go

---

[54] 1884, 110 U.S. 633, 4 S. Ct. 170, 28 L. Ed. 279; dissenting opinion of Justice Field. The case was approved in Cutler v. Kouns, 1884, 110 U.S. 720, 4 S. Ct. 274, 28 L. Ed. 305.
[55] Cit. *supra*, at p. 643.
[56] So Lieber, Fairman, Wiener, cit. *supra*, note 49.
[57] So Birkhimer, Randall, Willoughby, cit. *supra*, note 49; also Professor Glenn, in the first edition of this work.
[58] 1877, 95 U.S. 434, 24 L. Ed. 485.

to the extent of sustaining affirmatively the constitutionality of the acts of Congress in question, they did by the strongest implication." [59]

This sort of *ex post facto* legislation carries on its face the suggestion that Congress might just as well have made it precede the acts in question, and thus have made them lawful from the first. The officer who acts under orders is left in the position of a wrong-doer until, after the event, an act of Congress legalizes what, until the enrollment of the statute, was a wrong. And although the statute may not validate the act as to the officer who created the direction under which his subordinate proceeded, yet it provides for his benefit a short period of limitations. And we are told that the object of abbreviating the period of limitation is that, if judgment should be recovered against the defendant, then, for his act, "if done under a necessity or mistake, the government should not see him suffer"; it following that the government may not merely provide for the removal of such suits into the federal court, but may also prescribe a period of limitation.[60] This circumstance brings both classes of cases together. If, as to the officer acting under orders, Congress can, *ex post facto*, legalize what he has done, it can legislate in advance that such acts shall be lawful. If Congress can pay out public money in indemnifying the officer who creates the order, for the amount of a judgment recovered against him, based on the order being carried into effect, then Congress may properly legalize such orders in advance, and

[59] Birkhimer, cit. *supra*, note 49, at p. 578. There exist a number of state decisions construing similar state legislation, but these are not helpful since opinion on the constitutionality of the acts is divided, see Wiener, *loc. cit.*, p. 157.
[60] Mitchell v. Clark, cit. *supra*, note 54, at p. 641.

thus keep public money in the Treasury, or else pay the damage money direct to the injured party instead of standing as indemnifier for the officer.

No attempt was made to enact indemnity statutes after World War I. Indeed, the Act of April 18, 1918, which provided for the settlement of claims by citizens of friendly countries for damages caused by American military forces, specifically states that this in no way "diminishes the responsibility of any member of the military forces to the person injured or to the United States." [61] Whether it is intended to protect military and naval personnel for acts done in the present conflict we have no way of knowing, but if such is to be done, it would be well for Congress to consider the question now and not after the war, to devise a system of indemnity that would not be exposed to possible constitutional objection at the hands of a future Supreme Court.

[61] Sec. 3, 40 Stat. 532, 5 U.S.C.A. § 210.

10. CONCLUDING NOTE

THE final chapter of the first edition of this book was entitled "Martial Law at Home." It opened with a discussion of the nature of martial law, its recognized existence in the area of military operations, and its resemblance, in this aspect, to the French *état de siège*. Professor Glenn then turned to the more difficult question, whether it is possible to have a state of martial law in a domestic region which is not the seat of actual war. Two types of martial law must be differentiated in this connection, preventive and punitive. A study of English history demonstrates that preventive martial law has long been and still is recognized by the English courts, while punitive martial law is condemned only in time of peace, when common law process should naturally have full sway. A study of the history of martial law in our own country reveals that preventive martial law is fully acknowledged, while punitive martial law has not been recognized outside the theater of military operations. In conclusion, Professor Glenn looks forward to the acceptance of the minority view in *Ex parte Milligan*,[1] that is, the recognition of the power of Congress to establish complete martial law, punitive as well as preventive, in any areas of imminent danger when the nation is involved in war and exposed to invasion.

After much deliberation, and with the acquiescence of Professor Glenn, the reviser has decided to omit the chapter entirely. This, for a number of reasons. In the first place, a

[1] 1866, 4 Wall. 2, 136, 18 L. Ed. 281.

considerable number of books and articles, many of them first rate, have appeared since the publication of the first edition. It would entail much effort and fairly long treatment—which time and space forbid—to incorporate the ideas and information contained therein into the framework of Professor Glenn's chapter. Even more, the field of martial law, or martial rule as it has often been termed in recent years, is an exceptionally controversial one,[2] and the different viewpoints adopted by the various authors materially affect the treatment accorded and the conclusion drawn from the decisions of the common law courts.

Above all, however, the reviser believes that the chapter as it stands is not of primary interest at the present time. It is largely historical in character and primarily devoted to a consideration of martial law in time of peace. Today martial law in time of war is the vital aspect. The transference of civil power to the military in Hawaii, the removal of the Japanese from the West Coast, and the trial of the Nazi spies on the East Coast all have focused attention on problems entirely different from those dwelt upon by Professor Glenn. True, law reviews as well as non-legal periodicals are replete with discussions of these novel, yet significant, developments of martial rule. But judicial decisions upon the new problems are still few in number,[3] so inconclusive, indeed, as not to warrant

[2] Fairman, *Law of Martial Rule* (1930), pp. 245 ff., classifies his bibliographical references in three groups, articles which would restrain the exercise of military power within narrow limits, those which would concede greater latitude in the exercise of war powers or in the suppression of insurrection, and those which reflect the extreme authoritarian viewpoint.

[3] Ex parte Zimmerman, 1942, C.C.A. Hawaii, 132 F. 2d 442, upholds the validity of martial rule in Hawaii and the suspension of the privilege of the writ of habeas corpus; a strong dissent urges that the civil judge is entitled

consideration in a volume which otherwise, it is hoped, reflects the established views of the common law courts.

Consequently, the topic of martial law will be disposed of by reference to selected books of recent date on martial law generally, coupled with a listing of articles that deal with the subject in the light of the present conflict.

Recent Books on Martial Law

Fairman, Charles. The Law of Martial Rule (Chicago, 1930).
 The leading treatise of recent date, with full discussion of primary and secondary authorities, largely dispensing with the need of reference to earlier works.

Rankin, Robert S. When Civil Law Fails; Martial Law and Its Legal Basis in the United States (Durham, 1939).
 A picture of several martial law incidents in our history coupled with a detailed presentation of the views of practically all the writers on martial law.

Wiener, Frederick B. A Practical Manual of Martial Law (Harrisburg, 1940).

---

to determine whether the military action in detaining the petitioner is reasonably necessary to repel invasion or suppress insurrection. In two District Court cases, Ex parte Kanai, 1942, D.C. Wis., 46 F. Supp. 286, and United States v. Hirabayashi, 1942, D.C. Wash., 46 F. Supp. 657, the constitutionality of the executive order establishing military areas on the west coast, the military orders pursuant thereto, and the Congressional enactment imposing punishment for the violation thereof, is affirmed; but in United States v. Yasui, 1942, D.C. Ore., 48 F. Supp. 40, Judge Fee maintains that until martial law is established the proclamations and regulations of military commanders cannot be enforced by civil courts, and that any attempt by Congress to impose penalties upon American citizens for violation thereof would be unconstitutional. Finally, there is the well-known saboteur case, Ex parte Quirin, 1942,—U.S.—, 63 S. Ct. 2, 87 L. Ed. 1.

A forceful exposition of the state of the law just previous to the war.

Rich, Bennett M. The Presidents and Civil Disorder (Washington, 1941).

History of the role of the Executive in domestic disturbances involving armed forces.

Articles on Martial Rule in the Present Conflict

Anthony, *Martial Law in Hawaii*, 1942, 30 Calif. L. Rev. 371–96.

Comment, *Alien Enemies and Japanese-Americans; a Problem of Wartime Controls*, 1942, 51 Yale L.J. 1316–38.

Fairman, *The Law of Martial Rule and the National Emergency*, 1942, 55 Harv. L. Rev. 1253–1302.

Graham, *Martial Law in California*, 1942, 31 Calif. L. Rev. 6–15.

King, *The Legality of Martial Law in Hawaii*, 1942, 30 Calif. L. Rev. 599–633.

Smith, *Martial Law and the Writ of Habeas Corpus*, 1942, 30 Geo. L.J. 697–704.

Warren, *Wartime Martial Rule in California*, 1942, 17 Calif. S.B.J. 185–204.

TABLE OF CASES

Cramp v. International Curtis Marine Turbine Co., 163n
Crosby v. Cadwalader, 149n, 180n
Cross v. Harrison, 126, 127n
Cummings v. Deutsche Bank, 114n
Cummings v. Diggs, 147n
Cunningham v. Macon, etc., R.R. Co., 155n
Curtiss v. Witt, 57n
Cutler v. Kouns, 181n

Daimler Co. v. Continental Tyre & Rubber Co., 89n
Daniel v. Hutcheson, 132n
Davison, *In re*, 55n, 85n
Dawkins v. Lord Paulet, 65n, 67n
Dawkins v. Lord Rokeby, 65n, 66, 67n, 161n
De Lacey v. United States, 110n
De Lima v. Bidwell, 125n, 127n
Deming v. McClaughry, 55n, 70n
Despan v. Olney, 161n
Dewing v. Perdicaries, 136
Dick v. Tevlin, 74n
Dickey, *Ex parte*, 71n, 72n
Dinsman v. Wilkes, 61, 67n, 156
Dooley v. United States, 126n
Dostal, *Ex parte*, 26n, 28n, 31n
Dow v. Johnson, 92, 94n, 120, 131, 132n, 133n, 146n
Druecker v. Salomon, 159n
Dunakin, *Ex parte*, 27n
Dunn, *Ex parte*, 76n
Dynes v. Hoover, 52n, 56n, 59n, 69n, 70n, 71n

Egan, *In re*, 131n
Elphinstone v. Bedreechund, 121n, 122n, 123, 147n
Esmond, *In re*, 82n
Evans v. Richardson, 88n
Exchange, The, 117n
Exposito v. Bowden, 88n

Faber v. United States, 98n
Fair, *In re*, 81n
Farley v. Ratliff, 31n
Ferris v. Armstrong, 62n
Field, *Ex parte*, 164n
Fleming v. Page, 39n, 100n, 126, 127n
Fletcher v. United States, 45n
Ford v. Surget, 94n, 121n, 122, 174
Franke v. Murray, 31n, 33n
Franklin v. United States, 76n
Franklin v. Vannoy, 149n
Franks v. Smith, 161n
Fraser v. Balfour, 66n
Freeland v. Williams, 118n, 146n
Frye v. Ogle, 68n
Funk v. State, 78n
Furly v. Newnham, 103n
Fuston, *Ex parte*, 74n

Gallego, Messa & Co. v. United States, 121n
Gates v. Goodloe, 146n, 150n
Gavieres v. United States, 83n
Gerlach, *Ex parte*, 34n, 70n
Givins, *Ex parte*, 70n
Givens v. Zerbst, 70n
Government v. M'Gregory, 104n
Grafton v. United States, 82, 83n, 119n
Grant, Matter of, 153n
Grant v. Shard, 63n
Grapeshot, The, 131n
Gray v. United States, 86n
Greenberg, Application of, 75n
Griffin v. Wilcox, 159n
Grimley, *In re*, 3n
Griner, *In re*, 38n

Hall v. Howd, 61n
Hamilton v. Dillin, 11n, 90n
Hamilton v. Kentucky Distilleries and Warehouse Co., 86n
Harrison v. Myer, 146n
Hatfield v. Graham, 161n
Heddon v. Evans, 65, 67
Hefferman v. Porter, 131n
Henkle v. Royal Exchange Assurance Co., 88n
Herlihy v. Donohue, 161n

TABLE OF CASES

Herrera v. United States, 121n, 140n, 147n, 151n, 164n
Hewitt, Ex parte, 131n
Hines v. Mikell, 34n
Holmes v. Sheridan, 62n, 67, 159n
Hoop, The, 88
Hoskins v. Dickerson, 29
Hoskins v. Pell, 25n
Houghton, Ex parte, 55n
Houston v. Moore, 30n
Howe's Case, 81n
Hubbard v. Harnden Express Co., 94n
Hughes v. Techt, 102n
Hutton v. Blaine, 59n

Iroquois Iron Co. v. Industrial Commission, 3n
Isbell v. Farris, 126n

Janson v. Dreifontein Consolidated Mines, Ltd., 86n
Jeffers v. Fair, 21n
Jenkins v. Collard, 137n
Jochen, Ex parte, 34n
Johnson v. Biddle, 71n
Johnstone v. Pedlar, 104n
Johnstone v. Sutton, 63n, 65n
Jones, Ex parte, 129n
Jones v. United States, 6n
Juragua Iron Co. v. United States, 98n, 121n, 140n

Kahn v. Anderson, 33n, 70n
Kanai, Ex parte, 112n, 186n
Kawato, Ex parte, 112n
Keighly v. Bell, 58, 161n
Kennedy v. Cook, 8n
Keyes v. United States, 71n
King, Ex parte, 77n, 78
King's Prerogative in Saltpetre, Case of the, 169, 170n
Kirk v. Lynd, 137n, 138n
Kirkman v. McClaughry, 43n, 44n, 45n
Kitzerow, In re, 73n
Kneedler v. Lane, 21n

Koester, Ex parte, 78n
Koonce v. Davis, 147n
Kurtz v. Moffitt, 38n, 52n

Lamar v. Browne, 98n, 100n, 122, 140n, 141n, 143n, 149n, 150n
Laurey v. United States, 38n
Leitensdorfer v. Webb, 131n
Lewis v. McGuire, 148n
Lewkowitz, Ex parte, 55n
Lincoln v. United States, 148n
Lindo v. Rodney, 139n
Little v. Barreme, 58, 158, 161n
Local Draft Board v. Connors, 23n, 74n
Luther v. Borden, 36n, 158n

McCall's Case, 31n
McCall v. McDowell, 58n, 160 f., 166, 180
McCardle, In re, 131n
McClaughry v. Deming, 55n, 70n
McCollam, Ex parte, 29n
McKee v. United States, 90n
McKittrick, Ex parte v. Brown, 80
McLaughlin v. Green, 148n, 160n
MacLeod v. United States, 100n, 126n
McVey, In re, 28n, 71n
Maddux v. United States, 39n
Major William Smith, In the matter of, 38n
Mansergh, In re, 65n
Marais, Ex parte, 175
Maria v. Hall, 105n
Marks v. Frogley, 66n, 161n
Martin v. Mott, 30, 43n, 59, 69, 70n
Mason, Ex parte, 70n, 76n, 82
Meigs v. McClung, 162
Mikell, Ex parte, 34n
Miller v. United States, 90n, 98n, 137n, 150n
Milligan, Ex parte, 180n, 184
Milligan v. Hovey, 160n, 180
Mills v. Martin, 30n, 59n
Mitchell v. Clark, 118n, 165n, 179n, 181, 182n

TABLE OF CASES

Mitchell v. Harmony, 92, 115, 157, 162n, 173
Morgan v. T.V.A., 12n
Morrissey, In re, 3n, 24n, 26n
Mosher v. Hudspeth, 44n, 45n
Mouse's Case, 170n
Moyer v. Peabody, 156n
Mrs. Alexander's Cotton, 143n
Munich Reinsurance Co. v. First Reinsurance Co., 113n
Myers v. United States, 12n

Napore v. Rowe, 73n
Neall v. United States, 77n.
Neely v. Henckel, 125n
Neill, In re, 56n
Neu v. McCarthy, 58n, 161n
New Orleans v. New York Mail Steamship Co., 126, 132n
Nixon v. Reeves, 61n

Oakes v. United States, 141n
Ochoa v. Hernandez, 149n
O'Dell, In re, 27n
Oetjen v. Central Leather Co., 147n
O'Neill v. Central Leather Co., 147n
O'Reilly v. Brooke, 148, 149, 164n, 165n, 178n
Ortiz, Ex parte, 131n
O'Shee v. Stafford, 161n
Ouachita Cotton, The, 90n

Paradine v. Jane, 18n
Pennywit v. Eaton, 131n
People v. Denman, 78n
—— Wendel, 80n
Pepin v. Lachenmeyer, 131n
Perdicaries v. Charleston Gaslight Co., 136n
Perkins v. Rogers, 86n
Petition of Right, In re, 171n
Planters Bank v. Union Bank, 148, 150n
Platt, Ex parte, 74n
Poe, Matter of, 50n
Pollard v. Baldwin, 165n

Porret's Case, 43n, 44n
Porter v. Freudenberg, 98n, 109n, 113n
Potts v. Bell, 88n
Price v. Poynter, 147n
Prize Cases, 87, 93n, 100n
Puerto Rico v. Shell Co., 83n

Quirin, Ex parte, 130n, 186n

Ralli v. Troop, 169n
Rankin v. Tennessee, 81n
Rapid, The, 101n
Raymond v. Thomas, 134n, 135, 148, 175n
Reed, Ex parte, 83n
Reform, The, 90n
Respublica v. M'Carty, 106n
Rex v. Army Council ex parte Ravenscourt, 66n
—— Hampden, 170n
—— Lynch, 106n
—— Schiever, 103n
—— Vaughan, 106n
—— Vine Street Police Station Superintendent, 103n
—— Wall, 52n
Ribas y Hijo v. United States, 86n, 121n, 147n, 164n
Riggs v. State, 58n
Robson v. Premier Oil & Pipe Line Co., Ltd., 89n
Rose ex rel. Carter v. Roberts, 55n, 71n
Rothbarth v. Herzfeld, 109n
Runkle v. United States, 70n

Samborne v. Harilo, 170n
Sanford v. Robbins, 71n
Schaffenius v. Goldberg, 103n, 105n, 112n
Schuneman v. Diblee, 61n
Selective Draft Law Cases, 22n, 24n
Shimola v. Local Board, 73n, 74n
Ship-Money, Case of, 170
Simmons v. United States, 83n

TABLE OF CASES

Smith v. Brazelton, 147*n*
Smith v. Stewart, 93*n*
Smith v. Whitney, 43*n*, 44*n*, 71*n*, 75*n*
Soberman, Petition of, 74*n*
Sparenburgh v. Bannatyne, 104, 105*n*
Stanley v. Schwalby, 155*n*, 159*n*
State *ex rel.* Lanng v. Long, 52*n*
—— *ex rel.* O'Connor v. District Court, 158*n*
—— v. Rankin, 81*n*
—— v. Sparks, 5*n*
Steiner's Case, 82*n*
Stone v. Christensen, 23*n*, 74*n*
Stubbs, *In re*, 81*n*, 82*n*
Sumner, *Ex parte*, 78*n*
Sutton v. Johnstone, 64 f., 65*n*, 67
Sutton v. Tiller, 147*n*
Swaim v. United States, 39*n*, 45*n*, 70*n*, 71*n*
Swinton v. Malloy, 63*n*

Tarble's Case, 56*n*
Taylor v. Carpenter, 105*n*
Taylor v. Jenkins, 148*n*
Taylor v. Nashville & Chattanooga Ry., 147*n*
Techt v. Hughes, 102*n*, 110*n*, 112*n*
Terrill v. Rankin, 148*n*
Thirty Hogsheads of Sugar v. Boyle, 98*n*, 140*n*
Thomasson v. Glisson, 147*n*
Three Spanish Sailors, The, 103*n*
Tiaco v. Forbes, 179*n*
Totus v. United States, 74*n*
Townley's Case, 106*n*
Tyler v. Pomeroy, 148*n*, 158*n*
Tyson v. Rogers, 148*n*

Underhill v. Hernandez, 6*n*
United States *ex rel.* Bergdoll v. Drum, 31*n*
—— Diamond v. Smith, 31*n*
—— Drury v. Lewis, 82*n*
—— Errichetti v. Baird, 75*n*
—— Filomio v. Powell, 73*n*, 74*n*, 75*n*
—— French v. Weeks, 71*n*
—— Gillett v. Dern, 8*n*

—— Harris v. Daniels, 55*n*, 71*n*, 83*n*
—— Helmecke v. Rice, 31*n*
—— Pascher v. Kinkead, 73*n*
—— Pasciuto v. Baird, 75*n*
—— Pfefer v. Bell, 23*n*
—— Roman v. Rauch, 73*n*
—— Ursitti v. Baird, 73*n*
—— Wessels v. McDonald, 55*n*
United States v. Bevans, 77*n*
—— Block, 83*n*
—— Caparros, 128*n*
—— Carr, 77*n*
—— Cashiel, 77*n*, 81*n*
—— Cathcart, 94*n*
—— Chemical Foundation, 113*n*, 121*n*
—— Clark, 58*n*, 77*n*, 82*n*, 84
—— Cornell, 23*n*, 77*n*
—— Cottingham, 28*n*
—— Dunnington, 138*n*
—— Eaton, 38*n*
—— Eliason, 39*n*
—— Fletcher, 50*n*
—— Garst, 23*n*
—— Greiner, 106*n*
—— Herling, 23*n*
—— Hirabayashi, 186*n*
—— Hirsch, 78*n*
—— Huckabee, 141*n*
—— Klein, 138*n*, 142*n*
—— Lambert, 23*n*
—— Lee, 172*n*
—— Lipsett, *ex parte* Gillette, 81*n*
—— McIntyre, 31*n*
—— Mackenzie, 77*n*
—— O'Keefe, 101*n*
—— Pacific R.R. Co., 172*n*
—— Padelford, 102*n*, 138*n*, 141*n*
—— Palmer, 6*n*
—— Rappeport, 23*n*
—— Rice, 20*n*, 98, 99*n*
—— Russell, 164*n*, 172*n*, 173
—— Smith, 86*n*
—— Stephens, 22*n*, 73*n*
—— Sugar, 8*n*, 22*n*
—— Webster, 38*n*
—— Williford, 27*n*, 55*n*
—— Yasui, 111*n*, 112*n*, 186*n*

TABLE OF CASES

Vallandigham, *Ex parte*, 40n, 131n
Vance v. United States, 130n
Vanderheyden v. Young, 59n
Vavasseur v. Krupp, 163n
Venice, The, 150n
Ver Mehren v. Sirmyer, 33n
Vidal, *In re*, 71n

Wales v. Whitney, 55n
Wall v. Macnamara, 63, 65n, 67n
Wallace v. Alford, 121n
Wallace v. United States, 13n
Walt v. Thomasson, 130n
Warden v. Bailey, 49n, 62n
Webster, *Ex parte*, 71n
Weirman v. United States, 83n
Wells v. Williams, 112n
Wilcox v. Jackson, 162
Wilkes v. Dinsman, 61n, 82n

William Bagaley, The, 101n
Williams v. Bruffy, 136n
Wilson v. Franklin, 148n
Wilson v. Mackenzie, 67n
Winfield, *Ex parte*, 29n
Wingfield v. Crosby, 128n
Wise v. Withers, 56n, 69, 70
Wolfe Tone's Case, 106
Worthy v. Kinomon, 142n
Wright v. Fitzgerald, 176n, 178n
Wright v. White, 67
Wulzen, *In re*, 81n

Young v. United States, 100n, 101n, 139n

Zamora, The, 139n, 170n
Zimmerman, *Ex parte*, 185n

INDEX

Accountability, strict: doctrine of, 158-60
Act of March 3, 1863, authorizing selection by lottery or draft, 21
—— drafting militia into the national forces, 30
—— of July 13, 1861, on intercourse with enemy, 90
—— of March 8, 1918, for protection of soldier from court action, 153
—— respecting the restraint, regulation and removal of alien enemies, 168
Age limits, of draftees under Selective Service acts, 22, 23; under earliest statutes, 24; of minors, 25
Alien Enemies Act, 114
Alien Property Custodian, 91, 113, 168
Aliens, rights of: classes, 5; enlistment, 27, 28; property of non-resident, 101-3; return of enemy subjects to own country, 102; enemy dwelling within this country, 109-14, 168; foreign enemy cannot sue or claim damages, 109; governmental control of conduct, 110; interposition of army into affairs of, 110 f., 114; restricted or prohibited areas, 110, 111; under jurisdiction of the common law, 112; treatment of interned, 112 f.; *see also* Enemy
Allegiance to enemy government, 93-97, 124; during Civil War, 93; distinction between armed forces and civilians, 94-97; oath of, 124
André, Major, 108
Angary, rule of, 170
Appellate review of action of courts-martial, 72

Appropriation for army, time limit, 7, 14, 36
Areas, restricted or prohibited, 110, 111
Army, deemed a necessity: influence of precedent, etc., on law governing, 2; entry into, means change of status: and subjection to laws and customs governing, 3; common law plays part in law governing, 4; why the relation, 4-6; constitution of, 7-31; appropriation for, 7, 14, 36; reserve elements, 7-10; powers of Congress, 7, 11, 32, 86 (*see also* Congress); use of, 10; President and other ranks of command, 11 f.; manner and form of enlistment, 13 ff.; Anglo-Saxon institutions: inadequacy, 13; history of standing army, 13, 16 ff.; universal service, 14 ff. (*see entries under* Universal service); dual system still maintained in U.S. and England, 20; provision for formation of a National Army by draft, 22; viewed by courts as having distinct status in governmental system, 23; qualifications re enlistment, 24 ff.; minors, 24-27; fraudulent, 27; aliens, insane, and other disqualified persons, 27 f.; military courts and law, 32-53 (*see also* Courts-martial; Martial law); personnel to whom military code applicable, 33; right of self-regulation, 54-85; in its relations with the enemy in our own country, 86-114; against public enemy, may be used only in time of war, 86; how personnel affected by trade with enemy, 92; distinction be-

INDEX

Army (*Continued*)
tween members of, and private citizens, 94 ff.; dealings with enemy army are matters of military, not common, law, 108 f.; interposition of, into affairs of civilian alien enemies, 110 f., 114; jurisdiction over troops abroad, 116-23; military occupation, in matters of government, 123-35; in matters of property, 136-51; relation to civilian, in peace, 152-66; in war, 167-83; sphere of action enlarged during war, 167; personnel, *see* Commander; Officers; Soldier

Army Act, British, 35

Army Discipline and Regulation Act of 1879, 35

Army Regulations, 37; source: authority, 38; General Orders of same status as, 39

Arrest and confinement preparatory to trial, 55n

Articles of War, 12, 27, 45, 47, 49, 52, 68, 76, 77, 78, 79, 107, 116; when first prepared: successive statutes, 32; complete revision: is present military code, 33, 36; source in British Articles, 34; persons to whom applicable, 36; classification, 37; provision for removal of case from state to federal court, 56

Atkinson, Lord, quoted, 171

Authority, Army Regulations on, 1n; vested in military personnel, legal view, 155 ff.

Bibliography of martial law, 185n, 187 f.

Brooke, General, 149, 165

Captured and Abandoned Property Act, 122, 137, 138, 139, 150

Capture of property, *see* Property

Carter, Oberlin, 85

Chase, Chief Justice, quoted, 128n

Civilians, when soldier subject to liabilities of private citizen, 4; Military Code applies to retainers or persons accompanying forces, 33; military jurisdiction of civil population, 46; people as well as government, classed as enemy, 88, 93; status fixed by allegiance: location immaterial, 93; choice between status of soldier or that of citizen, 95; violations and consequences of this rule of law, 95-97; property in enemy country, 101-3; have no place in enemy country except with license to trade, 115; rule of law, where rights of are concerned, re exercise of military power, 134n; soldier's relation to, in time of peace, 152-66; in time of war, 167-83; orb of rights diminished, 167; age-old principle that rights of, must yield to those of state at the time of its peril, 169; *see also* Aliens; Enemy

Civil War, conscription, 21; drafting of militia, 30; Lieber's Code issued during, 40; ratification of intervening acts of executive, 87; question of allegiance, 93; confiscation of property, 101, 122, 136-39, 143, 145n, 146n, 149 f., 174; just treatment of enemy during, 135; districts not to be treated as theaters of war or as being subject to requisitions, 150; indemnity acts, 165, 166, 178, 179

Clausewitz, theory about enemy property, 142

Code, Lieber's, 40, 42, 142

Code, Military, 33, 40; *see* Articles of War

Command and obedience, 1, 23

Commander, legal question of power to act, 54; how affected by license to trade with enemy, 92; military government in occupied territory, 123 ff.; may prescribe jurisdiction over courts, 128, 130; supreme

INDEX

power, 132; just treatment of population, 133, 134; may not arbitrarily upset judgment of court given jurisdiction, 134; not liable for seizure or destruction of enemy property, 140, 147; acts during quiet government as distinct from full campaign, 148; liability for taking property a question of supreme emergency, 173 ff.; civil actions that may face him at close of war, 176; works under double pressure, 177; indemnity legislation for legalizing acts of, 177-83; *see also* Officers

Common Law, plays part in military establishment, 4; why the relation, 4-6; rights of aliens, 5; rules incorporated into military law, 44*n*; little flavor of, in courts-martial, 47; *see also* Courts, common law

Compulsory service, earliest advocacy in U.S., 21; defined by court, 24; *see also* Selective service; Universal service

Confederate government, conscription, 21; question of allegiance to, 93

Confiscation, statutes of, 136-39, 143, 150; *see also* Property

Congress, powers, 7, 11, 32, 86; may not impair President's authority, 39; question re giving jurisdiction to courts-martial, 77, 78 f.; may ratify unauthorized executive acts, 87; question of its power to ratify, 179; power to provide a statute of limitation for state as well as federal courts, 181; can, *ex post facto*, legalize what has been done, or can legislate in advance that such acts shall be lawful, 182; power to establish complete martial law, 184

Conquest, confers no sovereignty over occupied regions, 124-27; its effect upon titles to land and personal property, 136 ff.

Conscription, *see* Selective service; Universal service

Control and obedience, 1, 23

Cotton seized during Civil War, 122, 143, 150, 174

Courts, common law, rules of international law the subject of inquiry by, 6; validity of draft legislation upheld, 22, 24; view of army as having distinct status in governmental system, 23; Supreme Court's recognition of Lieber's Code as obligatory on armies, 40; judicial review of courts-martial, 54-72, 75-85; dual system of federal and state, 56, 81 f.; cases where inferior claims injury by conduct of superior, 56; ministerial *v.* discretionary acts, 57; whether act or decision is within scope of officer's authority, 60; cases of express malice, 62 ff.; ruling that no civil action will lie against superior officer for act done in course of duty, even maliciously, 65; asks only whether court-martial has jurisdiction and guides own conduct accordingly, 69; judicial review of draft-board determinations, 72-75; must look to statute for appellate powers, 72; extent of concurrent jurisdiction of courts-martial and, 75-80; effect of trial before court-martial, upon proceedings of, 82-84; no jealousy or distrust in scrutiny of court-martial jurisdiction, 84; view only state-recognized belligerency as war, 86; jurisdiction of prisoners of war, 104; civil litigation between enemy combatants impossible, 109; jurisdiction of resident civilian enemy, 111, 112; of interned alien enemy, 112 f.; view of capture of enemy property, 138; at sea, 139; on land, 140 ff.; distinction between military acts during quiet government and during full campaign, 148, 151;

Courts, common law (*Cont.*)
when cases of property seizure pass from domain of, into affairs of state, 149; questions as between soldier and civilian within jurisdiction of, 152 ff.; when power of decision held to carry immunity from its consequences, 156; rule of strict accountability applied to obedient subordinate, 158; modified by doctrine of illegality, 160; decisions in suits where government was offender, 163; distinction between destruction of property, and its use or taking, 172
—— military, 44, 46-53; factors making for creation of, 3; jurisdiction exclusive when army leaves national boundaries, 116-23; powers and limitations of war courts, 116, 129 f.; provost courts, 116, 128, 130, 131; provisional courts, 128 ff.; *see also* Courts-martial
—— in enemy country, army of occupation exempt from jurisdiction of, 118; except for trial of war crimes, 119; may handle civil and criminal business of own subjects, at will of army commander, 123, 125; new and provisional courts may be set up: their jurisdiction, 128
Courts-martial, Articles of War relating to, 37; procedure governed by custom of the service: principle of noninterference of courts of law, 44; system of: personnel, 46; defined general, special, and summary: persons subject to trial by them, 47; historical sources, 47; procedure and jurisdiction, 47-53; judicial review, 50 f., 54-72, 75-85; limited powers: not a court in full sense of term, 51; jurisdiction dependent upon status of delinquent and power of commander to act, 54; defendant's right to test its power over him, 55; liability of members acting without jurisdiction, 58*n*, 61*n*; question of jurisdiction the one issue of fact or law which it cannot conclusively determine, 69; errors reviewable only by way of appeal, 72; difference in nature of draft boards and, 73; extent of concurrent jurisdiction of common law courts and, 75-80; effect of a trial before, upon subsequent federal civil court proceedings: reverse of the situation, 82-84; no jealousy or distrust in other courts' scrutiny of, 85; jurisdiction of prisoners of war, 103; treason not within jurisdiction of, 107; jurisdiction over troops outside of own country, 116, 119; may be chosen by enemy, for trial of war crimes within its territory, 119; distinguished from provisional court and military tribunal, 129
—— British, 52*n*, 116*n*
Crimes acts of 1790 and 1825, 77
Cruelty, in exercise of authority, 63, 65*n*; denunciations of, 133

Damages, right to bring action for, 55; mitigation of, 160
Date of change of status, 30, 31
Deady, Judge, quoted, 160
Debtor, protection of, against court action, 153
Decision, actions involving power of, 156
Declaration of Paris, 39
Defense Act of 1842, British, 171
Deserters, enlistment, 27, 28; failure to report, 30, 31
Dicey, conception of rule of law, 4*n*; quoted, 14, 18, 165
Discretionary *v.* ministerial acts, legal view of, 57 ff.
Domicile of military men, 153
Draft, provisions of Selective Service acts, 22, 23; validity of, upheld, 22,

INDEX

23; *see also* Selective service; Universal service
Draft boards, judicial review, 72-75; statutory provisions, 72 f.

Emergency, power to decide whether arisen, 59; nature and extent of the justifying, 173 ff.
Emergency Price Control Act, 168
Enemy, persons giving relief or aid to, 36; military government applicable to, 45; defined, 87, 93; trading with, 88-92, 113; citizens as, 88, 93; question of allegiance, 93-97; the determining features of residence, 98-100; of situs of property, 100-3; return of subjects to own country, 102; treatment of those who come armed or as prisoners of war, 103-5; treatment of the traitor in arms, 105-7; litigation between combatants, 108 f.; dealings with armies of, are matters of military law, 108 f.; aliens dwelling within this country, 109-14 (*see entries under* Aliens); individual cannot sue or claim damages, 109; when civilian viewed as in same class with, 115; army in country of, exempt from jurisdiction of its courts, 118; country occupied, or under military government, 123-35; military occupation in matters of property of, 136-51 (*see entries under* Property); right to requisition service or labor of, 151; *see also* Civilians
England, *see* Great Britain
Enlisted Reserve Corps, 9
Enlistment qualifications, *see* Army
Espionage Act, 111, 168
"Excess" of jurisdiction, 63
Executive, *see* President
Exigency, *see* Emergency
Express malice, 62 ff., 176

Felons, convicted: enlistment of, 27
Field, Justice, quoted, 157

"Flogging Fitzgerald," 176
Fowler, Surrogate, quoted, 153n
France, universal service, 15; invaders' treatment of civilians, 95, 96
Fraudulent enlistment a military offense, 27
Frederick the Great, 16

General Orders, 39
Germany, universal service, 15, 17; thesis that laws lose binding force in case of necessity, 42n; correct in propositions of law: unfit ministers of justice, 95
Government, liability for property seized in enemy territory, 121; only source of redress for violation of the laws of war, 122; relief sought against officer acting only in behalf of, 162; can plaintiff turn to, for redress? 163; ratification of a wrong unauthorized in beginning, 164-66; constitutional powers widened during war, 168; age-old principle that rights of the individual must yield to those of the state in the time of its peril, 169; compensation for property seized, 171-73; not suable by petition of right, 172; taking of property by commander during supreme emergency, 173 ff.
——— military, defined, 45; in enemy territory, 46, 123-35; "at home," 46; principles by which it should be guided, 133-35; matters of property, 148-51
Grant, General, 135, 153n
Great Britain, constitution of army, 13, 14; Mutiny Act, 14, 18, 20, 34 f., 52; germination of universal service idea, 17 ff.; history of Articles of War, 34, 35; Army Act, 35; lack of permanent statutory code, 36; rules of war published by War Office, 41; court-martial, 52n, 116n; express malice cases, 63; proclamations re **trading:** nonintercourse acts, 88 f.;

INDEX

Great Britain (*Continued*)
return of enemy subjects permitted, 102; jurisdiction over treason, 107*n*; grants of exclusive jurisdiction over American soldiers, 117; enactments to further war efforts, 169; compensation for property seized, 171; suable by petition of right, 172; acts of indemnity, 177, 179; history of martial law in, 184

Habeas corpus proceedings, 55, 70, 74, 81, 103, 106, 130, 185*n*
Hague Regulations, 40, 96, 109; re treatment of enemy property, 140, 142, 145
Hawaii, martial rule in, 185
Heath, Justice, quoted, 104
Hierarchy, military, 1
Home Guard, 9
Hunt, Justice, 127

Illegality, doctrine of, 160-62
Indemnity acts, 165, 166, 177, 178, 179, 180, 183
Inflation Control Act, 168
Injunction of no avail when offender is government, 163
Insane, enlistment, 27
Instructions for the Government of the Armies of the United States in the Field (Lieber's Code), 40
International law, rules often subject of inquiry by courts, 6
Intoxicated persons, enlistment, 27

Jackson, General, 174, 179
Japanese, not permitted to depart, 102
Judge advocates, 45, 50
Jurisdiction, "excess" of, 63; of courts, *see* Courts
Justice of the peace, status, 70

Kelly, Chief Baron, quoted, 66
Kent, dictum re capture of private property, 143

Labor, right to requisition, 151
Land titles in occupied territory, 136
Law, rule of, advanced by Dicey, 4
Lawrence, Justice, quoted, 49
Laws of war, 42*n*; *see also* Articles of War
Lee, General, 124
Lieber, Francis, Instructions for . . . Armies . . . (Lieber's Code), 40, 42, 142
Limitation, statute of, 181 f.
Lottery, selection by, 21

McCardie, Justice, 66
McDowell, General, 160
Malice, express, 62 ff., 176
Mansfield, Lord, 65*n*, 68, 88; quoted, 5*n*, 63, 139*n*
Manual for Courts-Martial, 46*n*, 48*n*
Marlborough, standing army, 19
Marshall, Chief Justice, quoted, 5, 159
Martial law, history of: preventive and punitive types, 184; novel developments during World War II, 185; bibliography, 185*n*, 187 f.
"Martial Law at Home," why chapter on, was omitted, 184-86
Military areas and zones, 110, 111
Military Code, 33, 40; *see* Articles of War
Military commissions, 116, 128 ff.
Military courts, *see* Courts, military; Courts-martial
Military government, *see* Government, military
Military law, outline of branches, 32-47; codified portions, 32-42; uncodified, 43-46; common law rules incorporated into, 44*n*; military courts, 44, 46-53 (*see* Courts, military; Courts-martial); defined, 46*n*, 132; dealings between armies are matters of, 108 f.; enforcement and its requirements, 133; *Military Laws of the United States*, 37*n*
Military necessity, principle of, 43*n*

INDEX

Militia, constitution of, 7; portion known as National Guard ..., 7; subject to states, 8; uses, 9; English, 13, 18, 20; value of: satires on, 14; enlistment of minors, 28; calling forth into federal service effects change of status: failure to report: problem of date of change, 30; question of where right to draft, is vested, 59; *see also* National Guard

Miller, Justice, quoted, 179*n*

Ministerial *v.* discretionary acts, legal view of, 57 ff.

Minors, enlistment and disqualification of, 24-27, 28 f.; consent of parents or guardian, 25, 28 f.

Municipal laws of occupied country, 127

Murder, court jurisdiction, 76, 77, 80, 82, 118; by war prisoners, 104*n*

Mutiny Act, 14, 18, 20, 34 f., 52

Napoleon I, 16; quoted, 132, 133; code of rules re property, 144

National Army, provisions for, 22; *see also* Army

National Defense Act, 7*n*, 10*n*, 22, 23; recognition of National Guard, 7, 8*n*, 9*n*; terms re minors, 25

National Guard, distinguished from National Guard of the U.S., 8*n*, 9*n*, 29; state use, 9; voluntary service, 13; enlistment of minors, 28 f.; *see also* Militia

National Guard of the United States, 7, 8, 21; distinction between called into, and drafted into, federal service, 8*n*, 9*n*, 29; President the supreme head, 12; question as to whether federal or state law is to apply, 28 f.

National Guard while in service of U.S., 7

Naval establishment, 6

Necessity, military: principle of, 43*n*

Neutrals, property rights, 170

Ney, Marshal, 85

Non-intercourse legislation, 89 ff.

Obedience, and control, 1, 23; duty of, recognized by courts, 57; of enemy subject, 124, 125

Occupation, held by courts to be a question of fact, 98-100

Occupied territory, military government of, 46, 123 ff.; residents as enemy, 98-100; matters of property in, 100-3, 136-51 (*see entries under* Property); jurisdiction over army in, 115-23; what military occupation means, 124; conquest confers no sovereignty over, 124-27; cannot pass to conquer unless ceded, 125; principles by which administrators should be guided, 133-35

Offenses, defined by Articles of War: 36 f.; system of courts for punishment of, 46

Officers, Regular Army Reserve, 9*n*

Officers, reserve, 9, 10*n*; appointment and removal: non-commissioned, 12; ministerial *v.* discretionary acts, 57; liability for discretionary act, 59; right of inferior to maintain civil action against, 62*n*, 63-68; express malice, 62; may amount to "excess" of jurisdiction, 63; ruling that no civil action will lie against, for act done in course of duty, 65; legal question of authority vested in, 155 ff.; actions involving power of decision, 156; liability for carrying out illegal orders, 158 ff.; suits against improper, when relief should be sought against government only, 162; *see also* Commander; Soldier

Officers' Reserve Corps, 9

Organized Reserves, 9

Paley, observations of war and the military establishment, 17-20

Palpable illegality, doctrine of, 160-62

Parker, Lord, quoted, 89

INDEX

Patent infringement, 162
Peace Conference, codification of rules of war, 40
Perry, Justice, quoted, 44
Pershing, General, 116
Pillage, 141, 144
Platt amendment, 149, 166, 178
Pope, General, orders by, 96, 124, 145n
Posse Comitatus Act, 11
Prerogative, Royal, 169, 172
President, Commander-in-Chief of the Army and Navy, 11, 39; duties, 11; powers, 12, 30n, 38, 59, 60, 86, 90; Congress may not impair authority of, 39; confirmation of courts-martial cases, 50; unauthorized acts may be ratified by Congress, 87; regulation of resident aliens' conduct, 110; war powers fully authorized, 168; orders of, as defense in court actions, 179
Prince Rupert Articles, 35
Prisoners of war, status and treatment, 103-5
Prize court and law, 139
Property, military occupation in matters of, 100-3, 136-51; withdrawal of, 102; of interned alien enemy, 113; seizures in enemy country, 121, 136, 143, 150, 174; confiscation acts, 136-39, 143, 150; land titles unaffected, 136; capture at sea, 139 f.; on land, 140 ff.; distinction in classes subject to capture, 142 ff.; system of requisitions, 144-47, 170; principle that all property needed for army was legitimate subject of capture, 144, 146; captures during quiet government and during full campaign, 148, 151; when cases pass from domain of common law into affairs of state, 149; rule of angary, 170; government's compensation for, 171-73; legal distinction between destruction of, and its use or taking, 172; commander's liability for taking, a question of supreme emergency, 173 ff.; indemnity legislation, 177-83; *see also* Trading with enemy
Provisional courts, 128 ff.
Provost courts, 116, 128, 130, 131
Prussia, universal service, 16, 17
Public opinion, tribunal of, 120, 133
Punitive articles defined, 37

Railroad Strike of 1894, 11
Ratification, government's, 164-66
Regular Army, the standing army, 7; constitution, 7-31; *see also* Army
Regular Army Reserve, 9n
Removal from military office, 12
Reprisal, doctrine of, 43n
Requisitions for enemy property, system of, 144-47, 170
Reserve elements of army, 7-10
Reserve officers, classes, 9; when subject to military law, 10n; *see also* Officers
Residents of enemy countries, 98-100
Roman law, 41, 47
Rooke, Justice, quoted, 104
Rousseau, theory of war, 16, 88
Rules of Land Warfare, 40, 42, 97n, 103n
Rules of war, violations constitute "war crimes" punishable in military courts, 108; *see also* Articles of War

Sabotage Act, 111
Saxe, Marshal, 144
Schofield, General, 181
Scott, General, 129
Sea capture of property, 139 f.
Selective Service Act, 15; provisions, 21, 31, 72; constitutionality upheld, 22
Selective Service Regulations, 31
Selective Training and Service Act, 24, 72; persons inducted under as part of army, 7; on National Guard, 8n; universal service, 15, 23

INDEX

Soldier, entry into army, 3 ff.; statutes for protection against court action, 153; relation to civilian in time of peace, 152-66; status in civil suits, 153, 154; domicile, 153; necessity for pleading obligation imposed by official position, 154 ff.; liability when carrying out unlawful military orders, 158 ff.; relation to civilian in time of war, 167-83; *see also* Commander; Officers
Spanish army with Wellington, 96
Spy, Articles of War apply to, 36
Standing army, history of, 13, 16 ff.; fear of, 14, 18; *see also* Army
States, when militia subject to, 8; use of militia and National Guard, 9; authorized to provide Home Guard, 9; dual system of federal and state courts, 56, 81 f.; statutes for protection of military men, 153
Status, change of, with entry into army, 3; date of change of, 30, 31; soldier's, in civil suits, 153, 154
Statute of limitation, 181 f.
"Statutes, Ordinances, and Customs" of Richard II, 35
Statutes for protection of military men against court action, 153
Story, Justice, 30, 43; quoted, 59, 87, 99
Stowell, Lord, 88
Strict accountability, doctrine of, 158-60
Swinfen, Lord, quoted, 171

Taxation in occupied country, 125
Tenterden, Lord, quoted, 122
Territorial and Reserve Forces Act of 1907, 13
Territorial restriction on troop movements, 39n
Trading with the enemy, 88-92; how the military is affected, 92
Trading with the Enemy acts, British, 89; American, 91, 113, 114, 168
Traitors, armed: jurisdiction of, 105-7

United States, *see* Congress; Government; President
Universal service, 14; history, 15-21; beginnings in U.S., 20, 21; during World Wars, 21, 23; defined by court, 24; *see also* Selective service

Vattel, idea of war, 16
Volunteers, 7

War, once viewed as affair of state, not of people, 16; only state-recognized belligerency recognized as, by courts, 86; array of enactments to further, 168, 169; army's sphere enlarged, citizen's rights diminished, during, 167; constitutional powers of government enlarged, 168
War, Secretary of, 12, 39
Warbeck, Perkin, 105
War Powers acts, 168
Wellington, 96, 132
Willes, Justice, quoted, 58, 88

DATE DUE